Twenty-First Century Celebrity

Fame In Digital Culture

Twenty-First Century Celebrity

Fame In Digital Culture

BY

DAVID C. GILES
University of Winchester, UK

United Kingdom – North America – Japan – India
Malaysia – China

Emerald Publishing Limited
Howard House, Wagon Lane, Bingley BD16 1WA, UK

First edition 2018

Reprints and permissions service
Contact: permissions@emeraldinsight.com

British Library Cataloguing in Publication Data
A catalogue record for this book is available from the British
Library

ISBN: 978-1-78754-212-9 (paperback)
ISBN: 978-1-78743-708-1 (Online)
ISBN: 978-1-78743-965-8 (Epub)

CONTENTS

Part IV: The Future of Celebrity

PART I

CELEBRITY IN THEORY AND RESEARCH

1

CELEBRITY STUDIES AND THE CHANGING MEDIA LANDSCAPE

"There was no such thing as celebrity prior to the beginning of the twentieth century" (Schickel, 1985, p. 23).

"Celebrity must be understood as a modern *phenomenon, a phenomenon of mass-circulation newspapers, TV, radio and film." (Rojek, 2001, p. 16).*

If the phenomenon of celebrity is inextricably tied to cinema and television, what are we to make of celebrity in the twenty-first century? As I write, the number of Facebook members is starting to approach two billion–yes, almost a third of souls on the planet–and each month, various sources claim, over a billion people view video material on YouTube. Never mind the hundreds of millions of people using Twitter, Instagram, and Snapchat every day. The media landscape has changed beyond all recognition in the last two decades: these are mass, global communication systems like none before, spawning their own cultures of fame, and generating 'stars' with, it is claimed (Sehdev, 2014), greater social influence over younger generations than the movie stars and pop singers of 20 or so years ago. PewDiePie, the most popular YouTuber, has 62 million subscribers to his various channels, and many others have attracted over 10 million. But are these influential individuals really *celebrities* in the twentieth century sense of the word? In this book, I will argue they are, but to claim this requires us to examine what we really mean by celebrity, and to develop a concept of celebrity that is sensitive to cultural contexts, particularly in relation to their media landscapes.

The birth of 'celebrity studies' as an academic discipline is a thoroughly twenty-*first* century affair. When I produced my own early contribution to the literature, *Illusions of Immortality* (Giles, 2000), there was precious little academic literature to help me. Braudy had produced his exhaustive history of fame (Braudy, 1986), and, in a more sociological vein, there was Gamson's analysis of American fame from Hollywood onwards (Gamson, 1994). Film scholars had for some time cultivated their own sub-field of 'star studies', where Dyer in particular blended a semiotic reading of star texts with a sociological analysis of their ideological significance (Dyer, 1979). But at the turn of the millennium, only Monaco's (1978) *Celebrity* and Marshall's (1997) *Celebrity and Power* had focused explicitly on the concept. In producing a psychological account of fame and celebrity, I was forced to take my ideas from biographies and press interviews by celebrities themselves.

Things took off rapidly after the turn of the century. Rojek published *Celebrity* (Rojek, 2001), and then came Turner's *Understanding Celebrity* (Turner, 2004), followed by a slew of books and articles on the subject, culminating in the 2010 launch of the Routledge journal *Celebrity Studies*. This publication, and its associated biennial conference, have drawn together a wide international network of scholars from media, film, and television studies, right across the humanities and social sciences. There is plenty of contemporary writing on the subject. (For a comprehensive overview of the pre-*Celebrity Studies* literature, see Beer and Penfold-Mounce, 2010; see also Marshall and Redmond, 2015.)

Increasingly, scholars in the field are turning their critical gaze to the emergence of celebrity in digital media, with key studies on YouTube (García-Rapp, 2016; Smith, 2014 to cite just two), Instagram (Marwick, 2015), and Twitter (Marwick & boyd, 2011; Thomas, 2014; Kehrberg, 2015). Alice Marwick has argued that the digital explosion has brought about "two major changes in celebrity culture" (Marwick, 2016, p. 333): direct access to established celebrities via platforms like Twitter and the emergence of 'micro-celebrity', which is "a self-presentation technique in which people view themselves as a public persona to be consumed by others." I will argue in this book that this second change has evolved rapidly as the social influence of digital media has spread across mainstream culture, with individuals who would have remained 'micro' celebrities now competing with, and surpassing, many traditional celebrities in popularity, especially as far as younger audiences are concerned.

In this opening chapter, I dig into the rapidly expanding academic literature to unearth some clues as to how we might understand the nature of celebrity in its contemporary form. Is celebrity really something that originated with cinema and broadcast media? What about the claim that the cultural conditions for celebrity emerged as far back as seventeenth century Restoration Theatre (Studlar, 2015)? Is there actually one single, unitary concept of celebrity that covers all periods, media cultures, and spheres of activity? Or is celebrity one of those words, like 'community' (Potter & Reicher, 1987), which can only be understood through the rhetorical force of its actual use, which may vary from moment to moment, even in the mouth of the same speaker? It would seem that the best place to start is to examine some definitions of the term.

DEFINING CELEBRITY

How has celebrity been defined by those who have studied it? One of the first things that becomes apparent when surveying the many and varied definitions in the literature is that no single definition has succeeded in accounting for all the individuals we habitually lump together under the term. As Driessens (2015) points out, we should at least be grateful for those writers who make the effort, but something is always missing.

Celebrity as Talk, Text or Sign

Luckhurst and Moody (2005, p. 1) begin their historical study of theatrical celebrity with these words: "Celebrity, the condition of being much talked about". Definitions don't come pithier than that, but clearly "being much talked about" is insufficient to capture all aspects of the phenomenon. For a start, who does the talking? Where? And exactly how much is required to create the condition of celebrity? Maybe Luckhurst and Moody are wise not to over-complicate matters. After all, researchers commonly adopt quantitative methods to ascertain just how famous a person is. In one study, van de Rijt, Shor, Ward, and Skiena (2013) amassed a corpus of names cited in various media and found that, across different domains, a subset of names enjoyed remarkable durability over time. It could be argued, alternatively, that these researchers were examining *fame* rather than celebrity *per se*.

The terms 'fame' and 'celebrity' are, more often than not, used interchangeably. In Giles (2000), I argued that they constitute two different phenomena. Fame is essentially a *social* process, by which individuals (or even their names) become well-known outside their immediate social circle. You can have fame in a school, or any organization; the Head Teacher is the usually the most famous individual in a school, followed by the class teachers (whose individual fame will vary for all sorts of reasons), but an individual student may, for whatever reason, eclipse the lot of them. Celebrity, I argued, is primarily a *cultural* phenomenon, which is why it has so often been associated with the media.

This brings us back to Luckhurst and Moody's (2005) definition and the issue of *where* celebrities are talked about. "Modern celebrity," argues Turner (2004, p. 8), "is a product of media representation," and it is often assumed that, unlike fame more broadly, celebrity requires some form of mass communication, preferably an electronic one. But many authors are not content to see celebrity as simply a by-product of electronic media. As Gamson (1994, p. 16) argues, "the basic celebrity motifs of modern America were composed long before the development of mass cultural technologies". Ultimately, it is the cultural formation brought about by mass representation that creates the conditions for celebrity to flourish, which enables such processes to take place as 'celebritisation' (the influence of celebrity on fields such as politics) and 'celebrification' (the process by which a private individual becomes a celebrity) (Driessens, 2013a).

The idea that celebrity transcends any specific medium or form of representation has led authors such as Marshall (1997, p. 52) towards a semiotic understanding of celebrity as both sign and text. This is 'talk' of a kind, but rather more complex and elusive than simply the citation of names in a newspaper. The semiotic definition allows us to cut across the various media in any time or place to see celebrity as a *discursive construction*, infused with various cultural and historical significations. If celebrity is, for example, "an extensive, industrialised, and inter-textual mode of gossip" (Goldsmith, 2009, p. 22), it can be said to perform essentially the same function for YouTubers like Zoella as for the Duke of Wellington in nineteenth century Britain.

But like Luckhurst and Moody's talk-based definition, this broad brushstroke doesn't really identify the essential distinction between celebrities and non-celebrities. Though it neatly describes the form that celebrity takes, at what point do all these signifiers produce celebrity for one person but only simple exposure for another? Perhaps it is not the amount of talk that goes on about them as much as the *nature* of that talk. Christine Geraghty (2000, p. 187) has argued that a celebrity is "someone whose fame rests overwhelmingly on what happens outside the sphere of their work, and who is famous for having a lifestyle". This introduces a new dimension to the phenomenon: that of the 'work' the celebrity does. Rather than just being talked about, a celebrity needs to *do* something, whether or not it accords with our own particular work ethic.

This again, though, is only a partial definition because the nature of 'sphere' remains suitably vague. Geraghty is essentially talking about the distinction between a television personality, whom we always encounter in the workplace (the televisual sphere) and a sports performer like George Best who became a tabloid fixture long after his football career had nose-dived. Would Best have become a celebrity in the first place were it not for his extraordinary skill in his sphere of work? And, in such a media-saturated, high-profile sport as football, does the sphere of work consist solely of the pitch, training ground, and changing room? The modern footballer, in high-definition close-up on regular live television, is also (in England in 2018 at least) a permanent fixture on Twitter.

Geraghty's definition of celebrity makes it harder to fit to modern You-Tubers and influencers, whose sphere of work is inseparable from their lifestyle. The same limitation applies also to many modern television personalities, such as the late Jade Goody, whose private and public performances, including her intensely scrutinised terminal illness, were acted out on the same stage (Bennett, 2011). Either these new forms of media representation constitute something new and different from celebrity, or we need to rethink some of the category boundaries we have placed around the concept.

Celebrity as Lived Experience

Thinking about celebrities as *people* (rather than representations, signs or texts) who have jobs and lifestyles, we might favour definitions that emphasise its lived experience, such as Ferris's (2010, p. 393) claim that celebrity is "the experience of being recognized by far more people than one can recognize back"[1]. Ferris uses this definition to lay claim to the phenomenon of 'local celebrity' (celebrities who are famous only in a delimited geographical area), likening this to 'subcultural celebrity' (Hills, 2003), a category likewise constrained by shared (sub)cultural concerns. To these one could also add 'micro-celebrity', a term initially coined to describe the 'webcam girl' phenomenon of the mid-2000s (Senft, 2008) and later extended by Marwick (2013) and others to describe the limited fame of social media pioneers in the early Silicon Valley start-up scene.

On the whole, particularly in the emergent field of celebrity studies, the study of lived celebrity experience has not been the approach taken by researchers. It is undoubtedly the case that celebrities constitute a hard-to-access 'elite', yet it is still surprising so few scholars have engaged directly with the question of what it is like to be a celebrity. One exception to this is Rockwell and Giles (2009), where it rather helped that the first author (Donna Rockwell, a former media employee) had useful contacts in the entertainment industry. Our study of the phenomenology of fame identified several core elements, positive and negative, that best captured its lived experience: a loss of privacy, a sense of objectification ('entitization'), increased expectations from life, the gratification of certain 'ego needs', and the sensation of symbolic immortality. One could argue that these personal events arise out of the 'talk' already identified as constructing celebrity for society as a whole and which apply, to varying degrees, to all figures from international megastars down to Ferris's (2010) local celebrities.

Other definitions of celebrity have taken the watching audience, or 'public', as the focus. A kind of midway point is John Ellis's term for celebrity as 'being-in-public' (Ellis, 2015, p. 355), which extends the phenomenological theme by referencing Heidegger's concept of 'being-in-the-world'. For Ellis, media provide a public stage for individuals to act on, and the celebrity of the individual is that aspect of their performance

---

[1] This is a good example of my point earlier about fame and celebrity being used interchangeably because Ferris's definition maps closely on to my own definition of fame. In a later study of localebrity, Williams (2016) discusses the operation of low-key stardom in geographically bound communities where even a familiar local tramp may be talked about as a (non-mediated) form of celebrity. This fits with the idea that celebrity is primarily a talk-based phenomenon, in which case media are simply convenient channels for that talk.

visible to the audience. Like Geraghty's (2000) definition, Ellis's is rooted in the distinction between film and television stardom, the latter being more 'public' because the performer is acting in person rather than interpreting a character and a script. He has a little trouble applying it to digital forms of celebrity, however, arguing that social media enable everyone to have a public existence, but that "this does not mean that we are all celebrities now" (Ellis, 2015, p. 357). Celebrity, he suggests, still requires "the confines of the mass media", meaning radio, press, and television, and that social media can only perform an ancillary role.

Celebrity as Comparative Term

Ellis's differentiation between mass media and social media as two fundamentally different representational systems brings us to a central concern of this book. In chapter 2, I will develop a theoretical argument for treating social media first and foremost as media, but I want to turn briefly to sociological approaches that have defined celebrity in relation to its public status.

What constitutes 'the public', however, is no simple matter either. Rojek (2001, p. 9, his italics) has argued that celebrity is essentially about being "[tied] to a *public*" and how it involves "the attribution of glamorous or notorious status to an individual within the public sphere" (p. 10). So, this calls our attention towards another 'sphere', one that we all inhabit on a basis of inequality, certainly as far as glamour (or notoriety) is concerned. (These are, of course, those aspects of 'lifestyle' mentioned by Geraghty, but there is no sense in Rojek's definition of them being disassociated from the celebrity's sphere of work). The notion of the public sphere as a (mythical) place where celebrities become distinguished from 'ordinary people' is central to Couldry's (2003) theory of media rituals. The 'ritual media space' of traditional broadcast media allows these distinctions to be understood as 'natural', thereby reinforcing the essential powerlessness of the ordinary person.

Tolson (2015) has explored how this process operates in the promotional literature around media (in this case, television). Through a discursive analysis of terminology in *TV Times*, a British television listings magazine, he identified a trend whereby the preferred term for famous people on television shifted from 'personality' during the 1950s to 'celebrity' in the 1960s. He argues that this arose out of the increasing use of ordinary members of the public in gameshows and other TV formats, and that this constitutes evidence for Couldry's thesis that in these types of ritual events, the celebrity/public boundary becomes salient. Other studies of the inter-actional dynamics in shows where ordinary people participate under the control of a media professional (e.g. a presenter) have revealed the subtle ways in which this boundary is reinforced (Giles, 2002a; Smith, 2010).

How might celebrity in contemporary digital culture be understood as a function of media rituals? YouTube celebrity could be seen as a continu-ation of the trend whereby genres like reality TV reinforce the symbolic boundaries between celebrities and ordinary people. On the other hand, it could be argued that the various strands of social media have broken open the ritual media space to an extent that 'populist' politicians like Donald Trump can use Twitter and other outlets to attack 'the establishment'. In later work, Couldry has argued that social media have created a different mythical space conceived as "the place where 'we' come together" (Couldry, 2015, p. 621). As I will go on to argue in the next chapter, the success of Trump and other (apparent) political 'outsiders' may result partly from the failure, on behalf of voters and the mainstream press, to perceive social media *as media*.

Towards a Material/Discursive Approach to Celebrity

To recap, there seem to be three broad trends in defining celebrity that derive from different epistemological, or possibly disciplinary, positions. One is that celebrity is defined in terms of how it is talked about (a discur-sive definition); a second is that it is defined by its impact on the individual celebrity (a psychological or phenomenological definition); a third is that it is defined in terms of its impact on the public (a broadly sociological definition). To these we could add, finally, a more differentiated type of definition, which is conditional upon *where* celebrity is talked about, which I will consider in more detail in the next section.

I have been rather loose in my application of terms like 'discourse' and 'discursive' throughout this chapter so far, but there is such a range of interpretations in the literature (much of it disciplinary-bound, it must be said) that I did not think any further elaboration would be helpful. However, the closest theoretical position that can be identified to this definition of celebrity would probably be the 'material/discursive' approach of writers on psychological aspects of health and illness like Yardley (1996) and Ussher (1997). These authors see concepts like 'anorexia' and 'depression' as social constructions, existing primarily as language categories, meaningful only within a specific cultural/historical context. However, unlike purely relativist approaches to social construction (e.g., Edwards, Ashmore, and Potter, 1995), these concepts are acknowledged as material realities that constitute the lived, or 'embodied', experience of 'distress' for those individuals concerned. Applied to celebrity, the material/discursive approach enables us to treat it as simultaneously a discursive category applied to public (or famous) individuals *and* the condition of being-in-public (Ellis, 2015) for those individuals. It is this position that I will tend to favour throughout the remainder of the book. First, I want to try and disentangle one particularly thorny matter of terminology that has threatened the boundaries we place around the study of celebrity.

CELEBRITY VERSUS 'STARDOM'

One of the biggest problems in developing theory around celebrity, as Driessens (2015) has pointed out, is that nobody can agree on exactly which people should be considered celebrities. Of course, different definitions of celebrity will inevitably throw up different exclusionary criteria. It is quite possible, for example, if employing a discursive definition of celebrity, to consider non-human figures as celebrities, such as animals and fictional characters (Giles, 2013a). Ones that are based on broad ideas about cultural formation that override the communication potential of different media allow us to go far back in history to the Romantic era (Mole, 2007) or further still (Luckhurst and Moody, 2005).

Even definitions of celebrity tied to twentieth century media, such as Schickel's (1985), can generate debate around who is and who is not a celebrity. Is the President of the United States a celebrity? Donald Trump is indisputably a celebrity, having risen to fame as an entrepreneur and host of TV show *The Apprentice*, but Barack Obama? George W. Bush? Many authors attempt to put some meaningful distance between 'public figures' and celebrities, implying that the former are somehow necessary for society while the latter are an indulgence peculiar to post-industrial (or mediatised?) society (Boorstin, 1961; Friedman, 1999; Schickel, 1985).

But this overlooks the cult of personality that has developed around charismatic leader figures since Alexander, exploited most effectively of all in societies that ironically espouse a philosophy of collectivism, Stalin's Soviet Union and Mao's communist China, to cite but two spectacular examples (Edwards and Jeffreys, 2010; Pisch, 2016).

Even if we allow that politicians can be celebrities, we still need to differentiate between those politicians who are celebrities and those who are not, either because their fame is limited to their constituency (their sphere of work, perhaps), or because they have not (yet) acquired the degree of media representation that is the prerequisite of celebrity status. Street (2004, p. 449) has identified the 'celebrity politician' as one who "seeks to realise a form of political attractiveness through the gestures and images of popular culture". On the face of it, this would seem to fit with Geraghty's (2000) definition of celebrity, except that it ascribes an agentic role to the individual: for a politician, it suggests, celebrity is something that can be determined at will. But just how far do the "gestures and images of popular culture", for example appearing on stage with a rock group, take politicians from their sphere of work?

Celebrity as Vulgar Modernity

The idea that we could divide politicians into pure, noble representatives of the people and shameless, vote-grabbing celebrity politicians introduces another dimension into our attempts to define celebrity: the idea that there is something vulgar, and possibly immoral, about celebrity. As Turner (2004, p. 4) and others have pointed out, the word 'celebrity' is frequently used in a pejorative sense to signify "a culture that privileges the momentary, the visual and the sensation over the enduring, the written, and the rational". In the same way that the 'celebritisation' of fields like politics and the arts is used synonymously with other pejorative terms like 'dumbing-down', so many people's lists of celebrities would differentiate individuals whose fame is seen as worthy or meritorious from those who are well-known largely through their visibility in various media. Such is the nature of probably the most famous definition of all that has been applied to celebrity, Daniel Boorstin's (1961, p. 58) claim that a celebrity is someone who is "well-known for their well-knownness". Ironically, it could be argued that the fame of this definition is largely down to its ubiquity rather than its saying anything profound about the phenomenon.

Boorstin's work, *The Image*, from which this quote is taken, was the first of many books, scholarly and popular, that have identified the emergence of broadcast media after World War II as a turning point in Western civilisation. Prior to this point, it is argued, individuals earned fame through performing great deeds, be they military, political, artistic or philanthropic; beyond this point, seemingly anyone can earn fame through appearing on television, being talked about in the newspapers, or, in the present century. making a noise on social media. There are some, and I think it is fair to include Braudy (1986) in this group, who find it difficult to credit this high media visibility with the word 'fame' at all. (In Braudy's conclusion he suggests that 'modern fame' is essentially a vulgar parody of historical fame.) For these authors (see also Postman, 1985; Schickel, 1985; Rein, Kotler, and Stoller, 1987), fame is historical, timeless, and worthy; celebrity is modern, ephemeral, and generally worthless.[2]

Quite clearly, this understanding of affairs relies on a media-centred definition of celebrity that rejects the claims of Mole (2007), and others who have located the emergence of the phenomenon in the Romantic period or before. Either these authors have simply identified a celebrity-*like* culture residing in limited contexts (such as the Restoration theatre), or fame itself might not be quite so lofty a status as imagined. Braudy's (1986) history of fame makes it quite clear that from ancient civilisation onwards, fame is essentially *amoral*. At various points in time, the god-dess Fama is depicted with two trumpets: one for broadcasting noble deeds, the other for scurrilous gossip. Reputation has not always been well-earned. There is also a degree of randomness about the process by which great names become established: even an undisputed genius like J.S. Bach had to be 'discovered' (by Mendelssohn, who rewrote parts of the St. Matthew Passion to make it palatable to the early Romantic audi-ence; see Boyd, 2000).

Then there is Hollywood. Cited as the moment when the publicity machine really assumed the form that it was to take throughout most of the twentieth century, much of the discourse and iconography around celebrity can easily be traced back to the myth-making practices of the inter-war

---

[2] It is notable that these particular arguments were more prevalent in the 1980s, and are seldom voiced in serious literature today, particularly among scholars of celebrity. Perhaps one is unlikely to take up research in a field where one has such a poor opinion of the subject.

studios (Gamson, 1994). If, as Boorstin and others have argued, celebrity itself, in all its vulgar worthlessness, did not emerge until the advent of television, the birth of rock 'n' roll, and other allegedly debased cultural forms, what label should be applied to the famous pre-war Hollywood actors? The answer: *stars*.

Stars and Star Studies

If celebrity studies is a twenty-first century discipline, 'star studies' has been in evidence since the 1970s. Dyer's seminal (1979) work *Stars* is an obvious reference point here, but the disciplinary foundations had already been laid by Alberoni (1972) and Walker (1970)[3]. Dyer's contribution was, through the application of a semiotic/discursive approach, to foreground film stars' social and ideological function, arguing that they should not simply be understood in their filmic context but in their broader social context through their appearance in other media, such as magazines and billboard advertising. This approach enabled the study of stars to spread to other domains; to some extent, Dyer's work acted as the cornerstone for Marshall's (1997) broader study of celebrity.

Though most authors agree that the word 'star' was first applied to theatre actors in the 1820s (indeed Cavicchi, 2007, argues that it represents the moment that individual actors became renowned independently of act- ing troupes), film scholars have largely appropriated the term as the most appropriate label for movie actors. This is probably because the academic literature on stars has been developed in film studies and until recently has only been discussed further in relation to television. Scholars interested largely in film have tended to scoff at the idea that small screen perform- ers might be accorded star status. Indeed, Bennett (2011, p. 15) describes film scholars' beliefs about "the impossibility of television stardom" as a 'mantra' challenged by his own work and that of other television scholars (Jermyn, 2006).

What is so special about film actors that grants them an exclusive right to the star label? One argument is that film stars inhabit more than one identity; they perform as the characters they portray (in films) and as

---

[3] see also King (1985) and DeCordova (1990); a useful recent overview of the field is Shingler's (2012) *Star Studies: A Critical Guide*.

themselves (their representation in texts outside films). Therefore, their text has to be 'read' across more than one persona (Dyer, 1979). Television performers, typically thought of as the hosts or presenters of shows, only perform "as themselves" (Bennett, 2011). Even when they play a character, as in a soap, they are, as Butler (1991, p. 81) has argued, "practically treated as ciphers for the character". One counter-argument here is that, particularly in the United States, television drama has increased in quality over the years to be placed on an equal footing with cinema, and its stars can no longer be relegated to the status of soap actors (Jermyn, 2006).

However, both these arguments hark back to the fame/celebrity distinction deriving from Boorstin and others, whereby stardom, like fame, is elevated to something earned through merit based on an aesthetic hierarchy of dramatic art. Dyer (1979, p. 185) concludes his work by arguing that analysis can only go so far to explain the "beauty and pleasure" he derives from his favourite performers. Indeed the word 'star' itself carries with it so many elitist associations (e.g. the performer who burns, shines, shimmers, and dazzles, and who is brought into being through other light sources, such as flashbulbs, silver screens, spotlights) that one can see why it would be clung on to as a metaphor in preference to the mucky, debased celebrity.

But what about those of us who derive beauty and pleasure from cultural products other than cinema? The star label is routinely applied to performers in popular music and sport though not politics or the arts. It is true that the intertextual representation of film actors prompts different questions about authenticity from those figures in other media, and because of the association between actors and the roles they perform, film star celebrity has different elements to the celebrity associated with being a 'television personality', such as a presenter. However, the elitism suggested by film scholars' ownership of the star label is challenged by James Bennett (2011), who offers a powerful defence for the work of television performers to be seen as skill of a medium-specific kind ('televisual skill'). I will return to this important work in later chapters, when exploring the specific skills of performers in digital media.

Industrial Aspects of Celebrity

Ultimately, the distinction between stars and celebrities may not have anything to do with beauty and pleasure at all but with their terms of employment. As Graeme Turner has observed, "when we conceptualise celebrity as something to be professionally managed, rather than discursively deconstructed, we think about it differently" (Turner, 2004, p. 136). The "narrative of discovery" (Ibid, p. 98) around stars is very much tied to the studio system of Hollywood and the idea that stars are 'chosen' (Shingler, 2012). A similar logic could be applied to popular music where, at least traditionally, record labels are usually accorded the power to select a handful of would-be stars from a potentially unlimited supply of talent. As with film, there is an expectation that the star is loyal to the company (while under contract, that is). Sport also operates within a similar structure of talent scouting, selection, and company (club) loyalty.

It is perhaps no coincidence that the term 'star' gets attached to these three domains much more readily than others, and that film, pop, and sport may be profitably contrasted with forms of celebrity that are rooted fundamentally in media representation: television's personality system and that of the traditional press (newspaper/magazine). In these latter forms, the individuals concerned are relatively free-floating and autonomous and only temporarily (if at all) contracted to organisations like television companies. This distinction might offer a further explanation of the way different descriptive labels have evolved over time. As the media landscape becomes ever more fragmented in the present century, it would seem that 'celebrity' might be a more appropriate term than star for the popular figures it produces (although even here it could be argued that there are now talent and management agencies at work in media like YouTube to try and control the production of that medium's own stars).

At the start of this section, I suggested that a discursive construction of celebrity enables us to consider all kinds of figures, from political leaders to animals, as celebrities. Like the professional management companies of film, pop, and sport, zoos operate their own star system in which certain individuals are 'discovered' (in the wild) and then offered up for the gaze of the adoring public. The star text around such figures as Knut the polar bear and Paul the clairvoyant octopus (Giles, 2013a) draws strongly from the discourse around celebrity while at the same time working to promote the zoo (or parent entertainment company) with which the star is under contract. If animals, lacking any obvious agentic power, can be constituted as stars and celebrities, this suggests that both concepts are ultimately a matter of representation[4]. If we consider any system of representation, from coins, sculpture and painting through to electronic communication technologies, as a medium, we arrive at a definition of celebrity that includes famous individuals throughout history, human and non-human, in which the only unknown parameter is a quantitative one. How much (mediated) representation is required to render an individual famous or well-known?

The answer to this question depends entirely on the scale of interest. As Williams (2016) points out, even a familiar face in a village can attain a kind of 'localebrity' without any form of media representation beyond oral communication, but this means little to anyone outside that limited geographical area. One can define celebrity as contained by national boundaries or even regions, such as Flanders (the Flemish-speaking half of Belgium; van Gorp, 2014) where representation is restricted linguistically to the Flemish language press and broadcast media. Even on an international scale, the spread of any one celebrity's fame will be determined by common language and shared interest. Ultimately, then, any definitive list of celebrities will be shaped by the social and cultural context in which it is produced, but the pool of eligible names is wider than that conceived in most existing writing on the phenomenon.

THE MODERN DAY: WHAT DO WE MEAN BY THE DIGITAL ERA?

Having earlier worked up a material/discursive definition of celebrity that allows us to apply the term to anyone with sufficient media representation,

---

[4] Of course, there are other non-human figures besides zoo animals that are discursively constituted as celebrities. The representation of Mickey Mouse and other cartoon characters in theme parks such as Disneyworld and Peppa Pig World draws widely on celebrity discourse, and here, Geraghty's (2000) definition might be usefully adapted by substituting the term 'primary text' for 'sphere of work'. So, even though a representation of Mickey Mouse in a clearly defined text like a film or comic can be seen as confined to the primary text, a physical representation of Mickey Mouse (at Disneyworld, say) draws on a discourse of celebrity, meeting some of the requirements for Rojek's (2001) definition of celebrity as "tied to a public". This distinction could also be applied to extra-textual representations of non-human figures, such as a story that was widely reported in the British media when the yellow glove puppet Sooty, familiar to UK television audiences since the 1950s, was said to have hospitalised celebrity magician Paul Daniels by hurling a hot pizza at him while filming a TV show (Telegraph, 2011).

the task that remains is to specify the contemporary media landscape in which twenty-first century celebrity is manifest. Most of this work will be done in chapter 2, but I am aware that, as with the interchangeable use of terms like 'celebrity' and 'star', there is a danger of underspecification when glibly drawing on terms like 'the digital era', 'digital media' (as opposed to traditional or broadcast media), or, worse, increasingly obsolescent terms like cyberspace.

The problem with rapid technological and cultural change is that any all-inclusive term that differentiates the *now* from the *then* faces imminent death the moment it zips off to the printers. I have little alternative but to pick a convenient term and stick with it. At the same time, media theorists will argue that the distinction between these terms is non-trivial. For example, the use of digital media as a way of distinguishing 'new', social media from 'old' broadcast media has been criticised because radio, television, and cinema have not simply been supplanted by new media and are now themselves fully digitized (see Bennett & Strange, 2011). As will be discussed shortly, my use of 'digital' is more a matter of history than of technology. The same argument can be applied to discursive concepts like 'web 2.0', which fall apart once unpacked as technological definitions (Allen, 2012) but nonetheless serve as convenient cultural milestones for describing how different things started being done with technology past a certain point in time.

The authors of a recent cross-cultural ethnographic investigation into social media admit that the term social media is unfortunate because, like the telephone and telegram in the last century, they do not regard phenomena like Facebook as media at all; they have reluctantly adopted the term simply because it is in current usage and is widely understood in the very diverse populations they study (Miller et al, 2016). While I do not agree with the researchers' definitions of media (see chapter 2), I think this is a sensible position to adopt. One might even argue that the same is true of the word 'celebrity' as used in this book, and, indeed, much of celebrity studies.

So, to summarise, I use the term 'the digital era' to refer to the present century, during which all forms of media have necessarily become digitised to some extent; 'digital media' to differentiate contemporary media (including television, newspapers, and cinema) from broadcast media that are dependent on fixed schedules and limited scope for expanding beyond their primary texts; and 'digital culture' more broadly to describe the global cultural environment whereby anyone with access to the World Wide

Web can share, simultaneously, the same content irrespective of their geographical location (local censorship notwithstanding).

Given the above, I will argue that celebrity, as a form of representation tied in the last century to the 'discovery' narrative tied to the star systems of various artistic and media domains, is gradually shifting towards a system of representation that is more fluid and decentred, enabling different kinds of celebrity to emerge, with different relationships to their audiences. How these new kinds of celebrity are tied to emerging forms of media will be discussed in chapter 2. How they are tied to different kinds of audience, and the significance of their relationships with these audiences, is the concern of chapter 3.

2

TOWARDS A THEORY OF MEDIA AND AFFORDANCE

If celebrity is essentially constituted through the activity of media, one might conclude that Schickel is right: it is a twentieth-century phenomenon. However, this holds only if we believe media to consist solely of the holy trinity of press, radio, and television, a view that seems unsustainable in the twenty-first century (Couldry, 2009). But to what extent are 'new', 'social' media actually *media* in the twentieth century sense of the term? In this chapter, I will argue that the best way of understanding celebrity in the digital era is to think of social media as comprised of a host of diverse media that supplement, and often complement, traditional media, and that 'celebrity' will manifest itself differently according to the unique *affordances* of those media. This builds on ideas already discussed in chapter 1, notably Tolson's (2015) discursive approach to celebrity, incorporating two rather older theories that have not really informed celebrity studies to date.

The first of these is Marshall McLuhan's broad philosophy of media, in particular the ideas presented in *Understanding Media* (McLuhan, 1964). McLuhan is often cited in relation to digital media, typically by way of concepts like 'global village', but most often in passing, without much serious consideration of his work. He is often caricatured as a 'technological determinist' who believed that the influence of media could be divorced from all other social and economic forces, notably by Williams (1974) and Hall (1986), both key authors in cultural and media studies and instrumental in shaping those disciplines. In disciplines such as psychology, media are often reduced to vehicles for distributing timeless, universal content (typically unwelcome content, such as violence and prejudice). Media are simply embedded somewhere within the broad cultural landscape, one of several inseparable communication systems circulating meaning, inextricably entwined with the economic, ideological, and social forces which operate on them.

As Stevenson (1995) has argued, although many of McLuhan's ideas are either inconsistent or problematic, I believe it is important not to throw "the baby" out with "the bathwater" (Ibid, p. 126), and instead to retain those parts of his work that have held up across the decades. In relation to celebrity studies, I would argue that nobody else has offered a better account of the way that media enable (without actually *determining*) social change, and that the definition of celebrity outlined in chapter 1 is best understood within this framework.

Before I get on to McLuhan's work itself, I want to deal with the issue of technological determinism and its limitations with regard to the study of social media. In the last chapter, I briefly alluded to a group of anthropologists studying social media use worldwide (Miller et al, 2016) who claim that Facebook, YouTube, and others are not media at all, but 'social networking sites' whose aggregated usage they term 'polymedia'. Studying Facebook alone is pointless because its members do not restrict their activity to that one site, and the content endemic to one site may, over time, migrate to another. Social media, Miller et al argue (2016: x), "should not be seen primarily as the platforms upon which people post, but rather as the contents that are posted on these platforms". Anyone in agreement with Marshall McLuhan's famous claim that "the medium *is* the message" might reject Miller et al's suggestion on these grounds alone[1], though Miller is correct to point out that 'social media' is merely a colloquial term which has come to be adopted by the general population. Very little literature has

---

[1] Miller et al (2016) make a lot of good points following from their excellent comparative ethnographic research about the irrelevance of the online/offline divide, and the datedness of early theories of online behaviour, which were mostly based on the idea of user anonymity. They also claim, correctly, that social media are intrinsically about human behaviour, rejecting the fanciful and equally dated notions of the 'posthuman'.

considered the extent to which social media might be *media* in any traditional sense of the word[2].

Partly this is due to a broader reluctance to nail down media to a strict definition, the same kind of tangle that I tried to unravel around 'celebrity' in chapter 1. Miller et al's position on social media derives from their argument that, historically, media were either public or private (contrasting, say, television with the telephone), and that social media occupy some intrinsically interactive middle ground that serves communication and information needs. The title of Miller et al's 2016 book is *How the World Changed Social Media*, an explicit rebuttal of the regularly-trumpeted claim that social media have changed the world, itself a contemporary version of the 'dominant account' of technological determinism peddled by popular culture (MacKenzie & Wajcman, 1999). Miller et al's ethnographic research has detailed how Facebook is used in different ways across the world and by different groups within those locations, leading the authors to assume that it is society, in its various manifestations, that determines media use rather than vice versa.

A complementary argument to Miller et al's 'polymedia' theory is that social media are actually indistinguishable from traditional mass media, and the issues around 'interactivity' have been overplayed. As earlier writers on radio and television, such as Brecht (1932/1979) and Benjamin (1963) argued, even these media have the *potential* to be used interactively and indeed in some instances have been, such as CB radio. However, in Western culture at least, these can be seen as marginal issues well away from the mainstream. Ultimately, it is the prevailing cultural and political climate that shapes technological development, serving the interests of those in power. As Fuchs (2014: 11) puts it, "corporate, military or state interests often stand above the communicative interest of humans".

A way of escaping the equally deterministic trap of seeing media simply as a conjuring trick used by elites to maintain power is to introduce a

---

[2] At the other extreme, some scholars have argued that the term "social media" is merely clever marketing by the likes of Mark Zuckerberg, and that Facebook etc are simply "a proxy for social interaction" (Couldry & Van Dijck, 2015, p. 3). This position, in which interaction in social media is framed as exploitation by some all-seeing 'Big Other' seems to me as essentially reductionist as the traditional media effects construction of the media user as the passive victim of unscrupulous propaganda pushed by Hollywood and other media institutions for commercial profit.

second theory, J.J. Gibson's (1979) concept of 'affordances'. Affordance theory addressed a different kind of dualism, separating the human from the physical, or 'natural', environment. This might not seem at first glance to have much to do with social media, although surprisingly enough the concept of affordances is ubiquitous in writing about social media and technology more generally, largely because Gibson's ideas have been enthusiastically adopted within the field of design and technology (following the work of Norman, 1988), as well as in computer-mediated communication and new media (Hutchby, 2014). In the process, some of Gibson's original ideas have been rather distorted. In applying them to social media as media rather than as technology, I hope to reinvest affordance theory with some of its original intentions.

McLUHAN: PUTTING THE MEDIUM BACK INTO SOCIAL MEDIA

Though some of McLuhan's insights have not aged well, his fundamental understanding of a medium is relevant for the study of celebrity. His entire intellectual project was, in a sense, a reaction against the functionalist notion of the mass media as simply a series of technological advances that have allowed society to circulate the same 'content' in faster, more colourful and efficient ways. I will go on to illustrate this with some specific examples of functionalist thinking in relation to media and content, but essentially, McLuhan's theory requires us to understand media in historical terms, taking us back to the origins of human civilisation and the development of things like tool use. For McLuhan, objects like wheels, clocks, and electric lighting can be constituted as media because each enabled our ancestors to extend themselves, adapting and shaping those objects to bring about profound social change (McLuhan, 1964).

Seen as the twentieth century equivalents to a wheel (or, say, the printing press or the car), television and radio are more than mere 'windows on the world', circulating content in auditory or visual modes. They are catalysts for changing the way humans think about themselves and one another and about what is possible in the future. In McLuhan's (1964: 9) words, "the medium shapes and controls the scale and form of human association and action". Just to illustrate the point, the electric light was not devised to enable all-night clubbing, nor was the car invented to allow out-of-town shopping malls. Those uses (which we will go on to consider affordances of the electric light and car respectively) came later, once social change, driven by ideological and economic interests and allied to technological development, made them possible.

McLuhanism vs Functionalism

Much of the research in disciplines like psychology and communication derives ultimately from functionalist theories, such as the 'two-step flow' of mass communication (Katz & Lazarsfeld, 1955). In functionalist thinking, media are reduced to a set of intrinsic design features (meaning the 'technological affordances' that I will go on to critique in the next section). Functionalism argues that each new medium renders its predecessors redundant by making communication faster, easier, more lifelike and more amusing. Journalists write copy about a future in which the new medium has obliterated the old ways of life because this is how the medium has been marketed. But nobody really knows how successful the new medium will be because its cultural impact will take several years to emerge. Rather than waiting, the manufacturers will be working on another new medium that is intended to do something else.

Nevertheless, many media commentators and academics persist with functionalist thinking because their concept of media is subordinate to their concept of other things: neuroscience, society, ideology. These other things are seen as invariants (to draw on another Gibsonian concept): timeless, universal properties of the world, fundamentally the essence of human nature. People will always (want to) do the same things, and media are simply transitory tools for enabling them to do them faster, more easily and more amusingly.

> *Human beings are not sponges; they do not simply soak up the material presented to them online. At a bare minimum there is some level of interpretation of content to which they are exposed, and to which they respond or ignore. The internet is a two-way road; it can only thrive and exist through the content which people create and provide when using it. Think about websites such as YouTube which can only exist if people continue to post and share material. If no one uploads*

content, then there would be nothing to watch, nothing for a
viewer to perceive, interpret or respond to. (Attrill, 2016: 15)

The above passage, taken from a text in the series *Palgrave Studies in Cyberpsychology*, neatly illustrates the dualistic nature of functionalism, which constructs human nature and technology as separate entities, so the Internet represents an empty vessel, waiting to be filled with meaning in the form of timeless and universal content. This derives directly from the behaviourist tradition of media effects research, where cultural activity, or media use, is reduced to a series of inputs and outputs, or stimuli and response (Bryant & Zillmann, 1994). Seen from this angle, YouTube is the empty vessel to be filled with content that would previously have been broadcast on television or otherwise tweeted, e-mailed or telephoned.

Functionalist thinking leads to continual claims that the Internet is directly responsible for all manner of contemporary social ills, that its excessive use impoverishes human relationships, and that it is a 'substance' to which one can become addicted (Kuss & Griffiths, 2015, another book in the Palgrave series). Long before the advent of cyberpsychology, functionalist thinking was responsible for millions of dollars spent on researching the effects of media violence, and the same theoretical assumptions have since been exported from research on cinema and television to the study of computer games (Ferguson, 2015). Violence is an inevitable part of human nature, functionalism claims; it simply manifests itself differently according to the medium that represents it.

"The medium is the message" (McLuhan, 1964) is a chapter heading often quoted though rarely reflected upon by authors in the social sciences and humanities. When it does get quoted, it is often taken literally and used as a straw man (Edwards & Potter, 1992) to provide an easy target for a counter argument. In one longitudinal study that examined the relationship between television viewing at age five with subsequent adolescent behaviour, the straw man was knocked down as a kind of post hoc rejoinder: "Marshall McLuhan appears to have been wrong. The *medium* is not the message. The *message* is the message!" (Anderson et al., 2001, p. 134). However, the design of this study was fundamentally incapable of testing McLuhan's theory because the authors assumed that "the medium" simply meant "the technology" and so compared meaningful TV viewing (violence, etcetera) with overall TV viewing. A classic functionalist error.

From a media effects perspective, the message is violence even though the medium is simply the technology that broadcasts the violence (manifesting as a Hollywood action movie, a gangsta rap lyric, or a racist rant on YouTube). More broadly, functionalism leads us to castigate the medium itself for reproducing the message, and effects researchers worry about how best to prevent the message from reaching the ears and eyes of people more susceptible than themselves. But suppose the message turns out not to be the violence after all?[3]

What is a Medium?

The real significance of McLuhan's theory for studying twenty-first century celebrity lies in its definition of a medium. In its quest for the study of timeless universals, much social scientific research identifies the medium as *the Internet,* or even simply *online communication*. This is typically the approach of researchers interested in 'health information seeking' (e.g. Singh, Fox & Brown, 2016), where the Internet is cast as a risky, external space filled with unreliable content and is unfavourably contrasted with official health advice issued by authorities such as the World Health Organization (whose authority is undermined by this alien source). However, the Internet contains so much information, one is constantly prompted to ask "which bit of the Internet" is the real problem. Medical professionals, even in the midst of a consultation, commonly seek information online on those aspects of medicine in which they are not expert. The concept of 'the dark Internet' has been coined to deal with this problem, setting up another wholly unhelpful dualism in the process.

The question of whether the Internet constitutes a mass medium in itself was posed by Morris and Ogan (1996) at a time when worldwide adoption stood at a mere 25 million users and the computer-mediated communication (CMC) field was still in its infancy. The authors argued that communication researchers' failure to consider the Internet a medium prevented

---

[3] See Barker and Petley (2001) for a cogent critique of the 'media violence' literature, in which the authors make the reasonable point that one could chop countryside scenes out of films and probably claim, on their use as stimuli in laboratory experiments, that countryside images in media have a beneficial effect on viewers!

them from developing a theoretical literature on its communicational properties. One useful criterion for defining a medium as a *mass medium* is
the point at which a 'critical' level of adoption is reached in the population, typically between 10 and 20 per cent (Valente, 1995). With the global
Internet penetration rate passing 50 per cent in 2016 (Internet World Stats,
2016), this certainly qualifies the Internet in terms of critical mass.

However, it may be time to consider whether it is any longer *useful*
to consider the Internet as a medium when some of its constituent parts
have already passed Valente's (1995) critical threshold. In 2016, for example, over half the UK population (30–40 million, depending on source)
were members of Facebook, with Twitter and Instagram boasting around
half of that figure, still comfortably above 10–20 per cent of the population. Moreover, these platforms have become well-established, celebrating
their tenth anniversaries in recent years. Perhaps most importantly, following McLuhan's idea of media as 'extensions of [sic] man', each platform
affords its users unique communication features that foster multiple adoption, in the same way that television viewers have continued to listen to the
radio and read newspapers. If we think of Facebook as primarily a medium
rather than just an online community or a spectacularly big social network
(in which the technology simply enables people to do the things they have
always done), we can also think of it having its own distinctive culture and
history that can be explored for its own sake (Brügger, 2015).

Following on from this, we can see how thinking about Twitter as a
medium rather than simply a communication technology affects the way
we study people's behaviour on it. Perhaps its most characteristic feature
(until November 2017, at which point it was doubled) was the 140-
character limit placed on individual tweets. Twitter was originally modelled
on short message service (SMS) text messaging protocols, and short texts
were thought to be more compatible with cellular administration systems
(Rogers, 2014). It was initially conceived as a 'microblogging' platform
(and some authors still refer to it as such even though the company itself
has dropped the term) in that the character limit imposes restrictions on
the length of each communication. It is a deliberate element of the design
that shapes the content.

If (pre-2018) Twitter can be thought of as a medium with its own distinctive culture, the 140-character limit can be regarded as an *opportunity*
rather than a limitation. It has fostered the evolution of a unique style
of communication (the tweet) that, in turn, promotes a unique style of

interaction. However, authors in fields such as communication and linguistics have routinely referred to the 140-character limit as a 'constraint' that impedes communication, and demands "the need to abbreviate and omit elements of the messages" (Scott, 2015: 9). Clearly this was also the view of Twitter because the decision to allow tweets to double in length was presumably based on marketing logic. Notwithstanding this, in the trial period preceding the 280-limit rollout, 95 per cent of tweets remained within the original 140-character limit (Duckett, 2017).

Ultimately, the belief that Twitter's 300,000+ users felt 'constrained' by the 140-character limit is a functionalist assumption that regards face-to-face talk as an idealised model of human communication that is compromised by any kind of technology use. Even the term 'microblogging' suggests that what users really want to do is to blog, and are then forced to rein in their habitual verbosity to satisfy Twitter's perverse demands, like poets in a Haiku competition who would rather be writing *Paradise Lost*. Much the same assumption has been made for years by authors in the human-computer interaction (HCI) literature, where online communication is often portrayed as 'impoverished' because of the absence of non-verbal gestures and facial expressions (Siegel et al., 1986). If 140-character tweets are simply messages with certain 'elements' omitted, then Twitter users have thus far been trapped in an inefficient and cumbersome communication network, and it is a wonder that the platform still exists at all.

Alternatively, we could see the 140-character limit as an *affordance* of Twitter. This does not mean to say that the character limit enables its users to communicate in a better or more efficient way than on any other medium, but that through its limitations we have cultivated a new style of interaction that has, in turn, opened other possibilities for social action. It remains to be seen whether the 280-character limit will generate new affordances, or whether the gradual adaptation to a less distinctive style of communication eventually results in a loss of uniqueness (and, ultimately, a drift towards rival social media).

GIBSON: RESCUING AFFORDANCE THEORY FROM THE OBJECT-CENTRED PERSPECTIVE

The literature on online communication abounds with the term 'affordances'. Online communication generally is described as affording Internet users multiple opportunities to interact on a global stage, construct desirable and attractive identities, and have their contributions frozen for posterity in searchable form (boyd, 2010). But if social media can be broken down into discrete, distinctive, and complementary media, we can see each medium as possessing unique affordances that account for its distinctiveness, its commercial success and its corresponding cultural survival.

Although many authors cite Gibson's original writings (e.g. Gibson, 1979) as the source of affordance theory, it is far from normative practice in the social science and humanities. Even in psychology textbooks, Gibson's theories have often been hopelessly misinterpreted (Costall & Morris, 2015). In media and communication research, the work of Norman (1988) tends to be privileged, through which Gibsonian theory underwent some adaptation to be applied to systems design, or the enhancement of 'user-friendliness'. In this tradition, affordances have become properties of objects, such as 'grab handles', rather than the outcome of a reciprocal relationship between an organism and its environment. In much of the writing on social media, affordances are discussed as design features that platforms introduce to please their users, such as hashtags on Twitter.

We must not overlook that Gibson's original theory of affordances aimed to account for basic survival behaviours, such as the ability of gannets to swoop and spear fish swimming in a river. At the human level, many of the behaviours afforded by aspects of the environment are simple actions like grasping and climbing. Even in Norman's updated, object-centred adaptation, the human behaviours under consideration rank low in Maslow's (1943) hierarchy of needs: cooking, door opening, and so on. The application of affordance theory to communication media takes us a lot higher up the pyramid. Designing a platform like Facebook or Twitter is not like designing cooker knobs or door handles. To see Twitter as possessing 'reduced affordances' (Zappavigna, 2012, p. 95) because of its character limit again raises the question of what sort of user appeal one might expect it to have, or what other forms of communication it might be seen as competing against.

Looking at social media more generally (as compared to traditional communication practices in the work environment), Treem and Leonardi (2012) identify four affordances of social media, which are qualities that differentiate social media use from more general forms of CMC: visibility, editability, association, and permanence. These are, in a broad sense, technological affordances of all social media; they are the features of the various platforms which invite users to perform certain functions (and are generally used accordingly). Across such a wide range of media, this remains a largely object-centred approach. Though a broad overview may be useful in an organisational context (such as Treem and Leonardi's) or for researchers largely concerned with technological aspects of social media, it masks important differences between those media that may well be significant when accounting for the different forms of celebrity that each enables.

A more directly relevant development of affordance theory has been proposed by Hutchby (2001), who applies it more widely to technological forms or artefacts such as computers, as a way of negotiating another kind of dualism between social constructionism and technological determinism. From the former perspective, authors such as Grint and Woolgar (1997) have argued that technologies should be understood as texts, or *tabulae rasae* (blank slates), whose functions are only given meaning by the way they are used. On the face of it, this position is similar to McLuhan's: it allows a manufacturer to produce a new piece of software that is intended to compete against other social media but is then adopted by users to perform a unique and entirely different function. But Hutchby argues that any new technological artefact possesses *some* affordances even if they are not the ones that users eventually engage with. The telephone was initially envisaged as a broadcasting device: users would be able to listen to, say, a concert through their handsets (Hutchby, 2014). But once they found they could use the telephone to talk with one another, the affordance of broadcastability was trumped by the affordance of long-distance conversation[4]. (Of course, the development of mobile phone technology has since reversed this process, turning the telephone into a micro-computer for receiving online communication.)

Which qualities of media constitute affordances? Hutchby (2014, p. 87) defines affordances as "the practical uses that anything... makes available for participants... they enable (and constrain) the engagement in some activity; they shape the conditions of possibility associated with

---

[4] Occasionally through its history, the landline telephone has afforded broadcast of information: for instance, the General Post Office in the United Kingdom offered various services in the 1960s and '70s such as 'the speaking clock', the weather forecast, and Dial-a-Disc, where the current top 10 pop singles were broadcast in rotation, much to the annoyance of parents and others who had to pay the resulting bills.

an action". Though obvious features like anonymity have a clear impact on communication, because comment streams on online newspapers will inevitably contain more abusive communication than found in platforms like Facebook where users are named and photographed, the affordance concept can be applied more widely. Stommel and te Molder (2015), for example, compared the interaction in normal online (chat) counselling sessions with those sessions in which the clients had uploaded their answers to a 'pre-screening' question. They found that pre-screening information had a significant effect on the course the online chat took, not always for the best, and argued this could be regarded as an affordance of Internet Relay Chat (IRC).

One might argue this isn't quite the kind of affordance that Gibson had in mind when developing his theory. Indeed, he was notably reticent when it came to extrapolating his ideas to human behaviour more generally, aiming at a pre-linguistic concept that could extend to all organisms (Costall, 1995). If we were to adhere strictly to Gibson's own writings, we would not be able to apply affordance theory to any kind of social or technological issues. So, as with McLuhan, we must take what is useful and overlook the contradictions. For example, Gibson could never quite decide whether or not affordances existed independently of organisms although, ultimately, this is a metaphysical issue, like whether a falling tree makes a sound if no one is around to hear it.

At this point, I will bring together the theories of McLuhan and Gibson and explain their relevance to the study of media and, by logical extension, to the study of celebrity. McLuhan defined media as technologies whose meaning is generated by their cultural usage, which is a product of the characteristics of the medium itself rather than any 'content' it communicates through it. The social and cultural impact of television can be understood by comparing it to, say, the wheel or the electric light. Television's ability to broadcast moving pictures to the home has transformed the way that people perceive their position in society, their potential for action, and the kinds of people they can become. This is not simply because of the technical properties of television (which have evolved rapidly since its invention) but of the way television is used by its audience: as source of information, as topic of conversation, or even as meaningless, empty-headed entertainment. Bringing in Gibson here, these things are all the affordances of television.

Moving into the twenty-first century, we can use McLuhan's definition of media to identify the emergence of specific media among the many digital platforms available to Internet users. If we understand, say, Facebook as a medium in its own right, we can see how it has evolved from being an 'empty structure' to a cultural phenomenon with well over a billion registered users (Brügger, 2015). Along the way, its creators have introduced a multitude of technical and content-rich features, some of which have been spectacularly popular with users (the 'friending' concept perhaps being the most successful of all) even as others have failed, often because they simply mimicked an existing property of a rival medium (Hern, 2017). The former are, effectively, Facebook's affordances; some, like friending (or 'following' on Twitter) have become affordances of many other digital media even though others (like the 'Facebook official' relationship status) have remained unique to Facebook. The success or failure of a medium's technological features hinges precisely upon Gibson's notion of reciprocity: irrespective of the preferred affordances intended by the creators (or owners) of that medium, the actual affordances emerge out of the perceived match between user demand and technological characteristics. The complementary nature of this process, entirely consistent with McLuhan's definition of media, offers a resolution to any charge of 'technological determinism' that could be levelled at either theory.

One final point to make about affordance theory is that it is *relational* (Hutchby, 2014). A flight of steps affords climbing for one organism, but only if that organism is equipped with suitable apparatus. A non-swimmer cannot leave a sinking ship without any flotation equipment, so water does not by itself afford an escape route. What attracts one person to a social medium will repel another. The friending or following affordances of many social media provide a tremendous opportunity for self-aggradisement and the humiliating prospect of social rejection. Both outcomes emerge out of the relationship between the cultural or technological environment and the characteristics of the individuals that interact with it, and it is at this point that we can bring celebrity into the picture.

IMPLICATIONS FOR THE STUDY OF CELEBRITY

There is plenty of evidence from the celebrity studies literature that different media afford different kinds of celebrity. Whether *all* media afford some kind of celebrity is another matter entirely. The fact of illumination by an electric light does not enable individuals to become celebrated although, combined with the right cultural and historical conditions, it could be argued that celebrity began to emerge once individual performers could be picked out at a distance: the theatre spotlight has been identified as one of the technical innovations that led to the emergence of a celebrity culture in nineteenth-century theatre (Luckhurst & Moody, 2005). That certain social media, with their opportunities for glorifying the self and building an audience, afford celebrity is beyond doubt even if there has been a tendency to dismiss this as 'micro-celebrity'. It may be that the application of the description 'micro' derives from a reluctance to accept social media as media (and that *bona fide* celebrity requires coverage in the traditional media: newspapers and television). Here, I am arguing that contemporary forms of celebrity are no longer entirely dependent on the traditional media; indeed, the star of a television show on a little-watched channel may be more 'micro' than a YouTuber or Instagrammer with hundreds of thousands of international followers.

Perhaps the most striking comparison between celebrities operating in different media is the one made between televisual fame and cinematic fame by several authors (notably Bennett, 2008, 2011, and Ellis, 1982, 2015). I touched on the key arguments in chapter 1, but to incorporate affordance theory here, it could be summarized as cinema affording *stars* versus television affording *personalities*. As Langer (1981) first argued, the properties of the cinema screen (large, viewed at a distance in a public space) promote a different kind of celebrity from the small, intimate viewing environment of domestic television. Naturally, discursive borrowings occur from one to the other, so the iconography of film stardom is reproduced, sometimes ironically, in the context of television, the limo and 'red carpet' treatment for the at-that-point-unknown *Big Brother* contestants being one obvious example. But, as Costall (1995) argues, all objects have a social/cultural history, and this will always influence taking up their related affordances.

Marshall (1997) takes this distinction further by contrasting cinema and television fame in terms of those media's "various forms of signification" (p. 75), with the additional comparison of celebrities from the worlds of popular music and politics. Because Marshall is working in a semiotic tradition, with the 'sign' as his primary unit of analysis, he does not interpret the critical distinction between these forms of celebrity as the medium which enables the fame to take place. Like other cultural theorists wary of technological determinism, he warns that "making claims about the types of personalities that are produced by such a medium presents the danger of making an essentialist argument about the technology" (p. 122). Instead, he turns his attention to the "specific institutional sites of the culture industries" (p. 75), such as the Hollywood studio system and the record industry, which produce certain kinds of star owing to things like the rapid turnover of new and young pop performers required to satisfy the industry's demands for novelty.

Even though such economic concerns are undoubtedly important in influencing which types of individuals appear in the various media, my argument here is that the recording industry and political systems alone cannot generate celebrity without the considerable assistance of those media. Without the publicity of radio, television, and print media, it is hard to see how musicians and politicians would ever acquire anything more than a specialist audience. Even the origins of Hollywood stardom are usually traced to the emergence of the 'fan magazines' that cultivated public interest in actors and actresses in conjunction with the gossip columns of the established press (Gamson, 1992).

In the contemporary media environment, new forms of media afford their users the opportunity of celebrity without requiring representation in the traditional media of radio, television, and the press. As I will discuss in more detail in chapter 4, the kinds of celebrity afforded by the Internet as a generalized medium were initially described as micro-celebrity, largely because the potential audience was limited both in terms of population and sphere of activity. The original micro-celebrities were either 'camgirls' – that is prototype vloggers whose moment-by-moment existence was broadcast from their bedrooms via webcam (Senft, 2008) – or Silicon Valley entrepreneurs who had used their Twitter accounts to cultivate a following of over 50,000 members (Marwick, 2013). In the former instance, these were individuals who lacked a medium to promote them; in the latter, the nascent medium (Twitter, Facebook, or whatever) was still some way short of the 10–20 per cent population reach required to qualify as a mass medium. 'Micro' was an appropriate prefix for these figures. Genuine celebrity still required coverage in *The New York Times* and network television.

A decade later, the media landscape has changed. Social network sites are no longer the preserve of a few tech-savvy users, and YouTube is full of people broadcasting their 'ordinary' lives to an audience of many millions across the planet. Though micro-celebrity could, conceivably, be regarded as an affordance of the Internet *per se*, the enormous popularity of discrete online platforms forces us to separate the affordances into the relevant parts of the Internet. As Marwick (2015, p. 138) argues, Facebook does not afford celebrity, as it "[constrains] self-presentation within a rigid profile structure". Instagram, Twitter, and YouTube, on the other hand, allow individuals more flexibility for 'self-branding' and are associated with different kinds of fame. 'Instafame', for example, has emerged as a property of the visual nature of Instagram, where individuals express themselves photographically, particularly by means of the 'selfie'. This means that certain types of individuals are privileged, typically those who are "conventionally good-looking, work in 'cool' industries such as modelling and tattoo artistry... and emulate the tropes and symbols of traditional celebrity culture" (Ibid, p. 139).

YouTube, meanwhile, affords a different kind of celebrity: vloggers, game commentators and comedians, who each require a certain kind of performance skill to cultivate and maintain a global audience that potentially numbers many millions. YouTubers and Instagrammers can generate so much wealth through their share in their relative platforms' advertising revenue they scarcely need to expand their activities beyond those media. They frequently do, partly because celebrities have always used their capital to cross into other fields (Driessens, 2013b) and because contemporary fame-seekers would be unwise to restrict all their online activity to a single medium. (So, YouTubers will typically have profiles on Facebook, Twitter and Instagram, with additional 'followers' on each to add to their core audience.)

Media do not just afford the opportunity for individuals to become famous. They also afford the opportunity for individuals to incorporate those famous people into their extended social networks. In the next chapter, I will discuss celebrity from the point of view of audiences and argue that contemporary media have begun to blur the distinction between celebrities and their followers (or 'fans'). Even though the term 'micro-celebrity' may no longer be a meaningful description of the likes of PewDiePie, with over 60 million subscribers to his YouTube channels, the practice of micro-celebrity–or 'self-branding' through online promotional activities–is engaged in by millions of social media users who may never accumulate more than a few thousand followers. But this is a few thousand more than they would have attracted in the pre-social media era.

Meanwhile, traditional celebrity is holding on to its allure, partly through the strategic use of new media in keeping established audiences engaged in the day-to-day activities of film stars, pop stars, and sports performers. But here again the affordances of social media–notably the zero-entry point of profile creation (everyone has zero followers when they open their Twitter account)–enable a different kind of relationship between celebrities and their audience. These new forms of media challenge the celebrity structure of broadcast media just as television broke down some of the barriers separating film stars from their audiences.

In the next chapter, I will focus on the affordances of media for that major portion of their users that are traditionally referred to as their audience. An affordance of broadcast and print media was the huge range of (para)social opportunities they opened up for users, enabling them to form relationships with important and exciting people they would never have had the chance to meet face-to-face. An additional affordance of digital media is the opportunity of making direct (albeit merely textual) contact with these same people. How these new affordances potentially shape the practice of celebrity, and users' experience of media, is a central concern of this book.

3

CELEBRITIES AND THEIR AUDIENCE(S)

In communication, audience researchers have for some time been mindful of the threats that new, digital, social media pose to the intellectual tools that have crafted their theories and methods for most of the last century. As one communication scholar (Neuman, 2016, p. 2) puts it, "the revolution in communication technology… makes possible a paradigm shift in how human communication is studied". Less dramatically, it is still argued that "questions of how media practices are meaningful to audiences-as-practitioners need rephrasing and… other forms of contextualization" (Hermes, 2009, p. 133).

The concept of audience, its etymology reflecting the practice of *listening*, is tied to the tradition of broadcasting, an association that informs the communication and media literature. The established model of sender and receiver has only been challenged by work that constructs audiences as 'active', whether in the quasi-psychological tradition of 'uses and gratifications' (Rosengren, 1974) or the encoding/decoding model (Hall, 1980) that has dominated most work in cultural studies. But 'active' in this sense is largely relative, prioritising the meaning-making practices of readers, listeners, and viewers over the 'passive' subjects of the behaviourist tradition, who are just black boxes 'responding' to 'doses' of decontextualised 'stimuli' delivered under controlled experimental conditions (Biocca, 1988). The idea of the media user as more than active, as a person capable of generating content, had no place in mainstream communication and media theory.

In one sense, this is somewhat perverse because the content generators of media have always been first and foremost members of the 'audience'; indeed, they were some of the most active and engaged members. Only with the emergence of fan studies in the 1990s had this rather obvious point been brought into the scope of audience research, with much interest in 'fan fiction' (fanfic) and other creative practices (Hellekson & Busse, 2006). Even at this stage, however, the conceptual boundary between production and reception remained impermeable: fanfic was something dabbled in by members of the TV audience even when it was quite clearly being produced for a specialist portion of that same broad audience. It was not until the content-generating potential of social media became impossible to ignore that researchers of these new audiences came up with a new conceptual model: the 'produser' (Bruns, 2008).

Likewise, celebrity studies has not have always worked on the assumption that celebrities and their audiences inhabit entirely separate universes, a dichotomy that has informed the semiotic approach of Dyer (1979), Marshall (1997) and others, rooted in film scholarship, whereby celebrities, whatever their human characteristics, function primarily as texts to be read and interpreted by other people. It has not helped, particularly in cultural and media studies, that in writing about celebrities as individual human beings (rather than texts), academic authors risk being positioned as uncritical participants in the cultural phenomenon under interrogation (Holmes, Ralph & Redmond, 2015). Only with the growing interest in television's personality system (Bennett, 2011 and so on), and the emergence of reality TV in the early 2000s, do we start to get a sense of a celebrity as a *person* who has crossed the audience/production boundary (Turner, 2010).

The realm of digital media that celebrities are now obliged to inhabit urges a significant re-think of this dichotomy. When initiating a personal profile on a site like Twitter even the most lauded of international superstars begins with zero followers. Faced with so humbling a prospect, many established celebrities have been slow and reluctant social media adopters. Some have failed to take the process at all seriously (Thomas, 2014). Others delegated the work to minions until they were no longer able to ignore the changing demands of the celebrity industry. The necessity for celebrities to maintain an authentic profile on social media has even resulted in a new badge of celebrity status: the 'official' blue tick that denotes a 'verified' profile on Twitter.

In this chapter, I revisit some of the most important concepts from the communication and media literature that have described and (partly) explained the nature of the relationship between celebrities and audiences and suggest some ways in which these concepts can be adapted for use in the contemporary digital environment. I will start by outlining the concept of parasocial interaction, a much-cited term in the communication and celebrity literature but one which has been under-theorised throughout most of its history and, perhaps as a result, often dismissed as 'pathologising', particularly in media and fan studies.

Parasocial Interaction: Irrational Behaviour or Routine Audience Activity?

The terms *parasocial interaction* and *parasocial relationship* were coined in a paper by Horton and Wohl (1956) to describe the 'illusion' of intimacy between performers in radio and television and the at-home audience. It took another two decades before communication and media researchers were to follow up on their observations and to build a literature based around empirical research. This was largely due to the efforts of Marc Levy, whose pioneering study of regional newscasters in the United States (Levy, 1979) incorporated focus group discussions and the creation of a short psychometric scale devised to measure the strength of parasocial interaction. This scale was revised and extended by Rubin, Perse, and Powell (1985) and has been used subsequently in hundreds of communication studies. Respondents (typically undergraduates filling out questionnaires for course credit) are asked to rate a number of statements relating to their 'favourite' media figure – in some cases, a fictional character.

In recent years, communication scholars have attempted to address some of the limitations of the parasocial interaction literature, particularly the conceptual distinction between interaction—the moment-by-moment sense of intimacy with media performers—and relationships, the persistent sense of knowing a media figure solely based on one-way media use. This has led to the creation of a new psychometric scale, the Experience of Parasocial Interaction scale (Hartmann & Goldhoorn, 2011), which explores viewers' responses to an actor on video. It is argued that this scale taps the psychological processes that ultimately lead to the formation of parasocial relationships, which are themselves better captured by the Rubin et al. (1985) scale (Dibble, Hartmann, & Rosaen, 2016).

Meanwhile, the concept of parasocial interaction is routinely cited in other forms of media research and celebrity studies as the explanatory mechanism for how celebrity-audience relationships evolve (Holmes & Redmond, 2006; Turner, 2004; Rojek, 2012, 2016). However, the concept, with its roots in the psychology of audience activity, does not always sit comfortably with a cultural or sociological approach, and occasionally those authors will take it to task for 'pathologising' audiences, particularly in the context of fandom. Within the fan studies literature, Jenson (1992) and Duffett (2013) devote a whole chapter to the pathologisation of fans, in which parasocial explanations are lumped together with popular stereotypes and other unsympathetic media coverage as part of a general tendency to depict fans as psychologically inadequate. Horton and Wohl's original conception is critiqued on three grounds: that mere fandom is seen as ultimately insufficient to meet the complex needs of fans; that attempts to contact celebrities are the inevitable outcome; and that fandom is essentially parasitical – parasocial relationships are indulged in for a vicarious share in their objects' glory.

Much of the criticism of parasocial interaction derives from the notion that these relationships function as substitutes for 'normal', 'healthy', face-to-face relationships. But communication researchers have long dismissed this as a simple explanation ever since Rubin et al (1985) found that parasocial interaction did not actually correlate with scores on a scale of loneliness. The more usual interpretation is that parasocial relationships function as additional friendships, and that media users seek out these figures because they resemble the friends they already have (Perse & Rubin, 1989). Likewise, patterns of parasocial interaction tend to reflect attachment styles so that those who score highest are more likely to have attachment styles characterized by anxiety and those at the bottom end are most likely to be 'avoidant' – of all relationships, including parasocial ones (Cole & Leets, 1999). In any case, there is no reason to assume that 'substitute' relationships are inherently unhealthy. Individuals can intentionally use media to generate idealized relationships, as has been found in some fan research (Stever, 2017), and adolescents may use parasocial interaction as rehearsal space for incipient adult relationships, particularly romantic ones (Giles & Maltby, 2004; Greene & Adams-Price, 1990).

A more widespread belief is that parasocial activity, being 'illusory', is fundamentally irrational, leading to the idea that fans are somehow 'duped' into believing they are in an actual social relationship with the celebrity (Holmes, Ralph & Redmond, 2015). There are some grounds for seeing this as a valid critique of the literature. For example, one of the items in Hartmann and Goldhoorn's (2011) Experience of Parasocial Interaction scale asks respondents, following a video screening session, to rate the statement 'I had the feeling that [the performer] was aware of me'. People scoring this item 'strongly agree' would, arguably, be under the false impression that their one-sided experience was somehow reciprocal. But nowhere else in the literature is it argued that such a belief is a necessary condition for parasocial interaction (Horton and Wohl, for instance, suggest that this would only happen in extreme circumstances).

It is true that, over the decades, parasocial interaction has suffered from a lack of refinement by researchers interested in the concept. I addressed some of its limitations in Giles (2002b), a paper written at a time when print, radio, and television were still the only media worth considering, and the parasocial relationship could be easily defined as one in which no reciprocation occurred (and in the case of fictional characters, no possibility of reciprocation). I argued that the concept's reliance on a psychometric scale asking respondents to rate items relating to their 'favourite' media figure placed enormous constraints around its theoretical development. Firstly, there was little attempt to compare ratings of different types of media figure. Whether figures are alive or dead, real or fictional, opens up all kinds of implications about the feelings we have for them. Secondly, any meaningful theory must allow for negative parasocial interaction, since there are many figures (particularly politicians) that we hate with a passion. Thirdly, ratings of one individual figure tell us little about the lived parasocial experiences of individual media users, most of us enjoying multiple relationships with media figures, positive, and negative. There is the additional constraint of limiting parasocial activity to private, cognitive events when, much of the time, our media use takes place in the company of others, and so there is a dialogical aspect to parasocial relationships. (We discuss media figures with our friends and even strangers and these discussions shape our personal feelings accordingly.)

I concluded my paper by sketching out a theory of the parasocial that attempted to locate it as one end of a social/parasocial continuum

Fig 1.

Most Intimate   Most Parasocial

Situation
Sex   Date   Job interview   Seminar Lecture   Watching TV news   Reading novel   Fantasy film

Medium
phone call   e-mail   reciprocated Tweet   unreciprocated Tweet

Potential relationship between interactants
Partner   Employer   Teacher   Fan/celebrity   Fantasy relationship

(see figure 1 above). My thinking here was that each encounter, in physical space or in mediated space, defines the possibilities for any relationship that could develop as a result of that encounter. At the extreme 'social' end there are face-to-face, intimate dyadic encounters: sex between cohabiting partners, for instance. At the extreme 'parasocial' end, remote encounters occur where there is no possibility of reciprocation: reading about, or viewing, a character in a fictional text that may not even be human (existing only in cartoon, or animal form). In between come a whole range of ambiguous, partly mediated encounters: groups of students listening to a lecturer or spectators watching a concert or sports fixture, or TV viewers watching an all-night 'reality' show in which the cameras are trained on the same individuals (and who are unambiguously real and contactable even though the latter would require considerable effort for most viewers). So, each encounter can be evaluated according to four properties: the number and nature of individuals involved; the distance between the interactants; the formality of the encounter; and the potential relationship that could result from that encounter.

I will return to this model later when factoring in the emergence of social media; for now, though, it remains one of a mere handful of attempts by researchers to address Horton and Wohl's (1956, p. 225) recommendation that psychologists "learn in detail how these parasocial interactions are integrated into the matrix of usual social activity". An alternative theory to bind parasocial interaction into everyday social interaction is that of Rojek (2012), who suggested that three elements differentiate the parasocial from the social: access, utility, and labour. Celebrities, unlike our actual friends, are always available via various media; they are infinitely useful to us; and (possibly as a consequence) we are prepared to invest considerable labour in the relationship. Hills (2016) argues that these elements make it impossible to compare celebrities with non-celebrities because their access and utility are shared across multiple individuals (our actual friends do not offer all their friends the same degree of access), and much of the 'labour' invested by fans is, likewise, communal (e.g. running and participating in fan clubs).

Rojek has extended his account of parasocial interaction further in his more recent work (Rojek, 2016) where he casts it, in almost dystopian terms, as part of a contemporary social landscape where media audiences are manipulated for political and economic purposes by various institutions and elites. From this standpoint, parasocial relationships are merely 'second-order' relationships with 'screen apparitions' that are so numerous as to be overwhelming, blunting our emotional responses. Unlike most other parasocial research, Rojek extends the idea of the parasocial well beyond encounters with specific, favourite, figures, arguing that this kind of remote interaction incorporates all our social cognitive responses to human figures, including the victims of disasters and terrorist attacks with whom news bulletins invite us to empathise.

Though Rojek's extended model of the parasocial has some useful implications (e.g. parasocial interaction has been long neglected in accounts of media framing: see Giles and Shaw, 2009), it ultimately rests on the assumption that media offer merely "fractured aspects" (Rojek, 2016, p. 1) of the real, and that social media and other online communities produce nothing more than the "illusion of being connected" (Ibid., p. 5). This is a common position among contemporary social scientists (not to mention people working in the traditional media, such as journalists), a standpoint from which online interaction is essentially fake, mere 'simulation' (of the offline, presumably) and a poor substitute for 'real', 'natural' human activity (Couldry & Van Dijck, 2015). Ultimately, such a position leads to the construction of an artificial social/parasocial "binary" (Hills, 2016) by which 'the social' is reified and 'the parasocial' devalued, always an unsatisfactory simulation of the real.

The Fan Studies Perspective

Quantitative communication researchers seem, for the most part, to have been satisfied with a single (if superficial) measurement to stand for parasocial interaction in large-sample, multivariate studies. Meanwhile, there has been a tendency in media and cultural studies to dismiss parasocial explanations for celebrity-audience relations. Partly this reflects the kind of research question favoured in these disciplines where the object of interest is often the media text (including celebrity) in question, and audiences are more likely to be studied in the context of fandom than for their general media use. As Turner (2004, p. 94) suggests, "the term 'parasocial'… may be useful in highlighting the difference between face-to-face relations and those provided through the media, but there are limitations to the usefulness of the term as a means of describing the quality and cultural function of such relations". However, in the way I have outlined parasocial interaction in this chapter, I can see no reason why, as an overarching framework, it might not be able to satisfy these requirements.

Alternative accounts of celebrity-audience relations centred around fandom tend to privilege explanations that view fandom as essentially rooted in practices of meaning-making and self-reflection or even a technology of the self (Foucault, 1988), like keeping a diary or blog or mastering a new skill. Sandvoss (2005) sees fandom as part of a project of self-development, by which "individuals recognize themselves in the signs and symbols of fan objects" (p. 158), and then incorporate those objects into their own personal identity or self-concept. This kind of self-development is not necessarily limited to critical periods in the lifespan (adolescence, for example) but can extend right through the life course (Harrington & Bielby, 2010). In his study of David Bowie fans, Stevenson (2009, p. 850) found that the singer's constantly changing image and music acted as an "emotional resource that can be drawn upon in good times and bad."

Several authors have interpreted this kind of media use through psychoanalytic theory, notably the object relations school of Melanie Klein, Donald Winnicott and others (Hills, 2002; Sandvoss, 2005), whereby the fan object is seen as a 'transitional object' that provides ontological security, like Bowie's work inspiring fans through thick and thin. Although the transitional object idea was primarily conceived with child development in mind (exemplified by the comfort blanket or favourite teddy), Hills (2002) has argued that fan objects constitute a secondary transitional object, often containing a number of primary objects, such as recordings, memorabilia and official merchandise. They also need not originate in childhood nor need individual fans to cling to the same object over the years; Hills (2005) talks of 'cyclic fandom' as consisting of a continuous and deliberate search for new objects.

Of course, this account of fandom leads us partly away from celebrity-audience relationships into a broader realm of cultural interests and activities, and one of the problems with the fan studies literature is that authors have a tendency to become stuck when generalizing across different types of fandom and fan objects (Duffett, 2013, p. 3[1]). Much of the theory (Jenkins, 1992; Hills, 2002) was initially developed around fandom of 'cult' TV series such as *Star Trek* and *Doctor Who* where the attachments are mostly with texts rather than specific individuals. One of the salient aspects of Bowie fandom identified by Stevenson (2009, p. 86) was the ability of older fans to use him as "a model for how to grow old without shutting out new ideas and influences", a function unlikely to be attributed to a more closed textual object (although it would be fascinating to see how Stevenson's interviewees re-interpret their relationship with Bowie after his death).

All the same, it is easy to see why media and cultural scholars might regard the mechanism of parasocial interaction—if this is reduced simply to the moment-by-moment sensations experienced when encountering a person or figure through media use—as insufficient grounds for theorizing about the personal meanings that celebrities hold for individuals. But, of course, this is merely the tip of the iceberg: a fully developed theory of the parasocial, which incorporates the many social and cultural influences that build our relationships with media figures beyond those moments of direct media use,

---

[1] At the outset of Duffett (2013), the author defines 'media fandom', the object of his otherwise sympathetic and thoughtful book, as "the recognition of a positive, personal, relatively deep, emotional connection with a mediated element of popular culture" (p. 2). He distinguishes this from 'sports fandom' by dismissing the latter as "ultimately tribal and based on a controlled, competitive mentality" (p. 3). He illustrates this distinction ("one example should suffice") with an anecdote of a riot that took place in a city centre when large screen coverage of a football match failed. Such unashamed prejudice stems from the assumption that media fandom is necessarily positive, as well as the idea that media and sport inhabit entirely separate cultural realms. In an extended discussion of the academic disjuncture between research on fandom in popular culture and sport, Schimmel, Harrington and Bielby (2007) make the point that focusing attention on sport-related violence is equivalent to reducing fandom to the stalking, and attacking, of celebrities. Paradoxically, Duffett spends much of his book complaining about the latter tendency.

should be capable of explaining how those personal meanings develop and permeate our experience, potentially through the lifespan. It should serve equally well to explain those occasional relationships that become problematic, which fan scholars have sometimes been too quick to dismiss as solely the product of individual pathology, so that the celebrity ends up no more than an unlucky passer-by. To reiterate, not all parasocial relationships are positive ones, and even positive ones can turn sour, as undoubtedly many Jimmy Savile fans found to their horror when his terrible record of sexual violence against women and children became evident after his death.

Ultimately, it is perhaps most helpful to see fandom as a small subset of parasocial relationships, in which those relationships have gradually acquired meanings that transcend the type of "second-order relationships" that Rojek (2012) has argued constitute the parasocial. Even within this subset, we can distinguish fan relationships with fictional characters and historical figures from those with living celebrities. As will be seen later in the chapter, when considering online interaction, the possibility of receiving a tweet from a celebrity means that the experience of those relationships is notably different from those where reciprocal communication is impossible.

The 'Celebrity Worship' Perspective

The claim that parasocial theory pathologises media users might seem somewhat harsh given many authors' attempts to frame it as typical behaviour. It is harder, though, to defend the literature on 'celebrity worship' on those grounds. Firstly of all, the use of the term 'worship' immediately ruffles feathers among fan scholars, who are hostile towards any attempts to explain fandom as 'quasi-religious' (Hills, 2003; Duffett, 2013). Secondly, the celebrity worship literature has at times followed an explicitly clinical agenda. The original Celebrity Attitude Scale (CAS) (Maltby, McCutcheon, Ashe & Houran, 2001) was developed to distinguish pathological from nonpathological fandom even though nobody has yet identified a meaningful cut-off point in the measure. Nevertheless, in this and subsequent studies, researchers have registered associations between high levels of celebrity worship and various measures of pathology, such as depression and anxiety, obsessive-compulsive disorder, fantasy proneness, and dissociation (Maltby, Day, McCutcheon, Houran & Ashe, 2006) as well as aspects of personality relating to addiction and criminality (Sheridan,

North, Maltby & Gillett, 2007) and narcissism (Ashe, Maltby & McCutcheon, 2005).

Like with Rubin et al's (1985) measure, the CAS asks respondents to pick a 'favourite' and then rate a number of statements according to their agreement with each item with regard to their favourite celebrity. Research using the scale has consistently identified two or three underlying components, or factors, that account for most of the variance in people's responses. The first, and usually most dominant, has been termed 'entertainment-social'. This includes statements like "My friends and I like to discuss what my favourite celebrity has done", and might be regarded as a measure of conventional fandom, whereby celebrity worship is a communal, shared activity. The second component, or factor, identified in most studies using the CAS is 'intense-personal', which includes items relating to private cognitions and beliefs about the celebrity that are not shared with others, such as "I have frequent thoughts about my favourite celebrity, even when I don't want to". To identify a clinical usefulness for the scale, a third factor has sometimes been identified, labelled 'borderline pathological' although this is not as robust a factor as the previous two and has not been regarded as significant in all studies using the scale. A typical item that distinguishes this factor is "If someone gave me several thousand dollars to do with as I please, I would consider spending it on a personal possession (like a napkin or paper plate) once used by my favourite celebrity". These last two elements of the CAS are those that have caused most concern for fan scholars because they seem to reinforce some of the negative stereotypes around fandom: that fans are delusional, socially isolated and obsessive, particularly about trivial details.

I will come back to this last issue in a moment, but it is worth investigating the celebrity worship literature in more detail to see exactly which aspects of 'nonpathological' celebrity worship might give way to those behaviours of real concern, such as stalking and violence towards celebrities. Most of the studies have attempted to account for their findings through an 'absorption-addiction model' first described by Maltby et al (2001). This model argues that celebrity worshippers, through a process akin to hypnosis, develop a "heightened sense of reality" about their favourite celebrity that leads to a "delusional belief that they have a special relationship with the celebrity" (McCutcheon, Lange & Houran, 2002, p. 81). This is then reinforced by obsessions and compulsions more typical of addictive behaviour. Why should celebrities in particular trigger this psychological process? The authors suggest they are (perhaps inadvertently) chosen in the quest "to establish an identity" (Sheridan et al, 2007, p. 570) perhaps as the result of "a compromised identity structure" (McCutcheon, Scott, Aruguete & Parker, 2006, p. 290), itself deriving from insecure attachment to parents. Naturally, these claims are somewhat speculative because they are based entirely on one-off studies using psychometric self-report measures. The absence of data on the life histories of celebrity 'worshippers', pathological or nonpathological, places clear limits on how far this kind of model can be supported.

After a hiatus of publications in the 2000s, celebrity worship research has gone rather quiet. Most of the authors have retired, gone into consultancy, or moved on to other, non-media-related subjects, and, despite the celebrity phenomenon continuing to expand in the same period, the baton has not been passed on. Even within Psychology, there is a sense that the literature has gone a little too far in its attempts to link routine fan behaviour to psychiatric disorder. As Stever (2011) has argued, the concepts of fandom and celebrity worship are conflated in the literature (presumably the CAS was intended to differentiate them in terms of high and moderate scores, but this has never been fully articulated), and the lack of any specific detail about what constitutes a problematic level of celebrity worship leaves just the vague impression that celebrity fandom is a 'slippery slope' (Duffett, 2013). Most studies using the CAS have been conducted with university students, many of whom will not be fans of anyone and might have struggled to identify a 'favourite'; when Stever (2011) administered the measure at two different fan conventions, she obtained only moderate scores on the two main subscales even though several of the entertainment-social items relate to communal fan activities. Finally, there is little in the wording of the CAS items that seems to indicate any religious dimension to the practices described. In retrospect, it may be that the authors would have done best to omit the 'worship' element altogether[2].

---

[2] The one exception to this rule is the study by Maltby, Houran, Lange, Ashe, and McCutcheon (2001), which found a negative relationship between CAS scores and a measure of religiosity, which could be taken as evidence that celebrity worship is a functional substitute for religious worship (or at least shares psychological roots).

Parasocial Relationships in the Digital Era

From the earliest days of Twitter, there has been speculation about the opportunities the medium affords for enabling direct contact between celebrities and their followers. A report in *The Guardian* in 2008 compared the Twitter feed of tennis star Andy Murray with that of entertainer Stephen Fry. The former displayed no interaction with followers, while Fry replied to direct tweets on a regular basis. "It's a real two-way conversation", argued the author of the piece, "intermediated by the Internet, visible to everyone" (Arthur, 2008). Since then, Twitter 'spats' between celebrities (Fry included) and other users have become regular, almost routine, news items.

Nevertheless, seven years later a paper in *Celebrity Studies* made the rather extraordinary claim that "social interaction between fans and celebrities on Twitter... is not in practice taking place" (Kehrberg, 2015, p. 93). What planet was the researcher living on, one might ask; the answer is, almost certainly, that she had chosen to study celebrities who simply do not use Twitter like Stephen Fry, having selected the five most followed Twitter users, none of them with a following of fewer than 30 million people. Perhaps not surprisingly, these figures had most likely delegated operation of their accounts to management lackeys who just used the medium as a noticeboard for informing fans of upcoming tour dates and record releases.

Of course, the wide variation in social media use by celebrities makes it harder to say whether direct interaction *is* actually taking place on a vast scale, but the point is that it has become a distinct possibility for anyone following a celebrity on Twitter, Instagram or any medium that affords direct contact. I will say more about the specific behaviours of celebrities on social media in chapter 5, but for now it is worth citing Stever and Lawson's (2013) analysis of the timelines of 15 celebrities and (samples of) their fans. The authors found that between 23 and 74 per cent of celebrity tweets were addressed to individual fans, in most cases as responses to direct communication. Those celebrities with the lowest percentage of fan-directed Tweets tended to be the most successful and popular (Katy Perry, Tom Hanks); those with the highest rates were actors from *Star Trek*, a series with a long history of fan activity and frequent encounters between stars and fans at conventions (Jenkins, 1992).

Stever and Lawson's (2013) study is not only important for its broad overview of celebrity Tweet activity, but also for providing examples of specific exchanges. By examining the profiles of fans as well as stars, we discover celebrities not only thank fans personally for their interest, but also on some occasions, pursue unwelcome interaction. Elswehere, Stever and Hughes (2013) report the case of a television actor who sent a critical tweet to a fan, who then indignantly relayed the communication to fellow fans, accusing the star of 'trolling [her] timeline'!

For some authors, this kind of direct contact via social media is enough to sound the death knell for parasocial interaction. As Marwick and boyd (2011, p. 148) have argued:

> *While parasocial interaction is largely imaginary and takes place primarily in the fan's mind, Twitter conversations between fans and famous people are public and visible, and involve direct engagement between the famous person and the follower. The fan's ability to engage in discussion with a famous person de-pathologises the parasocial and recontextualises it within a medium that the follower may use to talk to real-life acquaintances.*

Once again, the limits of parasocial theory, and the degree to which it pathologises media users (especially fans) is dependent upon which elements authors choose to prioritise. For Marwick and boyd, its pathologising properties are rooted in the idea that the imaginary (or cognitive) nature of parasocial interaction is somehow problematic. It also assumes that the *opportunity* for reciprocal communication is sufficient to kill off all parasocial activity, as if all we needed to do when fancying a chat with our favourite celebrities was to send them a request via social media. Nevertheless, the 'recontextualisation' of celebrity-audience relations on Twitter is an important point (that they refer to elsewhere as 'context collapse'). It effectively brings celebrities closer to our actual social networks like distant relatives from whom we cannot always guarantee a reply.

Hills (2016) makes a similar point in relation to digital implications for parasocial theory. He argues that the recontextualisation endemic to Twitter serves to reveal the long-standing limitations of the parasocial construct. Hills argues that parasocial relationships are fundamentally social in that they are shared amongst fans of media figures, who then use them as "[resources] within their self-narratives" (2016, p. 471). The idea, promoted in the work of Rojek (2012), that there is a sharp divide between the social and parasocial is dismissed as "unsustainable from any perspective... which accepts the multiple, social and divided nature of the self" (Hills, 2016, p. 478): instead he prefers to talk of "multisocial interaction".

This is an important observation and I will return to it shortly when introducing the roles of language and discourse to parasocial theory.

At this point, however, I would like to refer back to my own (Giles, 2002b) attempt to extend the concept of parasocial interaction into what Horton and Wohl (1956) referred to as "the matrix of usual social activity". I found it most helpful to break the social/parasocial binary by locating *all* encounters along a social/parasocial dimension. This allows for some encounters to be more or less (para)social than others, but the distinction is not absolute. It also takes into account the medium through which the encounter takes place, comparing the dyadic intimacy of a phone call to the experience of watching a remote figure on a screen along with an unseen audience of millions. Somewhere in between these two extremes lies Twitter.

One might see all these encounters as comfortably accommodated within Hills's (2016) concept of "multisocial interaction", although there is still the awkward issue of the ontological status of the individuals involved. Marwick and boyd's (2011) recontextualisation argument is significant here because it forces us to move away, to some extent, from the idea of celebrities as 'sign' or text, and to think of them merely as common-or-garden variety media users like any others. This is a big step in the history of celebrity studies, which until the present century has been dominated by the 'star text' approach of film studies, whereby the agency of individual celebrities, and their personal beliefs and desires, have had to be interpreted through indirect encounters in print and broadcast media. It also has implications for the status of fans, as I will go on to explain in chapter 5, whose position in the hierarchy, until the present century, was certain. Like all other non-celebrities, their noses were permanently pressed against the glass, separated from their fan objects by the remoteness of broadcast media.

Perhaps one of the biggest objections by fan and other media scholars to the concept of parasocial interaction is its apparent reduction of meaningful relationships (such as those experienced by fans) to private, cognitive events. Hills (2016) takes this problem to an interesting place. He argues that fantasy elements, interpreted in psychoanalytic terms as projection and transference, are not just involved in media use but help constitute many of our social, face-to-face relationships in general. If we relegate parasocial relationships to a second-order level, what about those 'social' relationships transformed through cognitive events where we wrongly believe the boy or girl next door (or attractive friend or colleague) is interested in us simply because we are infatuated with them? Even our most intimate relationships can be subject to this kind of misalignment as we discover when we are deceived by a friend, cheated on by a partner, or sacked by a boss we trusted.

This blurring of the parasocial and social boundaries is entirely consistent with Giles (2002b), where the idea of the parasocial is more flexible than in a binary model such as Rojek's (and indeed most research in the communication literature). However it would make little sense to describe, for instance, a marriage as parasocial because one of the partners is deceived by the other (in thinking he or she is faithful, when he or she is having an affair). This is where the concept of 'multisocial interaction' must take into account the ontological status of the individuals involved, their personal histories, and the nature of their mediated or face-to-face interaction.

However, there is another way round the 'pathologising' problem that also helps to preserve parasocial theory in the digital era, and that is to move away from the notion of the parasocial as located only in the private, mental events of the individual consumers of broadcast media. In line with the position taken thus far on celebrity, I would like to introduce a discursive aspect to parasocial interaction that accounts for the role of language and mediated context.

A Discursive Psychological Account of Parasocial Relationships

One of the most striking phenomena described in Stever and Hughes's (2013) study of celebrity-fan exchanges on Twitter was the claim by a fan that television actor Brian Dietzen[3] was "trolling [her] timeline"! This kind of exchange constitutes a complete *volte-face* in the history of celebrity-audience relationships, whereby Hollywood stars become stalkers of their own fans, a breach of the 'fourth wall' only seen previously in fields like sport, such as soccer star Eric Cantona's kung-fu kick on a Crystal Palace supporter in 1994[4]. On another level, however, we might see the fan's announcement as part of what Hills (2016) describes as the thoroughly

---

[3] Star of CBS series Naval Criminal Investigative Service (NCIS); Dietzen plays an autopsy assistant called Jimmy.

[4] This incident is best understood as an attack on an *anti-fan* because Cantona was playing for Manchester United, Palace's opponents.

'social' nature of parasocial interaction because it generated much discussion among NCIS fans on Twitter. The key element here, though, is that the exchange between Dietzen and the fan, and the subsequent discussion, all took place in written (or typed) text, one of the more obvious affordances of Twitter (and social media in general). There is no need to speculate here about the private cognitive events of the fan or, indeed, the star: the relationship is, first and foremost, a discursive one.

A discursive theory of the parasocial is not a way of shoe-horning digital relationships into a redundant model. It can also address many long-standing audience phenomena relating to broadcast media. Much of the parasocial literature (indeed much audience reception research generally) works on the assumption that the media user interacts in complete isolation with the figures on screen. But radio and television have rarely been consumed by isolated listeners and viewers: before, during, and after episodes of parasocial interaction, audiences discuss celebrities and other media figures (Giles, 2002b). What on earth is he wearing? What a stupid thing to say! Oh, isn't she gorgeous? In these moments our own private cognitions about the celebrities are confirmed, or troubled, by the discursive contributions of our co-viewers. (I hadn't thought of her as gorgeous before, but now you come to mention it....)

A focus on the discursive elements of parasocial interaction also helps tidy up some of the more ragged edges of the concept. It allows us to dissolve the binary imposed by authors such as Rojek (2012), whereby the online is merely an 'illusion' of the real because the language that constructs online relationships is broadly consistent with that which is used to construct any other kind of relationship. The idea that even our most intimate relationships are socially constructed (through notions of romantic love, for example) has been long prevalent in some fields of social psychology and relationship theory (Braithwaite et al., 2010; Baxter, 2004).

The discursive model of the parasocial does not resolve the ontology problem (that is, the actual existence of the celebrity), but then this is the dilemma that confronts all social media users: how can we be sure that the people who tweet us are the actual people represented by their Twitter profile? The 'verified' profile status introduced by Twitter and Instagram is social media's attempt to resolve this issue, but there is certainly nothing new about non-celebrities masquerading as celebrities, often for commercial gain (Giles, 2017a). However, looked at in more traditional media terms, a discursive focus addresses some of the more seemingly 'pathological' behaviour of fans who transcend the fiction/reality divide by locating their logically inappropriate responses within the narrative framework of a soap opera, or as intertextual play.

As much as anything, a discursive focus opens up the whole celebrity-audience distinction in social media. When every Twitter user is a 'follower' of another, how do we separate the 'celebrities' from the 'fans'? Authors such as Marwick and boyd (2011) have addressed this issue through the concept of micro-celebrity, and the argument that all celebrity constitutes a 'practice'. These are some of the questions that I will be exploring in chapter 4 when I navigate a path through the extraordinary cultural events of the first two decades of the twenty-first century and their implications for the study of celebrity.

PART II

THE TWENTY-FIRST CENTURY AND THE DIGITAL IMPERATIVE

4

THE 2000s: REALITY TV AND 'MICRO-CELEBRITY' — WEBCAM GIRLS AND BLOGGERS

"I don't call us celebrities—you have to work *to be a celebrity, all we've done is been in a house": Jade Goody, cited in Holmes (2004)*

I have chosen in this book not to talk about 'digital celebrity' or 'online celebrity' for several reasons. The first is to avoid charges of technological determinism by arguing that contemporary forms of celebrity have not arisen solely because of the affordances of different Internet-based media. Even though those specific affordances might enable us to differentiate between celebrity as it has emerged within such diverse media as YouTube and Snapchat, there is nothing uniquely 'digital' about a twenty-first century celebrity *per se*. Digitisation has become obligatory for all traditional celebrities even though traditional celebrity practices have inspired the 'micro-celebrity' practices of the emergent digital generation. 'Micro' or not, the celebrity afforded by media like YouTube and Instagram balances the traditions of 'stardom' with the thoroughly *offline* phenomenon of the 'localebrity' (Williams, 2016), the kind of restricted fame long enjoyed in communities such as schools and workplaces (Giles, 2000).

The second reason for avoiding the term 'digital celebrity' is to maintain a historical perspective on the nature of celebrity that allows us to see YouTubers and others as an extension of what Turner (2010) calls 'the demotic turn' in twentieth-century media: the increasing visibility of 'ordinary people' in the media, now taken up to a point where the ordinary people have begun to supplement, if not replace, the traditional celebrity caste. For reasons I will go on to explain, this development would have been impossible without social media but should not be seen as the inevitable outcome of social media. There is too much continuity across the history of media for it to have occurred solely because of digital culture.

In this chapter, I would like to trace these historical developments as they have unfolded over the first two decades of the present century. I will start with a bit of twentieth-century media history before moving on to the explosion of 'reality TV' in 2000 and its various manifestations, moving on to the micro-celebrity phenomenon of 'webcam girls' and Californian tech entrepreneurs in the mid-2000s. On the one hand, these developments showcase the rise of celebrities who are renowned for nothing more than their unique personalities and associated lifestyles. On the other, they indicate the way audiences for such forms of celebrity do not have to be 'mass' in the traditional sense (at the national or international level) but through digital culture can nevertheless become 'global'.

A Brief History of Audience Participation Media

Right from the earliest days of radio and television, 'ordinary people' have been an essential ingredient of broadcasting. A popular format on BBC radio in the 1940s involved a celebrity presenter, such as Wilfred Pickles, visiting munitions factories and other locations where working-class people were engaged in wartime production (Scannell, 1996). In the 1950s, the quiz show, featuring members of the public as contestants, became one of the most popular genres in US television. Both formats constitute 'media rituals' as described by Couldry (2003): the interface where social categories are constructed, segregating the 'you' from the 'us' of broadcast media. The shows' success depended on audiences' identification with the public participants, who were carefully chosen to represent the average viewer while simultaneously promoting certain moral values (smart appearance, modesty, industriousness, and other middle-class virtues).

The same kind of ritual is enacted in contemporary lifestyle television, where typically the presenter (a media employee) interacts with 'experts' (representing the authority of a specific domain outside the media) and the participants (ordinary people, representing the audience). Authenticity is the defining characteristic of this last group, and lifestyle shows, epitomized by the 'makeover' genre, are structured so as to provide moments in which the ordinariness of the participants is realised via displays of spontaneous emotion, such as "the point at which the newly made over room… is revealed for the first time to its owners, and their reaction is presented to the nation in closeup" (Moseley, 2000, p. 299). Any suggestion that participants' lines are scripted or that they are media employees in disguise brings about considerable disapproval. When they first appear on television, at the very least, they must be portrayed as thoroughly ordinary, one of 'us', and certainly not one of 'them'.

Notwithstanding the need for representativeness, the 1950s US quiz show producers did not want contestants to be simply a rotating cast of nobodies. They knew, or at least sensed, that audience figures could be boosted by attractive, sympathetic, and above all recognisable champions, who would reappear week after week until finally defeated. In this time, they could expect to receive considerable coverage across the media, providing valuable publicity for the show. In their quest for ratings, producers gradually began to manipulate participants' celebrity appeal, sometimes interfering in the contest itself by feeding the correct answers to contestants who were seen to have greater public appeal.

This strategy was eventually unmasked by the great quiz show scandal of 1959 when, amid other revelations, it transpired that the producer of *Twenty One* had engineered a contest between six-week champion Herb Stempel and university lecturer Charles Van Doren so the latter would inherit the champion's crown. Audience ratings had dipped during Stempel's reign and the producer accredited this to his suspicions that Stempel, a Marines veteran, was regarded as unattractive and unsympathetic by viewers. As Van Doren (2008) later alleged in a personal reflection on the events, "Stempel's posture and gestures were awkward, his clothes were too tight – he seemed to be almost choking in his shirt". Van Doren, by contrast, was considered "well-spoken, well-educated, handsome – the very image of a young man that parents would like their son to be". He remained the show's champion for four months, amassing hundreds of dollars and acquiring the kind of celebrity then more associated with Hollywood actors, appearing on the cover of *Time* magazine and being "seen in public with movie starlets" (even these appearances were orchestrated by the show's producer). By the end of the run, he had become, at least according to his own father, "one of the most famous people in the country", before he was instructed to allow a popular new contestant to usurp his title.

With the demise of the quiz show (a central element in the scandal was the role of monetary prizes), television producers devised ever more creative formats for involving members of the public. These have ranged, across the world, from prank-type shows based on the earlier *Candid Camera* to dating contests and other studio-based game shows, 'lifestyle' series in which members of the public usually undertake some kind of skills training (following, say, medical students or learner drivers), 'makeover' series whose subtext is the cultivation of aesthetic appreciation or style (Giles, 2002a; Smith, 2010), and studio talk shows such as *Oprah* and *Kilroy*, which enjoyed particular popularity in the 1990s (Livingstone & Lunt, 1994).

Some of these formats have, like the 1950s quiz shows, involved repeat appearances by contestants that have resulted in brief celebrity, where again the issue of authenticity has arisen. One example, described in more detail in Giles (2000), was that of the *Blind Date* 'love rat' Paul Nolan, a 1980s dating contestant who amused the studio audience with his impressions. Though everything about his identity as a window cleaner was authentic, his eligibility for the series had one major problem: he was not single. Nevertheless, his brief period in the limelight included an invitation to host, with little success, a popular TV music show.

Rojek (2001) has described figures such as Paul Nolan as 'celetoids'. These are individuals who enjoy all the trappings of celebrity but only for a time that is restricted by the actual reason for their fame. Singers or footballers retain their celebrity status for as long as they continue to sing or play at the highest level unless, in the process, they acquire some other reason for publicity – a notorious personality or an unrelated skill that involves them crossing a field boundary (Giles, 2015). Celetoids lack any of these credentials, and so their fame is forever linked to the show they appear in or the brief period of news coverage that follows the events that brought them into the headlines (such as Robert O'Donnell, the US paramedic who saved a child who had fallen down a well and later committed suicide after losing his fame).

If television was capable only of turning its public participants into celetoids, this book would probably be about the constraints of 'ordinariness' and the supreme power of media rituals that only ever allowed the public access to screen time when their roles were heavily circumscribed. But over the last two decades, swift changes in global media culture have turned the conventional notions of 'audience' and 'participation' inside out

(Bird, 2011; Livingstone, 2013). Above all, we have seen the emergence of media that enable celetoids to take up residence at the top table of celebrity, by providing them with a variety of platforms through which they can sustain their celebrity status long after the show has ended.

But, first of all, there was reality TV.

Reality TV

Over time, the definition of 'reality TV' has fluctuated as much as that of 'celebrity', 'media', 'social media', and other terms dissected in the previous chapters. Initially, it was used to signify a kind of post-documentary trend in 'factual TV', including such formats as 'docusoaps' and dramatized versions of real-life events (Holmes & Jermyn, 2004), but in recent years, it has become largely confined to gameshows and related series involving both public contestants and celebrities in which they are continuously filmed either in their natural habitat or in a specially designed environment.

Though most authors today would agree that the intrinsic feature of 'reality' programming is its "self-conscious claim to the discourse of the real" (Murray & Ouelette, 2009, p. 3), this claim is probably best understood as the "present-ist timeframe" in which the production of all these diverse shows is set, which gives the impression of "immediacy, coincidence and liveness", even if the package itself is a tightly edited narrative drama consisting of carefully selected scenes (Kavka & West, 2004). Of course, this package has been supplemented from the early days of *Big Brother* by tabloid and magazine gossip and online content (providing apparently 'backstage' access – "the bits TV didn't show" – Couldry, 2002). More than a show, *Big Brother* and other series have become 'meta-texts' (Holmes, 2004), which, like the gradually unfolding narrative of test match cricket, become ingrained in the everyday lives of the audience. As Turner (2010) has argued, reality shows have more to do with 'our' reality than that of their participants.

Kavka (2012), one of the leading authorities on the phenomenon, has identified three generations of reality TV: the 'camcorder generation' of audience participation media from *Candid Camera* in the 1950s to MTV's *The Real World* (1991), really the precursor for modern-day reality series; the relatively short-lived 'competition generation' that spawned *Big Brother* and *Survivor*; and the 'celebrity generation', from 2002 onwards, where the primary goal of the show became the production of celebrity itself, or, in the case of celebrity reality TV (Holmes, 2006), the resurrection of celebrity for struggling D-listers. These last two generations have, inevitably, become entwined, and a case could perhaps now be made to add a fourth generation based around the popularity of shows like *Jersey Shore* and *Made in Chelsea*, which apply the format of celebrity-based 'docusoaps' like *The Osbournes* and *Keeping Up With The Kardashians* to casts of ostensibly 'ordinary' participants who represent specific social class-based lifestyles.

It is fair to say that three contexts exist in which reality TV is most closely associated with celebrity: the traditional gameshow (Kavka's second generation); the later lifestyle-based series; and celebrity reality TV, in which the entry qualification for the show is that contestants are already recognisable to the audience. I will next discuss each of these three contexts in turn.

Big Brother (UK): The Emergence of Celebrity Through Reality TV

Although the show was first produced in the Netherlands (the original Dutch production company Endemol still owns the franchise) and several European variants had aired prior to Channel Four's version, *Big Brother*'s impact on British media culture was unforeseen and profound. Even though it would not be true to say the show failed to generate celebrities elsewhere[1], the powerful influence of tabloid newspapers in Britain (Johansson, 2007) pushed its participants into the national consciousness in a way that generated huge coverage across the national press and broadcast media.

---

[1] Space (and ultimately the purpose of this book) does not permit a fully comparative analysis of *Big Brother*'s various national manifestations, but the German version had produced the first bona fide celebrity several months before the UK launch. Zlatko Trpkovski was, in Kavka's (2012, p. 159) words, an "...uneducated, tattooed auto mechanic from Macedonia who was outspoken and had never heard of Shakespeare" and went on to have at least one hit single (the twentieth-century equivalent of owning your own clothing range) and his own short-lived MTV show. Without the equivalent of the UK's tabloid press to sustain it, however (the popular gossip magazine *Bild* is really a one-off), media interest in the show declined quickly thereafter.

As much as anyone, the participants themselves were unprepared for the fame they were to receive for taking part in the series. Aside from the cheers (and occasional boos) reverberating around the house on the weekly eviction night, the contestants had no idea they were generating tabloid headlines and continuous discussion throughout all forms of British media during the nine weeks they remained in glorious isolation. As one of them later recalled, "we would often sit around talking about how weird it would be if no one was watching" (Crace, 2009). Unlike in subsequent series, contestants' concerns centred firmly on the game element itself: who was going to win, and why (Couldry, 2002). Perhaps for this reason, the biggest star of the first series was 'Nasty' Nick Bateman, who was evicted by the producers for passing notes to fellow contestants to manipulate the contest. The evening show featuring Bateman's confrontation with the others (notably eventual winner Craig Phillips) following their discovery of his duplicity attracted the ratings and blanket media coverage of a soap opera cliffhanger.

By the time of the third series, the show's function in generating celebrity had transformed the perceptions of the viewing public and the contestants, with much suspicion about the sincerity of their motivations for taking part. With several participants from the first two series now seemingly installed as regular TV presenters and journalists, much talk in the house revolved around the effects the fame earned through appearing on the show would have on them subsequently. Over time, contestants developed "a self-conscious awareness of the conventions of the programme" (Holmes, 2004, p. 118), whereby they would speculate about the contents of that evening's highlights show and even imitate the TV voiceover to provide a running commentary on events in the house.

Whatever the various ambitions of its cast, *Big Brother 3* produced the show's biggest star of them all, Jade Goody. Like Bateman, she did not even have to win the contest to reap the largest share of media attention. Her popularity with a substantial part of the audience eventually saw her become the show's first millionaire participant, with a full set of traditional celebrity trappings including an autobiography, fitness DVDs, and a range of high street perfume. But Goody was far more than just a popular contestant. She was effectively used by the British press as a symbol of everything that was wrong about modern Britain or, more precisely, working class Britain. As Jones (2011, p. 123) claims, "There can be few more shameful episodes in the British media's recent history than the hounding of Jade Goody."

The 'hounding' to which Jones refers began during the *Big Brother 3* series, when Goody's personality was routinely ridiculed in the tabloid press (and, as is the British way, replicated by the broadsheets too) for her excessive behaviour in the house (seen as coarse and ill-mannered) and her professed ignorance of British geography. Despite the moral censure of the media, enough people clearly identified with, and enjoyed, her performance to sustain her celebrity over the following three years, during which time she appeared in other reality shows until she was selected for the 2007 series of *Celebrity Big Brother*. On this particular show, she (and some fellow housemates) came into conflict with Indian actress Shilpa Shetty, and although not the only (or worst) culprit, Goody was again turned on by the media, the *Sun* newspaper describing her as "a vile, pig-ignorant, racist bully" (Tyler & Bennett, 2010).

Only when it was revealed, the following year, that Goody was terminally ill with cervical cancer, did the media begin to stop treating her as a scapegoat for society's ills. The same journalists who had sneered at her now praised her 'bravery' and 'dignity' as she invited national TV to film her final weeks. Her subsequent funeral was widely covered, even on the BBC. Goody was later proclaimed, in Channel Four's final series in 2011, 'the ultimate *Big Brother* contestant'. In this respect she, like Charles Van Doren, had fulfilled TV's ambition to 'grow its own' celebrity (Turner, 2010), but at the same time, the broader media recoiled at the access this gave to individuals perceived as undesirable and unworthy. The idea that celebrity warrants something identifiable as *labour* (expressed by the early Goody herself in this chapter's opening quote) was to become a recurrent theme in the traditional media's coverage of online celebrity a decade later.

Fourth Generation Reality TV?

Wood (2017) argues that the last two generations of reality TV can be distinguished by those elements that most successfully engage the viewing audience. For the competition generation, the watchword was 'authenticity'; the most successful *Big Brother* contestants (at least the winners) were those who were deemed to be the most 'true to themselves' and often the most unassuming, ordinary participants on show. Although these individuals generated enormous media coverage around the period of the series' screening, their celebrity tended not to last long; within a year, they would be forgotten, supplanted by the next group of contestants. In this respect, they fit perfectly Rojek's (2001) description of the celetoid.

The third (celebrity) generation, however, has traded on excess and exaggeration. As Wood (2017, p. 45) says of *Geordie Shore*, "all of the women have excessively long 'mermaid' hair extensions, extended false finger nails, eyelashes, high-definition and exaggerated eyebrows, some breast augmentation and deep orange tans... they work hard to *reveal*, rather than *conceal*, fakeness". She argues that, in this show at least, gender and class are 'flaunted' to make visible the self-defining 'labour' that has supplanted traditional work for uneducated young people in an economically deprived region of the United Kingdom. The same kind of self-labour and flaunting of gender and class are equally evident in the affluent participants of *Made in Chelsea* (UK) and *Rich Kids of Beverley Hills* (US), albeit with a focus on the consumption as much as the production of wealth.

Unlike the unassuming, celetoidal *Big Brother* winners, these reality stars have more staying power in that they are 'durable' (Curnutt, 2011). Distributed carefully across various media, the participants of *Geordie Shore* and *Made in Chelsea* alike are fully fledged career celebrities, with clothing and cosmetic ranges, apps, nightclubs, and modelling contracts. Whatever their social origins, most are millionaires by the time the second series rolls. There are no accusations of careerism or fakery because the entire cast of the show is shamelessly concentrated on self-branding.

It is surely no coincidence that this second generation of reality stars is coterminous with social media, since their continuous performance of celebrity most closely resembles that of micro-celebrity as described by Marwick and boyd (2011). The early *Big Brother* stars, by contrast, had few outlets in which to maintain their celebrity status beyond the decaying interest of the tabloids after each series' conclusion, resorting mostly to personal appearances in nightclubs and the opening of supermarkets.

Celebrities in Reality TV

In addition to two generations of reality TV celebrities, we should consider a third category, represented by people who participate in reality series with some form of celebrity already established; who are, from day one, recognised by a significant portion of viewers. Of course, Ozzy Osbourne fits this category. But since the beginning of the century, there have been a substantial number of reality TV series across the world in which the participants are not ostensibly individuals selected to represent the 'general public' but are people who are already understood to have taken up residence in the mythical centre of the media sphere.

In some respects, a *Celebrity Big Brother* (CBB) must have seemed like an obvious programming choice because all the work the audience needed to do to develop parasocial relations with ordinary participants has already been done where the contestants are recognisable celebrities. The first CBB series followed hard on the original, airing in 2001. Its success inspired a second explicitly celebrity-themed UK show, *I'm A Celebrity... Get Me Out of Here!* which has proved to be even more durable, broadcasting annually for the last 15 years. Rather than drafting celebrities into an existing and familiar format, this show pioneered its own (albeit loosely based on the Japanese contest *Endurance*), with contestants being airlifted into a remote rainforest setting and set a sequence of unpleasant or potentially humiliating tasks. The notable thing (at least for our present purpose) about CBB and *I'm A Celebrity* is that, in foregrounding the status of the contestants as celebrities, they establish their own definition of the term.

In 2009, CBB featured, for the first time, a participant whose fame had arisen out of reality TV itself: Jade Goody. At this point, *Big Brother* seemed finally to have acknowledged its role as a producer of bona fide celebrities rather than being a game show for ordinary people (Couldry, 2007, makes a similar point about the impossibility of contestants retaining their ordinary status on entering the house). As if to reinforce this function of the show, the following year *Ultimate Big Brother* brought together the winners of CBB and the non-celebrity version: It was won, appropriately, by Brian Dowling, who, since his *Big Brother 2* (BB2) victory, had become an established TV presenter.

Although casting existing celebrities as reality contestants might seem to be nothing more than an expedient way of guaranteeing media and viewer interest from the outset, it has been argued that shows like *I'm a Celebrity* also tap into a twenty-first-century predilection for 'celebrity baiting' arising out of resentment at the 'spoiled rich' (Sconce, 2004), specifically in relation to a US series that pitted celebrities against one another in the boxing ring. However, a consistent theme in celebrity reality shows is the relative lack of fame enjoyed by the participants at the point they enter the series. Such shows are routinely derided as a means to revive flagging careers rather than opportunities to tar and feather current A-listers. The archetypal contestant on *I'm a Celebrity* is someone who is recognised as a *former* celebrity or a minor celebrity whose profile could only benefit from exposure to a prime-time TV audience. In some cases, the celebrity contestants hope to reinvent their public image, so political figures are commonly among the participants, especially those on the fringes of power (or perhaps looking for an escape route).

The same process can be seen to operate in the large number of reality talent shows featuring celebrity contestants, such as UK shows *Celebrity Masterchef, Celebrity Bake Off, Strictly Come Dancing* and its Australian counterpart *Dancing With The Stars*. As in CBB, the participants are assuming the role of those ordinary contestants with whom the viewing public are invited to identify. By stripping them of their everyday professional roles, celebrities in reality talent shows are effectively reduced to their 'true', private selves, discursively constituted as ordinary alongside the celebrity presenter(s) and the 'experts', who, in some cases, can exploit their status to deliver stinging criticism to contestants who are perceived to be under-performing (Bonner, 2013).

Webcam Girls: The Origins of Microcelebrity

The first signs that the Internet might be able, like television, to manufacture its own celebrities came with the 'webcam girl' phenomenon of the late 1990s. This began in 1996 when Jennifer Ringley, an undergraduate student living in college accommodation in Pennsylvania, attached a webcam to her home computer and uploaded images every 20 minutes to her personal website JenniCam (initially www.boudoir.org) alongside a regular blog, several short videos, some original poetry and, eventually, a fan forum (or 'bulletin board'). Curious visitors passed the word around, and within a few months, she was able to charge a fee for regular updates (a fresh webcam image every two minutes). At one point, JenniCam received five million hits per day (Senft, 2008).

By the end of the century, JenniCam had spawned a host of imitators, such as Ana Voog (AnaCam), Lisa Batey, Kristie Alshaibi (ArtVamp), Cera Byer (SeeMeScreaming), and Auriea Harvey. Terri Senft (TerriCam) turned hers into a PhD thesis and later produced the definitive account of the phenomenon (Senft, 2008). Most distributed their productions via Usenet and Internet Relay Chat (IRC) before moving on to blogging services (notably LiveJournal) around 2000. Despite ending up as a guest on the David Letterman chat show, and being hailed as the 'inventor of reality TV', Jennifer Ringley shut her site in 2003 and currently has had no public web presence. Few of the original camgirls are still broadcasting.

Today, type 'Webcam girls' or 'camgirls' into Google and you will be offered a mountain of porn sites. Ringley and the others now tend to be described as 'lifecasters'[2], a term coined by Justin Kam, the founder of *Justin.tv* in 2007. *Justin.tv* offered Internet users more than occasional glimpses of Justin's life; it fed them a continuous live stream. However, whereas JenniCam's fans watched Jenni and her home, Justin's fans were immersed in Justin's own visual experience, relayed through mobile webcam attached to his baseball cap. Within a year, *Justin.tv* was host to 700 such channels although, with social media on the rise more generally, its appeal did not endure and in 2011 it gave way to *twitch.tv*, the now successful gaming platform.

What was so special about JenniCam that it made her the first true Internet celebrity? Novelty would explain most of her appeal; after all, a webcam trained on a Cambridge University coffee machine had gathered two million views following its launch in 1991 (Senft, 2008). But Jenni promised more than the occasional brew and refill. Viewers were drawn into her lifeworld, seeing her wake up, dress, leave the room, return, entertain guests, and retire to bed each night. One British fan even devised a 'JenniCam activity graph' to publish daily logs of her activity over the previous 24 hours (Jimroglou, 1999). Two early academic studies simultaneously hit upon the same Freudian explanation for JenniCam's popularity (Jimroglou, 1999; Burgin, 2000). Fans were enjoying a kind of 'fort-da' game that infants play by making a toy disappear and then reappear, the toy said to represent the mother. Fans repeatedly watched the empty room buoyed by 'the promise of return'.

---

[2] Even though lifecasting has long existed as a convention in the fine arts, the 'year zero' approach of social media has ridden roughshod over that convention by refusing to consider alternatives; instead, the online porn industry has appropriated the term '(web)camgirls' solely to refer to females who offer nothing other than sexual content (and most of whose earnings end up in the pockets of a digital pimp).

More exciting still was the prospect of almost live nudity and, eventually, sex. There is little doubt that much of Ringley's celebrity (and notoriety) can be attributed to the frequency with which she appeared unclothed on camera, and later she made sure the webcam captured images of sexual activity. All of this was done, claimed Ringley, in the interests of capturing 'reality': as she told ABC news, "what we see on TV – people with perfect hair, perfect friends, perfect lives, is not reality. I'm reality" (Senft, 2008, p. 16). Certainly part of the thrill lay in viewers' belief that they were catching a glimpse of a young woman's private life, like spying on an attractive neighbour: Jimroglou (1999) reports a fan alerting others that "Jenni is naked on jennicam.org just now!"

Inevitably, much of the mainstream media's coverage of Jennicam dwelt on the prurient aspects, with frequent charges of 'voyeurism' and 'exhibitionism' levelled at Ringley. But, as Jimroglou (1999) argues, the term voyeurism is not really warranted because Ringley is a willing spectacle; likewise, Burgin (2000) refutes the charge of exhibitionism on the grounds that the camera is not a window. This is a media production the audience can choose to participate in, and, as Ringley herself might have argued, it is only pornography if the viewer treats it as such. At the same time, just how many minutes *does* it take a 'real' college student to strip off and change into her nightwear? The chances of a webcam capturing pornworthy nudity in such a setting must be slim indeed. The selective nature of JenniCam's reality show is borne out by the fact that, despite later installing four cameras around her Washington apartment, she neglected to invite viewers into her bathroom.

Micro-Celebrity: The Evolution of a New Concept

In some respects, the webcam girls set the mould for online celebrities to come. Perhaps the broad affordances of web 1.0 were not entirely different from those of web 2.0. In particular, the degree of control the camgirls had over self-presentation and the ways they used their online presence to build an audience resemble those of YouTubers and other figures over the following two decades. This point was not lost on Senft (2008), who coined the term 'micro-celebrity' to describe this type of self-promotion which, along with the fandom it generated, had all the appearances of traditional celebrity but was fundamentally different in several important aspects.

Senft considered the term 'micro-celebrity' to be a category exclusively linked to Internet technology and, along with camgirls, included in it some of the most popular figures on the new social networking platform MySpace (launched 2004). She argued that the celebrity enjoyed by these figures was constrained by the size of the potential audience and the profits and influence they could make from their celebrity as well as their inability to export their celebrity to traditional media. She cited, by way of illustration, the example of Tila Tequila, 'the Madonna of MySpace'. Tequila had a MySpace following of 1.7 million, and so chose to launch her singing career, after spurning several offers from record companies, by releasing her first single on MySpace. It was downloaded a mere 13,000 times. Even D-list celebrities, argued Senft, can make more money than these web-based stars. Furthermore, she added, "unlike film and television audiences, Web viewers don't seem particularly interested in purchasing products endorsed by Web stars" (Senft, 2008, p. 25).

Ten years later, some of these differences between micro-celebrity and conventional celebrity seem considerably less important or even reversed. Not only has the global explosion of social media created audiences many times bigger than those achievable by any television network, but the commercial power and cultural influence of online celebrities has also, at least for younger audiences, begun to outstrip that of conventional stars. As a result, the need for online celebrities to export their talents to conventional broadcast media has dissipated considerably. If the recent example of reality TV stars in shows like *Love Island* and *Made in Chelsea* is anything to go by, the reverse is now the norm. Those individuals are now using television as a springboard for online stardom. The prefix 'micro' seems inadequate to capture the state of online celebrity in 2018.

Nevertheless, it has become almost customary in celebrity studies and other disciplines to refer to YouTubers, Instafamers, and other online figures as micro-celebrities regardless of the actual extent of their audience and influence. Much of this can perhaps be attributed to the popularisation of the term by Marwick (2013) and other authors, who applied Senft's definition to the emerging generation of well-known figures in California's technology industry and who were, at the time, the most popular members of the Twitter network following its 2006 launch. For this reason, it is worth spending some time looking at Marwick's work and some of the individuals studied in her research on the industrial culture surrounding the rise of social media.

Micro-celebrity in Silicon Valley and Elsewhere

Marwick's (2013) ethnographic study was conducted in the San Francisco Bay Area between 2006 and 2010, a time when many young entrepreneurs, inspired by the rise of companies such as Google and MySpace, were competing furiously (as now, but presumably with the wide-open imagination of a new culture) to launch the next big start-up. Those who succeeded inevitably acquired a cachet within the industry, as in any successful industry, as important people to know and be known by. But word of mouth was no longer the medium for spreading their fame: they had social media. The online profiles afforded by Facebook and the newly emerging Twitter gave these figures a stage on which to perform a kind of limited stardom, and they began to acquire fans who viewed them with the kind of reverence usually associated with film stars and rock musicians.

One such tech star was Kevin Rose, the founder of *Digg*, a technology news site popular with Silicon Valley employees, and presenter of *Digg-Nation*, an online TV show. Marwick describes him as having "no name recognition outside of the tech scene and his college-aged fan base. But within the scene, Rose was a superstar. Fans stopped him in the street and mobbed him at tech parties" (2013, p. 113). Another is Shira Lazar, who established a YouTube channel (Partner's Project) through which she presented a daily show 'What's Trending', which discussed the viral videos of the day that earned her channel 223,000 subscribers.

Based on this type of online entrepreneur, Marwick took Senft's definition of the micro-celebrity and adapted it somewhat. She saw it as comprising two separate phenomena. First, following Rojek's (2001) taxonomy of celebrity, the *ascription* of celebrity to online figures such as tech entrepreneurs like Kevin Rose; second, the *practice* of celebrity on social media such as Twitter. The former group's fame is limited by the reach of the Internet (or any specific platform at a given time); the latter group need not have any kind of audience at all but are actively establishing one through an online profile.

As an example of micro-celebrity-as-practice, she cites the case of Adam Jackson, a new arrival in the San Fransisco Bay Area, who, at the time of her study, was investing enormous reserves of youthful, sleep-refusing energy in self-promotion. He talked of using existing online celebrities as models ("I use [Ryan Block's] day to day actions to kind of sculpt my life") and spending a year and a half "changing the way I tweet" to find "that algorithm of success" (Marwick, 2013, pp. 126–127). Several years later, ground down by trolls and abuse, his Twitter following never rising above 3,000, Jackson had left the Bay Area and was enjoying a stress-free, Web-free life in the country "keeping chickens". Practising celebrity is no guarantee of acquiring fame no matter how hard you work at it.

The Future of Micro-Celebrity

The concept of micro-celebrity has informed much of the growing literature on online celebrity, where much of the time it seems to stand for fame acquired solely through social media (Abidin, 2016; Jerslev, 2016; Mavroudis & Milne, 2016). The fact that micro-celebrity does not really capture online figures with followings in the tens of millions has led to Marwick in particular dropping the 'ascribed' aspect and focusing solely on its performative elements: "micro-celebrity is something one *does*, rather than something one *is*" (Marwick, 2016, p. 339). For its more successful practitioners, it constitutes a 'mindset': providing fans with round-the-clock access and intimate disclosure while privileging authenticity (i.e. independence from the showbiz world). An enduring requirement for micro-celebrity is that the audience is 'niche', and at the same time, an assumption exists that the traditional entertainment industries and broadcast media sit above digital media in the cultural hierarchy. However, Marwick does conclude that the gap is narrowing, and that, particularly in reality TV, digital culture is beginning to infiltrate the mainstream at least for younger celebrities.

I believe it is important to urge caution on the indiscriminate use of the use of micro-celebrity to describe all digital celebrities. Current definitions rest on three assumptions that, even within the first decade of its coinage, are no longer true. The first concerns the constraints on online fame noted by Senft (2008) that restrict the audience share and profitability of micro-celebrities. Ten years on, these constraints surely no longer apply. As argued earlier, (global) online audiences now far outstrip television audiences, and through the patronage of various grooming, talent and management companies, and revenue-sharing agreements with the various media, online celebrities can acquire substantial profit from their activities.

The second assumption, which follows partly from the first, is that the world of broadcast media and the entertainment industry are beyond the reach of micro-celebrities, who are confined to niche audiences and are "unknown to most and ignored by mainstream media" (Marwick, 2016, p. 334). Though, in the early days, social media occasionally acted as a launching pad for conventional celebrity (e.g. Justin Bieber), online celebrities have rarely made what might be regarded as 'the step-up' to conventional media and entertainment. And mainstream media has tended to ignore, or in some cases patronise, online celebrity. But it is worth considering now whether the relationship between the online and the traditional is as hierarchical as it was ten years ago and whether online celebrity might be regarded as a goal in itself. When you have 40 million followers on YouTube or Instagram, who needs 'mainstream media'?

The third assumption, rooted in the 'practice' aspect of micro-celebrity, is that online celebrities are cultivating relationships with fans and followers that are fundamentally different from those enjoyed by traditional celebrities. This assumption undoubtedly held true in 2008 when most traditional celebrities were avoiding social media like the plague. It may also hold true if we compare an Instagram fashion blogger or YouTube prankster to a long-standing Hollywood star or pop musician. But over the last decade a generation of young practitioners in traditional fields such as music, drama and television, has grown up with social media as an almost obligatory tool for career management. These individuals enter their respective fields with the same audience demands for intimacy as an aspiring gamer or blogger. Whether this is changing the nature of traditional celebrity remains to be seen.

In the context of celebrity studies, then, the term 'micro-celebrity' needs a bit of a rethink. I will discuss some alternative constructions when I come to consider the figure of the social media influencer in chapter 9, not least the intermediate category of the 'meso-celebrity' proposed by Pedroni (2016). Of course, hundreds of thousands of social media users are still building their own niche audiences through social media, and these will be discussed in more detail in chapter 10 in the context of 'persona studies'. But these micro-celebrities are no longer the defining image of twenty-first-century celebrity; it would be like representing twentieth-century film stardom with an aspiring film starlet flipping burgers while waiting for that lucky break with the nearest studio.

5

TWITTER AS 'FUNDAMENTAL': THE OBLIGATORY USE OF SOCIAL MEDIA BY CELEBRITIES

If the last chapter was about the way that 'old' media began to generate new kinds of celebrity in the first two decades of the present century, this chapter, for the most part, is about the challenges that 'new' media have created for established celebrities. It takes us through an important point in recent history, somewhere around 2010, during which the existing stars of stage and screen were no longer able to dismiss social media as a playground for wannabes and no-hopers, and their management teams dragged them kicking and screaming into the digital age. Some kicked and screamed harder than others, but now, like it or not, they are all there, competing for attention with beauty vloggers and Instagram 'influencers'. In the process we see how traditional celebrity, founded on the affordances of broadcast media, has adapted to a set of media with entirely different affordances, most notably regarding audience relationships.

This process took place roughly in three stages from the mid-1990s up to 2010. The first stage involved the emergence of online fan communities, which, as Jenkins (2006) and others have documented, began to exert considerable pressure on the entertainment industry because of fan activism. Celebrities themselves, particularly from the field of popular music, began to respect the power of these communities and those with close audience relationships even invited online fans to participate in the creative process (Shrayne, 2010). The Internet generally had appeal to musicians. With the arrival of the MPEG format, file-sharing websites became a useful place to disseminate new music even if the same affordances for illegal uploading eventually deprived them of a vital source of income.

In the second stage, which saw the emergence of social networking, other kinds of online affordances became apparent to celebrities. As Marshall (2010) puts it, social media instigated a shift from representational media (television, press) to presentational media. The creation of personal profiles on sites like Facebook and MySpace gave individuals a platform not only for communicating with fans but also taking direct control of their image. The final stage arrived at the end of the decade with Twitter, which stripped away all the image-building materials of those earlier networks and threw the emphasis completely on to the written (typed) word. Now it was celebrities from television, sport, and all other fields who leapt into the fray, who were able to pass opinion and poke fun at anything they chose without needing the intermediary assistance of a press interview or management statement. This new-found freedom has brought with it the burden of responsibility, and some of the keenest Twitter users have also been the most critical of the medium.

In the following section, I am going to discuss two documented cases in the celebrity literature that illustrate the pitfalls of online engagement for established celebrities.

Giles (2013b): Morrissey Falls Out with His (Online) Fanbase

(Steven) Morrissey, former Smiths vocalist turned solo artist, has inspired intense devotion from his fans since the mid-1980s. As one of them confesses, "[Morrissey] is the brother I never had, the father figure I always longed for" (Maton, 2010). At times, the relationship between Morrissey and his fans has drawn so much on religious imagery that it has been a perfect illustration of the concept of 'celebrity worship' (see chapter 3). Morrissey has been adored for the intimate nature of his lyrics, his controversial statements against royalty, the erosion of Englishness, the meat industry and his witty and articulate persona presented in music press interviews.

But the arrival of the Internet, and a series of disappointing recordings, introduced a new element into Morrissey fandom: the devoted fan as critic. His largest online fan forum, morrissey-solo.com (henceforth 'Solo') was a huge success in 2004, around the release of the well-received album

You Are the Quarry, with 100,000 posts in 19,000 separate threads in that particular year. Almost a decade later, although the site was still active (17,000 posts in 2012), many Solo members had jumped ship to set up a rival site, All You Need Is Morrissey (henceforth 'AYNIM'), claiming the atmosphere on Solo had become toxic, full of fans complaining about the quality of recent releases and attacking the singer for his increasingly offensive remarks, leading to numerous accusations of racism over the years (Snowsell, 2011). AYNIM presented itself as a haven of calm, a "happy little bubble" as one member put it, where diehard fans could shelter from the "bullying" from the "haters" on Solo (Giles, 2013b).

Though this particular online community opens up all kinds of questions relevant to fan studies more generally (what constitutes a 'true fan', for instance – blind acceptance or constructive criticism?), its relevance to the present chapter concerns the reaction of Morrissey. After one particular flurry of criticism, he appeared onstage in a T-shirt reading 'Fuck morrissey-solo.com' and banned the founder of Solo from attending a concert in Copenhagen after he had travelled all the way from his home in Los Angeles. It is notable that, at this point in time, Morrissey had not been personally involved with either fan site. The closest thing to an official Morrissey website was True To You, an information-based site which occasionally disseminated 'official statements' by the singer and his entourage, and a mysterious Twitter account, @morrisseysmum, which seemed to relay tour dates, and other news earlier than the fansites (Giles, 2013b).

The case of Morrissey illustrates the potential difficulties facing celebrities in the digital era. Through the lens of affordance theory, we might conclude that, for some celebrities, the gulf between representational media and presentational media is practically unbridgeable. The affordances of broadcast media – where a celebrity (or their management) can hide from their audience, issue occasional statements in the press, meet fans through the printed word (interviews) and through carefully staged conventions and other events – are no longer tenable in an age when fans have such a vocal presence (and power) and when other, more approachable, celebrities can be seen enjoying relatively intimate relationships with their audiences.

Of course, many fans, particularly older ones, will continue to value remoteness and untouchability as hallmarks of idolised stars. One Solo member claimed that she never wanted to meet Morrissey because she would be "too shy", and "bad company" (Giles, 2013b). Nevertheless, the intimacy fostered by social media is clearly not one of its affordances for celebrities whose image is founded upon the Hollywood tradition. As Beer (2008) wrote in an early discussion of celebrities on social media (in this case MySpace), how does a "rock god" manage the transition to becoming a "familiar friend"? In Morrissey's case, it seems, by refusing to engage with the process at all.

Thomas (2014): John Cusack Goes Incognito, then Cognito Again

The second case study that I want to use to illustrate the difficulty of embracing presentational media is the Hollywood actor John Cusack, star of *High Fidelity* and numerous other films around the end of the millennium. For a fairly conventional Hollywood actor, Cusack was unusually early to embrace social media, setting up a MySpace site under his own name in 2008 on which he uploaded articles about political issues (Cusack had been a long-standing critic of George W. Bush) with brief comments. The following year, he migrated to Twitter although here he disguised himself as an online avatar named 'Shockozulu', leading to much debate amongst fans as to the authenticity of the account. Conforming to Twitter's condensed communication affordances, his commenting style became more personal and interactive, but his comments were often gnomic or unintelligible, with "weirdly framed political diatribes" (Thomas, 2014, p. 251).

As more Cusack fans followed @shockozulu, and began to challenge his communicational style, he started to behave rather like Morrissey, retweeting complaints and blocking their authors (some of whom took their protests to YouTube in the form of video critiques). Finally, in 2010, he changed the name of his account to @johncusack, and, whilst maintaining the political edge, modifying the content to reflect accounts of other celebrities from the film world, with "details of favourite bars, music and quirky artworks, and retweeting positive responses to the films he aligns himself most with" (Thomas, 2014, p. 252).

Thomas's conclusion is that Cusack regarded @shockozulu as "an authentic representation of self, an online identity that reflected who he felt he 'really' was in contrast to the coolly affable star image presented through film roles and publicity" (Ibid, p. 252) and that @johncusack represents a "compromise between these two elements". For Thomas, doing social media well requires celebrities to experiment with online personae, just like the micro-celebrities considered in the previous chapter, except with a potential risk to relations with their existing, and often long-established, fan base.

In the remainder of this chapter, I am going to examine the relatively small literature on celebrities' use of Twitter and consider how its potential technological and social affordances have been picked up or rejected by different individuals.

A Brief History of Celebrities on Twitter

HI TWITTERS. THANK YOU FOR A WARM WELCOME. FEELING REALLY 21ST CENTURY.

With these words, Oprah Winfrey dipped a toe in the waters of Twitter back in 2008 and opened up a channel through which thousands of celebrities were to flow over the following decade. Many of these paddled gingerly without daring to take the plunge, but within a few years, they were off, gliding through the water, some more gracefully than others. Twitter had gone from being seen as an idle indulgence on the part of narcissistic preeners[1] to being an indispensable publicity tool. By 2014, Graeme Turner updated his key work on celebrity by adding (p. 74): "At the moment, a professional engagement with Twitter is fundamental for virtually anyone interested in managing their public persona".

Much of this has to do with the sheer scale of Twitter's success. The medium's expansion had much to do with two events in 2008: its role in the successful electoral campaign led by Barack Obama and the mainstream news bulletins' coverage of live updates on the terrorist attacks in Mumbai (Bennett & Thomas, 2014). From being seen as another social network in the tradition of MySpace and Facebook, Twitter was now being credited with political influence and as an instantaneous source of news, either supplementing or threatening traditional news media, leading to popular claims that it was creating 'citizen journalism'. Millions signed up.

---

[1] Just as an example of this attitude, London daily newspaper the *Evening Standard* described Twitter in September 2009 as a "home of vacuous celebrities... filled with endless chatter about what users had eaten for lunch."

By May 2009, it boasted 18.2 million users; this had risen to 27.2 million by the following January (Marwick & boyd, 2011).

As the Twitter membership grew, so inevitably did the numbers 'following' individual celebrity accounts. Never mind citizen journalism; this was great publicity for those seated at the top media table. Hollywood star Ashton Kutcher demonstrated the power of the medium for audience-building by successfully challenging the CNN television network in a race to obtain a million followers (Marshall, 2010). As far as Twitter is concerned, by 2010, the micro-celebrity era was over, with Kevin Rose and other tech entrepreneurs being swiftly overtaken by the "conventionally famous" names of Barack Obama and Britney Spears (Marwick & boyd, 2011). Even stars who had established themselves on social media like MySpace and Facebook were crossing over to Twitter, whose 'soundbite' form of communication was seen as more of an affordance than the chattier, more intimate style of 'status updates' and 'wall posts' of those earlier media.

Of particular appeal to celebrities, the Twitter audience consisted of *followers*, not *friends*, a much more fitting appellation for the legions of fans they imagined to be associating with their accounts. One crucial difference between Twitter and earlier networks, however, was that members did not choose their followers; even though they could 'block' individual members, they were unable to prevent hordes of 'anti-fans' (Gray, 2003) from showering them with abuse. The exposure to abuse and criticism has led to many celebrities developing a love/hate relationship with Twitter, with frequent threats to 'quit', even if this simply took the form of migrating to a different medium (like Instagram) or returning, several months later, tail firmly between legs, simply unable to cope with life after complete withdrawal.

British comedian Stephen Fry is probably the best example of a celebrity who seems unable to fully work out what Twitter affords him. One of its earliest and most enthusiastic adopters, he raced to a million followers as early as 2009 but has since closed and re-opened his account on numerous occasions. Despite this, he continues to be one of the most generous celebrity users, responding regularly to individual tweets sent by fans. Another British celebrity who found himself in deep water is the writer Richard Dawkins, whose various 'spats' with Twitter members taking issue with his criticisms of religion often make news in the mainstream British press.

Not all celebrities have been quite so enamoured of what Twitter appeared to offer them. Ashton Kutcher is a rare example of a film star who has fully embraced the medium; others have steered clear. Harry Potter star Daniel Radcliffe argued that its use was incompatible with having a private life (van den Bulck, Claessens & Bels, 2014). George Clooney branded anyone famous who uses Twitter 'a moron' (Brady, 2013)[2]. Emma Stone and Keira Knightley opened and closed their accounts; as yet, neither has reopened them. Julia Roberts opened an account in January 2011, which is currently followed by over half a million people, but she has never posted a single tweet. Others use Twitter sparingly, to promote work or issue the occasional bland statement, usually an endorsement of a fellow celebrity. It is easy to see why because, for many celebrities, the risks posed by frequent Twitter use outweigh its positive affordances.

Risky Business: When Tweeting to Millions Simply isn't Worth it

In 2010, US figure skater Evan Lysacek ought to have been a pretty popular figure. Gold medallist in the Vancouver Winter Olympics, and praised as "an outstanding ambassador for the United States and the Olympic movement worldwide" by the CEO of the US Olympic Committee, he had everything going for him until one day a follower sent him the following tweet:

> Hey Evan, is Johnny Weir really a guy? Hard to tell from the photos I've seen, LOL;

You might think that, even if Johnny Weir, a fellow American figure skater, were not a bitter long-term rival, it would have been sensible simply to ignore this comment. After all, most celebrities manage to ignore most personal slights directed at themselves. If you are going to respond to an offensive remark about your rival, it might have been politic, in full view of the

---

[2] Plenty of others have denounced Twitter and other social media to the press but have subsequently succumbed to the temptation: Stephen Fry's former sidekick Hugh Laurie is one (Brady, 2013).

public, to bury the hatchet momentarily and take issue with the question. What Lysacek did was to reply:

Verdict is still out.

Several hours later, the chastisements from other followers, some of them claiming to be long-time fans, ringing in his ears, Lysacek tried to make amends. Someone had hacked into his Twitter account, he claimed on his Facebook wall, and was sending messages on his behalf. Just ignore them. It was hard to ignore the offending tweet though because, twelve hours later, he had still failed to delete it, allowing all and sundry to copy and paste the screen capture into multiple online locations. Despite all evidence to the contrary, Lysacek persisted in repeating the hacking claim, so that "a simple faux pas" became "transformed... into a communicative breakdown" (Colapinto & Benecchi, 2014). After 36 hours, he finally relented, an issued an apology to Johnny Weir for his "insensitive, hurtful and offensive" comment.

The main point to be taken from this incident, as Colapinto and Benecchi (2014) argue, is that Lysacek's initial attempted cover-up and eventual apology reflect the seriousness, which such 'faux pas' or slips of the mask are now taken in the digital era. Apart from anything else, it demonstrates how quickly Twitter content can become news even in the mainstream press. As Marshall (2010, p. 45) writes, Twitter content "travels quickly back into the representational media." We have become used to reading headlines in established news outlets about a 'Twitter spat' between two or more celebrities, between sports stars and their management. Of course, in 2016 Donald Trump became the first major world leader to use Twitter as his (un)official mouthpiece for issuing policy statements. Whatever the public at large might think, for the traditional press, Twitter is now as credible a news source as anything.

Academic authors have dwelt mostly on the element of risk that social media poses to celebrities who continue to "dabble" with it (Bennett & Thomas, 2014). It is "a hazardous balancing act" (Van den Bulck et al, 2014), unstable, methodologically challenging for researchers, and it effectively constitutes a "third space" somewhere between the traditional media and entertainment industries and the (broadcast) audience (Bennett & Thomas, 2014). In studying strange new spaces, one of the biggest challenges thrown up is *authenticity*: on one hand, Twitter promises greater authenticity, appearing to give the stars control over their presentation; on the other, the instability of the online environment means that audience readings of Twitter material are an important consideration. Only through careful analysis can audiences be confident they are privy to the authentic voice of the celebrity they follow.

Concerns over the authenticity of Twitter accounts has long been a concern for academics, reflecting early claims by psychologists and others that online communication was characterised by anonymity and potential deception (Joinson, 2003) and deriving probably from a more general "hermeneutics of suspicion" (Ricouer, 1970) throughout the humanities and social sciences. In his discussion of MySpace profiles, Beer (2008, p. 232) puts the emphasis on audience "*perceptions*, as we already know it is relatively easy to pass yourself off as someone else in a virtual environment", citing examples of record companies funding account curators as a reason to be wary. By the time of Marwick and boyd's (2011) analysis of celebrity Twitter practice, an orthodoxy was taking shape; of 144 "highly followed" accounts in their study, 105 showed clear signs of authentic authorship, based on criteria such as tweets that are "personal, controversial or negative" (p. 149) and contained idiosyncratic signs, such as spelling errors that would be screened out by a careful account manager[3]. Suspicions that fake accounts were masquerading as authentic ones were allayed by sites such as truthtweet.com (which 'outed' the fakes) and by Twitter and other social media's uses of 'verified' accounts.

Verified accounts in Twitter (indicated with a blue tick next to the account name) are awarded to applicants who can demonstrate their account is 'of public interest' and they have made some 'impact in their field'. The list of fields that verified users might be drawn from includes music, acting, fashion, government, politics, religion, journalism, sports, media and business although 'other key interest areas' are also considered (presumably to account for newer forms of celebrity). There is an additional requirement that the account name '[reflects] the real or stage name of the person' and that the biography 'specifies an area of expertise'

---

[3] Nevertheless, Dare-Edwards (2014) cites a case in which fans interpreted spelling errors as a deliberate double bluff on behalf of an account curator to lend it a false air of authenticity, so presumably this criterion had a short shelf life.

although it appears that this latter requirement is waived once the award has been made because many celebrities on Twitter, particularly comedians, prefer quirky or enigmatic biographies.

Though fake accounts and alleged hacking of verified accounts are still broad concerns in popular and academic discussions of social media, consensus has at least settled on the assumption that most celebrities have a Twitter account, and where it consists of a bit more than marketing (announcements of tour dates and so on), the celebrity's authentic voice is speaking most of the time. Nevertheless, the perception that celebrities are merely 'dabbling' in social media suggests it is not really their environment, a view that contrasts sharply with Turner's (2014) claim that Twitter use is "fundamental" for any contemporary celebrity.

Preserving the Star/Fan Hierarchy: Twitter as 'Nothing New'

Over the past decade, the hermeneutics of suspicion in academia seem to have moved away from reading Twitter accounts as inauthentic to reading them as hierarchical. In the last decade, something of a backlash against the Internet has occurred in the social sciences and humanities whereby it has become almost *de rigueur* to downplay claims that social media represent anything new, radical, or 'democratic' (e.g. Fuchs, 2014). Much of this may be an understandable reaction to hyperbolic claims about the Internet's democratic potential, particularly by tech companies, but it has become almost obligatory to qualify any academic accounts of changing or transforming culture with a caveat about how social media are ultimately run for profit and are unable by themselves to challenge the power structures served by neoliberal economics. Any deviation from this position is either dismissed as naive 'technological determinism' or, worse, tacit endorsement of neoliberal politics (and occasionally, bias[4]).

---

[4] Many of the most enthusiastic claims, made on behalf of social media's 'democratic', emancipatory potential, have come from authors employed by the tech industry. While not denying the possibility that such authors are, if not consciously promoting their employers, at the very least the products of a culture of hyperbole, one imagines that a significant proportion of academically minded tech enthusiasts deliberately choose to work in tech environments rather than academic ones. Therefore, a bias in any other direction would be surprising.

In celebrity studies, two recent articles have made the same claims about the use of Twitter by celebrities: it is just another medium for acting out the same unequal power relationships between audiences and celebrities (as representatives of the entertainment industry). One of the articles is Thomas's (2014) case study of John Cusack's online profile across time, which along with other evidence, is used to argue that Twitter use reveals aspects of the "conservative" celebrity-audience relationship which date back to early Hollywood. "The close inclusivity between star and fan that Twitter invites does not represent a shift into a new realm of star interactions but an evolution of existing frameworks that reflect new convergence and technologies" (p. 247).

The second article is an analysis of the tweets sent to the five most-followed celebrities on Twitter during 2013 by Kehrberg (2015). Working on an analogy between tweets and fanmail (or, more generally, letter writing), the author analysed the structure of 200 such texts that included some kind of "message" (typically of 'adoration' or 'goodwill'). Critically, not a single one of the 200 tweets received a response from the celebrity concerned, a neglect that she describes as "alarming" (p. 95). This leads her to conclude that "while scholars laud the possibility for social interaction between fans and celebrities on Twitter in theory, it is not in practice taking place" (p. 93). Moreover, the structure of the tweets suggested that fans did not expect a reply to their messages, and that they were content to occupy a subordinate position in the medium. She concludes by comparing Twitter to the fanmail of Joan Crawford and baseball star Jackie Robinson, arguing that "both accessibility and hierarchy may be dependent on the star being addressed, and not on the medium of communication" (p. 96).

The first point to make about these two studies is that neither author arrives at a conclusion entirely unsupported by her data. There is good reason to place social media in a historical context as I have argued throughout this book so far. Clearly, celebrities from traditional domains such as cinema and music will be the most reluctant to close the gap between stage and audience (and are still supported by a global industry that sees them fundamentally as brands). However, both articles make a number of assumptions about celebrity and social media that lead them to dismiss Twitter's 'newness' (Thomas, 2014) as nothing more than a technological tweak to a timeless practice.

The first is the assumption that celebrity is a phenomenon with a distinct character that was formed by early Hollywood and has persisted unchanged throughout the twentieth century (Thomas, for example, deliberately switches between 'star' and 'celebrity' throughout because for her the distinction is unnecessary). I have already discussed definitions of celebrity at some length and I refer readers to the first chapter to see how problematic this simple equation is. The second assumption, in relation to media themselves, is essentially the position of 'functionalism' critiqued throughout chapter 2. For Kehrberg, Twitter is just letter writing with bells and whistles; for Thomas, it is a new kind of community platform like radio, which produced new stars who did not have to conform to the visual expectations of cinema.

Both analogies are clever but inappropriate. Radio is a broadcast medium; although early supporters (like Bertolt Brecht) considered it to have democratic potential, and CB radio shows some superficial similarities with YouTube (rather than Twitter), the technology for 'broadcasting yourself' ultimately lay far beyond the reach of most users. Anyone can open a Twitter account and send a tweet to any other Twitter member within seconds. Unlike fanmail, which had to be posted to an intermediary (fan club, management) and would only ever get replied via that intermediary with an authentic signature at best, Twitter members can reasonably expect to get a reply from most celebrities, and sometimes they do. This makes Twitter unarguably new in the historical context of celebrity.

Celebrity-Audience Interaction on Twitter

To underline this last point, I will now discuss the literature that has specifically focused on interactions between celebrities and other Twitter members (fans, mostly, but as I will go on to explain, fandom on Twitter and other social media differs from pre-Internet fandom). Two of the most important studies of this topic are those conducted by Gayle Stever and colleagues (Stever & Lawson, 2013; Stever & Hughes, 2013). In the former, she analysed the tweets sent by 12 celebrities; in the latter, she explored fan tweets as well, paying particular attention to specific interactions between celebrities and fans.

In a grounded theory analysis, Stever and Lawson (2013) coded celebrity tweets on two dimensions: whether the tweet was an original announcement in the style of a Facebook 'status update' (e.g. "Enjoying a beautiful Monday morning"), or whether it was a reply or re-tweet, and whether it was addressed to a fellow celebrity, or to a non-celebrity (typically, fans in general). They also coded each tweet for its content, categorising them as either 'serious' or 'funny'. The results show quite a wide range of practices that are not directly related to the size of the celebrity's following or to their field of activity. Tom Hanks and Lady Gaga issued mostly original tweets, while William Shatner and Katy Perry showed a more mixed pattern. Interestingly for claims of hierarchy, most celebrities tweeted more to fans (or the public) than to specific celebrities. In the case of *Star Trek* actor Brent Spiner, only 6 per cent of his tweets addressed fellow celebrities; for Tom Hanks and Lady Gaga, 10 per cent and 11 per cent respectively. In general, celebrity tweets tended to be serious rather than funny.

Stever and Hughes's (2013) closer inspection of celebrity-fan interaction threw up some surprising data. As reported in chapter 3, fan reactions to receiving tweets from celebrities ranged from excitement to indifference and even, in one case, irritation. Some celebrities were found to have very high levels of interaction: another *Star Trek* actor, Jeri Ryan, sent 96 per cent of her tweets to individual fans, sharing experiences of children leaving the family home and other personal issues. All but one of the 20 Jeri Ryan fans in their sample received at least one reply from her during the period. Other celebrities had less positive relationships; Brent Spiner, though responsive, tended to give "sarcastic" replies to fans and received quite a lot of abuse in return.

One notable phenomenon identified by Stever and Hughes (2013) was the high number of fan tweets "favourited" by celebrities; as high as 90 per cent of all "favourite" tweets sent to rapper Ke$ha, and 60 per cent of those "favourited" by Roseanne Barr. Even as big a star as Justin Timberlake sent 24 per cent of his tweets to individual fans, displaying "humour and gratitude" at their (typically positive) messages. In the case of singer Josh Groban, fan interaction did not just involve his personal account but those of his backing band, tour manager and security guard, who were all equally responsive and the majority of who found their own personal numbers of followers exceeding well over a thousand, turning them effectively into online (micro?) celebrities in their own right.

A slightly more recent study (data were collected in 2014) is Usher's (2015) analysis of the 20 most followed celebrities on Twitter. She found a similarly divergent pattern in terms of the ratio of original (here, "broadcast") tweets to replies and retweets, and likewise suggested that this reflects very different uses of Twitter. 81 per cent of Barack Obama's tweets were original and not one was a reply, while over half of singers Rihanna and Harry Styles' tweets were replies, indicating a more dialogic pattern of Twitter use. Indeed, the latter pattern was more typical of her sample than the former, painting a different picture of Twitter use to Kehrberg (though it must be noted that Kehrberg only studied tweets sent *to* celebrities).

While acknowledging that Twitter affords dialogue between celebrities and audiences, Usher (2015), like Thomas (2014), argues that the style of that dialogue is often rather formal and reflects the broadcasting tradition that most of the biggest Twitter celebrities have emerged from. One example of this tradition is the Q&A format that many celebrities use as a vehicle for communicating with individual fans (17 of the 20 figures studied by Usher used this format). Typically, Q&A sessions are initiated by the celebrity either by alerting followers in advance, using hashtags, or spontaneously by announcing them (Katy Perry, for example, tweeted "Okay: 5 questions, 5 answers. Go"). Some of the sessions in her sample were formulaic, with only the blandest questions answered. Britney Spears used hers to perform careful impression management (to counteract the media stereotype of her as 'bad parent'); of five permitted questions, Perry only replied to five individuals, four of whom had Twitter handles that directly referenced her name (so clearly fans).

For these (very) popular celebrities, it seems that Q&A sessions fall into Couldry's (2003) category of 'ritual' event that serves to delineate the boundary between 'media people' (celebrities in this case) and the 'public'. It would seem strange, and not a little presumptuous, for a non-celebrity to invite his or her followers to ask them questions in this way, but the convention is not challenged by those who are comfortable playing the role of fan. As Marwick and boyd (2011, p.139) claim, "in order [for celebrities, presumably] to successfully practise celebrity, fans must recognise the power differentials intrinsic to the relationship". Usher (2015) argues that, like most effective Twitter practice, it derives from the conventions that celebrities and their fans are used to from previous (broadcast, press) media experience. Taking a similar perspective, Thomas (2014) likens the Q&A format to the (offline) press conference, although of course it is (largely) fans asking the questions rather than reporters. But the point is that the convention is recognised and respected. An alternative explanation is that they are convenient ways of managing huge numbers of followers, bolstering fans' expectations of direct personal access in a concentrated burst of activity during a quiet moment.

One motive for high levels of celebrity-fan interaction on Twitter, argues Usher (2015), is that it can be seen as part of the "intertextual performance" of certain celebrities. This is particularly true for comedians, whose high level of 'banter' with the Twitter audience reverses the serious/funny pattern reported in Stever and Lawson (2013). Usher cites the case of British TV personality Jonathan Ross (@Wossy), whose interactive style builds on his existing success as a witty presenter with a keen interest in popular culture:

Fan: '@THR: Dark Knight returns' No 2 Cover features £478,000
            at Auction #batman @Wossy? You been splashing out again?
            [*link to news article reporting story*]
@Wossy: @[*fan name*] not me. Never liked that cover. Batman looks
            constipated. We've all been there.

Ross did not feature in Usher's main sample (his actual number of followers at the time is not mentioned but is presently 5.4 million). He represents a different type of celebrity from the likes of Katy Perry and Justin Bieber, being largely recognised by a national audience (the UK), in a slightly older age group (having risen to prominence in the 1980s) and arguably having more time to use the medium. He is one of the most prolific celebrity Tweeters, averaging over 10 messages per day, 75 per cent of which are replies. Usher argues that this pattern of use reflects his background in TV chat show interaction, and indeed this returns us to the issue raised earlier by Beer (2008): how does a "rock god" manage the transition to "familiar friend"? Arguably, with a lot more difficulty than a laddish, affable TV personality.

Fans and fellow celebrities are not the only Twitter users that celebrities reply to. As early as 2011, Marwick and boyd (2011) were reporting instances where celebrities had been been goaded or otherwise provoked into replying by an abusive or critical tweet. In one instance, right-wing US politician Newt Gingrich contested a tweet disagreeing with his claim about Ronald Reagan's part in the downfall of the Soviet Union, telling the tweeter to read a specific book on the subject. Singer Trent Reznor replied twice to a critical tweeter, the second time 'shaming' her by revealing her personal (offline) identity, place of residence and her "criminal record". Some of these responses demonstrated surprising restraint; despite being called a "cunt", Lily Allen explained, in measured terms, why she doesn't just "accept" anyone on her MySpace page.

One of the most unlikely affordances of Twitter has been the ability of certain celebrities to turn critical or abusive comments to their advantage by developing a reputation for cutting-edge humour. British singer James Blunt is an example of this; regularly hailed as 'king of Twitter' in gossip magazines, tabloids, and websites, he has kept his career in the spotlight by re-tweeting negative comments along with sarcastic replies. Someone tweets: "James Blunt could give me £1000 and I still wouldn't like him", to which Blunt replies: "OK, I'll just take the £20 rubdown with happy ending then, please". Even when music sharing site Spotify used his image in an advertisement, he retweeted the image asking its creator "How much have you had to drink?" Despite, like John Cusack, not appearing to take Twitter seriously, his pattern of use seems to have enhanced his profile among his 1.5 million followers. Gordon Ramsay, celebrity chef, has over three times this number but is still happy to interact with followers who seek his typically abrasive opinion by tweeting him photos of unpleasant-looking airline food or even their own less-than-stellar creations. As with Jonathan Ross, this kind of 'banter' reinforces the authenticity of Ramsay's television persona while maintaining his status as (culinary) expert.

Twitter Use as 'Normal Social Interaction'

One of the claims that has been repeated about Twitter use by celebrities is that it offers them an opportunity to perform the 'true self', unfettered by the industrial restrictions imposed by managers, record companies and other professional gatekeepers. In its early days (before its adoption became practically obligatory for celebrities), it allowed adopters to create the impression they had "'bucked the system' and undermined the publicity process by speaking honestly and directly to their fans" (Turner, 2014, p. 75). Perhaps the most successful celebrity who has used Twitter in this context is Lady Gaga, whose professional image relies on her being accepted by her fans as a rebel and an outsider. She was one of the earliest celebrities to fully exploit the medium, reinforcing her fans' belief that she is 'different' and that she genuinely cares about her 'little monsters' as they are known. One of Click, Lee, and Holladay's (2013, p. 374) participants makes the claim that even though 'other stars' use social media for marketing, "Gaga actually communicates with her fans". By 2013, she had over 37 million followers (68 million at the time of writing).

In many respects, Lady Gaga's relationship with her fans is more reminiscent of Hills' (2015) concept of 'multisocial interaction' than the more intimate banter style of Jonathan Ross or Gordon Ramsay. As Click et al (2013, p. 375) say, "Lady Gaga need not reply directly to each fan for them to feel as though she is talking to them", quoting one fan as saying "when one Little Monster tweets [Gaga] and she tweets them back, that monster represents us as a whole and it means the world". Despite the occasional direct communication, however, Gaga manages to retain an otherworldliness that maintains her remote, star persona. Another 'little monster', cited by Bennett (2014) argues that "it would ruin the whole Lady Gaga image if we discovered she was... just like the rest of us".

Of particular importance to Lady Gaga fans is the impression that she personally authors her own tweets: "it seems... like she's there on her phone right now", says one of Bennett's (2014) participants. This sense of immediacy does not "ruin the Lady Gaga image" because her popularity is based entirely on her remaining autonomous of the vulgar requirements of the entertainment and media industries. Gaga is in control, making artistic decisions and expressing her individual opinion. Therefore, Twitter is the ideal platform for her, offering her fans a personal channel that circumvents managers, TV stations, fan club owners, burly security guards and all the other faceless nobodies standing between stars and their adoring public.

It is not just rebels and outsiders who benefit from the impression of autonomy. Thomas (2014, p. 245) cites a tweet by actor Jim Carrey claiming that "my people called... [asking me to] tame my tweets a little". Not only does this disabuse sceptics of any notion that his "people" are authoring his account, but it also strengthens the idea that Carrey is offering the Twitter audience his personal, uncensored, and sincere observations about life. When those observations concord with the familiar persona known from television, cinema or other media, they reinforce this impression, creating the perception that the public has direct access to the star's intimate day-to-day existence[5]. What matters is "the coherence of the celebrity per-formance" (Van den Bulck et al, 2014). The ultimate goal is to make this performance appear seamless, so that, as Stever and Hughes (2013) say of Josh Groban, "his Twitter interaction [looks] just like any other social interaction between… acquaintances".

Because celebrity presentation on Twitter is so bound up with notions of 'impression' and 'performance', it is not surprising that many authors in the humanities and social sciences have returned to the work of Goffmann (1959) as a frame of reference. Marwick and boyd (2011) and Usher (2015) both discuss Twitter presentation as a balancing act in which celebrities need to manage the difference between the self they enact in 'frontstage' areas (when on show, for example, in a meeting at work) and that presented in 'backstage' areas (in intimate surroundings such as the home, or relaxing with colleagues at lunch). In traditional media, this distinction is preserved by the conventions (and limited access) of broadcasting; in the entertainment industry more generally, by the physical separation of actors and audience and the spaces in which they perform.

Online, of course, the distinction is a discursive one, concerning subject matter and conversational style. It is "neither neat nor easy" (Marwick and boyd, 2011). Keeping the two realms separate is difficult when celebrities reply to tweets on a whim and later regret the ramifications their response has had for the coherence of their performance. The most obvious exam-ple of this is the Evan Lysacek gaffe discussed previously. Colapinto and Benecchi (2014) also interpret this incident in Goffmanian terms, citing his concept of 'disruptions' to the continuity of self performance. Such disruptions are also evident in the many 'Twitter spats' where celebrities lapse into slanging matches with fellow celebrities (or others), revealing

---

[5] I am being cautious here using terms like 'impression' and 'perception', partly from an epistemological angle in that we can never *really* know who authors the tweets on a Twitter account any more than we can tease apart the relative contributions of authors, editors and ghostwriters in traditional publishing. The more sceptical authors talk of Twitter autonomy, and the notion of fan access, as an 'illusion' (Dare-Edwards, 2014). To my mind, this is every bit as pathologising as describing parasocial relationships as 'illusory' and is simply not true, because there is now so much evidence that celebrities *do* tweet directly to fans and other non-famous Twitter users.

elements of the backstage self that, on reflection, they wished they had kept under wraps.

Marshall (2010) has argued that Twitter presentation takes place at three levels of self. The 'public self' is the traditional frontstage performance, heavily policed, revealing little other than professional announcements. We can see this self-presentation in a number of established celebrities who use social media mostly for announcements about tour dates and releases. The second level is the 'public private self' where followers are offered carefully selected snippets of backstage areas and is perhaps best exemplified by Lady Gaga's use of the medium. The third level is the 'transgressive intimate self', where backstage material leaks into the public performance: Marshall (Ibid, p. 45) cites Liz Taylor's reaction to her friend Michael Jackson's death: "what might have appeared appropriate for one's closest friends is... shared with hundreds of thousands who pass it on virally to millions."

Almost a decade later, the first kind of Twitter presentation has become the exception, especially for younger celebrities. Third-level presentation has become the norm, and the most successful Twitter users are arguably those who are best able to manage the occasional 'disruption' or have become adept at turning disruptions into opportunities for mirth-making and publicity. Even the second-level presentation is largely confined to established celebrities from the pre-social media era. It raises once again whether Beer's (2008) rock gods are an endangered species, along with other remote, supernatural stars whose aura relies on distance, aloofness and mystery. Bennett (2014) interprets Lady Gaga's appeal by citing Dyer's (1979) concept of the ordinary/extraordinary "paradox" surrounding traditional film stars. While deriving 'beauty and pleasure' from them as untouchable, remote icons, even in the days of early Hollywood, magazines sold them to the cinema-going public as mere mortals who ate breakfast and went shopping like the rest of us. Having arrived just in advance of the social media era, perhaps Lady Gaga is the last 'rock god(dess)'.

'Social Media Natives' and Twitter

I want to conclude this chapter by bringing the discussion of Twitter celebrity up to date and consider its use by aspiring celebrities who have grown up with the medium. I call these "social media natives", the generation for which social media use is as seemingly natural a part of contemporary daily life as running water, refrigeration, incessant car travel and electricity itself. That is to say, what television, radio, and daily newspapers were to the late twentieth century.

The important point here is that people seeking a career in the media and/or entertainment industry in the present (2010–2020) decade will probably have at least one active social media account in operation *before* the moment at which they become famous. This changes the whole picture of celebrity use of social media as discussed so far in this chapter because, for this generation of celebrities, there is no need to adopt social media as a publicity vehicle, communication mouthpiece, or soapbox: these celebrities are already experienced users of social media, as are their audience. In this respect, they are more like the micro-celebrities discussed in chapter 4, who were using social media (or the Internet generally) as their *only* publicity vehicle back in the first decade of the century except that, now that almost everyone in the Western world under 40 uses social media to a greater or lesser extent, they are no longer a 'niche'.

In terms of field, or domain, of activity, contemporary celebrities encompass everything from the modern-day celebrity categories of vloggers and influencers to the time-honoured practitioners of traditional arts and entertainments (singers, actors, writers, athletes, TV stars). In this chapter, I have been focusing on the latter group of individuals because, of course, the vloggers and influencers are uniquely twenty-first-century categories and will be discussed in depth in the next few chapters. What I am concerned with here are the emergent performers in these traditional sectors, those who practise pre-social media celebrity *via* social media. However, as I will go on to argue later in the book, direct comparison is difficult if not impossible because the two generations of celebrities have evolved in different cultural contexts, and these contexts are critical in shaping the kind of celebrities at any given point in history. I have chosen to concentrate almost entirely on Twitter in this chapter because of its popularity with established celebrities, which makes for a closer comparison between the social media use of the two generations (those who had to adopt and adapt to social media, and the "natives") though, as I have said earlier, this is a somewhat arbitrary distinction.

I will illustrate these points first by focusing on young musical celebrities who have risen to success since 2010 and with a discussion of some of my own research looking at aspiring crime authors.

Digital Pop Stars: Lorde, Stormzy, and the Next Generation

A young singer-songwriter from New Zealand whose first album has sold two million copies worldwide and topped the charts in several countries, Lorde's success owes much to digital media. Although signed to Universal Music Group (UMG), when she uploaded the tracks on an EP to the music network SoundCloud, she generated sufficient online interest to encourage UMG to release it commercially. It reached number two in the New Zealand and Australian charts and effectively launched her career. Very much the contemporary pop star, Lorde has an online relationship with fans that is more intimate and intense than many of the celebrities discussed in this chapter.

She opened her Twitter account in 2011 before enjoying any major success, which qualifies her for the social media native generation (i.e. she was using social media *before* becoming famous). At the time of writing, Lorde has 5.7 million Twitter followers although, without a high level of activity (only 3,800 tweets in six years), she is interactive, finding time every few days to retweet fan messages, seemingly the preferred way for celebrities to engage with fans today (as opposed to replying directly). Not coincidentally, she receives many hundreds of replies to almost every tweet, many of which hold out hope that she will receive (and read) them:

> *[Sep 9: selection of responses to set of stills from video along with the words "graceless night" (lyric from the song in the video)]*
>
> *…my dad wants me to ask you if melodrama [LP] will be out on tape!? He found his cassette player n he's super excited about it!!*
>
> *Text me later!*
>
> *Hi lorde you are so very linda [pretty] do you querer ser [want to be] my friend?*
>
> *Please notice me!*

In many respects, Lorde's followers resemble those of Lady Gaga's, with many gushing replies to every tweet; almost half contain a simple message of adoration (endless variations on "I love you" or "you are so beautiful"). So, from a historical perspective, it would seem that acquiring fame during the social media era has not markedly changed the basic relationship between audiences (fans) and celebrities. Indeed, the intimacy offered by Twitter seems to have intensified this relationship to the point where even a retweet by Lorde can generate tremendous excitement among her followers. In the following example, a fan has tweeted two photos of a pair of trainers with scribbles on them and the message:

> *@lorde SIGNED HER SHOES AND HANDED THEM RIGHT TO ME???!!! I LOVE HER SO MUCH WTF*

Lorde retweeted this along with her own message:

> *For the girl with the sweet face. Loved playing to you folks [emojis]*

In reply, several dozen appreciative messages came from other Lorde followers, some of which were responded to by the fan herself, with a series of exclamatory tweets, such as these:

> *@lorde I'M CRYING WAHT (sic) IS HAPPENING*

> *@lorde I WAS LITERALLY BRUSHING MY TEETH AND DROPPED MY TOOTHBRUSH HAHAHA*

Another fan is so starstruck at having had her tweet 'liked' and retweeted by Lorde that she posts a celebratory tweet on its first anniversary:

> *It has been a year since this happened wow "Lorde liked my tweet"*

This high level of interactivity comes at a cost, however, and among the many replies to Lorde tweets are to be found various cries for attention that border on the obsessional. One particular fan appears to have created two additional accounts from which to pester her and repeatedly replies to Lorde asking her, for no apparent reason, to "call me a stinker". Other fans seem to be in favour of this venture, also pestering Lorde to grant the fan's request, such as: "@lorde please call [fan's name] a stinker, make their dreams come true". As yet, this has not happened. "I wonder when Lorde will block me for spam", tweets the fan at one point.

British artist Stormzy became the first performer from the grime genre to achieve a number one album in early 2017. He currently owns two Twitter accounts, a small protected one with only 1,500 followers and an 'official' one, #GSAP named after his debut album *Gang Signs & Prayer* (951,000 followers). Unlike Lorde, Stormzy does reply to other Twitter users, but mostly to those with verified accounts. It is not a highly active account, but he follows the Lorde practice of occasionally retweeting fan tweets along with a personal message:

> @Stormzy1 four months on and we're still talking about your show back in Brixton, we were truly #blessed that night x

> Was one for the history books, love [emoji]

The fan subsequently tweeted:

> And a retweet from Stormzy, I'll take that

A few days later, Stormzy retweeted another fan message:

> Love how @Stormzy1 was worried about playing in Philadelphia but the crowd are there singing along [emojis]

> Was so sick [emojis]

Again, the fan's next tweet made reference to this:

> Stormzy quote tweeting me makes me a little bit gassed.

Further down the hierarchy, aspiring musicians in their first flush of minor fame still appear to use the same Twitter strategies as their more successful counterparts. Even artists with small follower numbers refuse to be drawn into interaction with fans, using the medium as a mouthpiece for announcements, links to other media and so on. Others have an interactive style similar to Lorde, with many retweets of supportive fans (albeit without generating the same level of excitement in the fans they have retweeted).

Overall, however, it seems that Twitter has less appeal to up-and-coming musicians (and those social media natives who have made it) than one might expect. Instagram is preferred by some; even media such as YouTube, which allow musicians to upload music, do not seem particularly popular at the level of the individual artist. Some groups shun social media altogether, preferring to promote themselves using their own stand-alone websites and the time-honoured publicity outlets of radio and specialist music media (online magazines for example). A recent study of unsigned musicians suggests there is some scepticism within the industry as to the perceived benefits of social media (Haynes & Marshall, 2017), although the study focused on artists working in fairly traditional musical genres (rock, indie).

As I will discuss in chapter 6, different kinds of musical artists have opportunities to succeed within YouTube without requiring the professional management of record companies although musical success within digital media looks different from traditional musical success. As Haynes and Marshall argue (Ibid, p. 11), "traditional income streams (sales of tickets, music, and merchandise) remain the building blocks of an independent musician's income". A powerful discourse of authenticity underpins genres like indie in which the maintenance of traditional practices (such as live performance and sales of recordings) are fundamental to performers' integrity. Indeed, it could even be argued that such artistic genres are meaningless without these practices and the media that (traditionally) support them, such as radio, and specialist press[6].

From the perspective of affordance theory, it could be argued that Twitter does not afford musicians the same benefits as media that allow users to compile an easily accessible archive of recordings, such as YouTube or SoundCloud. MySpace was popular with musicians because the prominence of sound files on the interface was one of its primary affordances. Facebook, in a continual attempt to mimic all the technical affordances of its rivals, has only recently enabled members to archive video material. Twitter has remained primarily a medium for verbal communication, which is why it has appealed most to established celebrities who have a ready audience for their personal thoughts and opinions, along with media employees and academics whose primary tools are words rather than sound or visual imagery. Most musicians would rather have their music do the talking for them.

Crime Authors and Their Followers

Giles (2017b) is a study that set out explicitly to examine the followers of a group of social media natives who had first enjoyed success as crime authors (publication of a first novel) after 2010. I used crime authors as a

---

[6] The name 'indie' refers to the decision by artists in the 1970s and '80s to release recordings through small, independent record labels rather than multinational entertainment companies such as EMI and Warner Brothers. Over time, the distinction has become blurred due to various marketing and distribution deals (and the success of some 'indie' labels), but the term has stuck as a descriptive label for traditional guitar-based groups.

proxy for celebrity in general, for slightly spurious reasons (I was, at the time, studying crime fiction in a different context) but it is nonetheless true that authors of fiction have enjoyed a fair amount of celebrity over the years (Moran, 2000; York, 2007; Braun & Spiers, 2016). Crime fiction now accounts for one in every three books sold (Knight, 2010), so it is reasonable to suggest that some new authors in the genre can expect to attain celebrity status at some stage if they become successful.

I focused on seven specific authors whose Twitter accounts had attracted between 800 and 13,000 followers and, on the basis of the biographical information provided on their accounts, categorised their followers into eight groups:

1. Published crime author

2. Published author in other fictional genre

3. Publishing industry professional (e.g. agent, editor)

4. Other kind of professional (e.g. academic, media)

5. Commercial account (not related to publishing industry)

6. Aspiring author (i.e. yet to publish first novel)

7. Book fan or blogger (depending on biography and other links)

8. Other (none of the above)

Between 28 and 48 per cent of authors' followers fell into the last (Other) category, which might be expected given that biographical detail is not always available. Membership of this category tends to indicate the Twitter member has no professional relationship with the author, and so it is within this group that one would expect to find people that can be identified as fans (as opposed to being a generic 'book fan'). It is also a category in which one might expect to find long-standing friends and family members though, as follower numbers increase overall, these will presumably constitute a smaller percentage of 'Other' followers.

For all but one author, the second largest percentage (12–22 per cent) of followers was represented by the second group (authors from other genres). This might seem surprising given that contemporary authors tend to be strongly identified with a specific genre, but may reflect relationships developed in creative writing courses and online writing circles where aspiring authors support one another regardless of genre. Only one author had over ten per cent of followers in the 'crime author' category although they had the smallest overall following (only 800). Membership of other categories varied between authors; for example, 17 per cent of one successful author's followers came from the publishing industry, and the book fan/blogger category accounted for between 2 and 15 per cent of total followers.

One of the aims of the study was to examine in detail the exchanges between authors and their followers, and here the practice of fandom could be observed even when followers did not identify as fans explicitly. One example here is the posting of a selfie with a favourite author or the following exchange in which a 'book fan' receives an unexpected reply from an author in response to an announcement of her husband's birthday: the comment "he will be thrilled" suggests that both are effectively fans of the author.

Book fan: Happy birthday to lovely [husband], my main man for ever [*emojis*]
Author: Happy birthday to [husband]! Have a great day!
Book fan: Thanks [crime author], he will be thrilled by this tweet!

Other exchanges between authors and followers concerned the release of new material, discussions about potential cover artwork for forthcoming novels, ideas for character names and general discussion about characters and other creative elements involved in writing fiction. Though most of these exchanges involved followers in the 'Other' category (thereby mirroring traditional celebrity/fan interaction), a significant number of exchanges involved followers from the 'book fan/blogger' group. Closer inspection of the members of this category shed an interesting light on contemporary publishing and digital practice because it transpired that some of the book bloggers had quite intimate relationships with the authors and had amassed a serious numbers of Twitter followers, pushing them towards micro-celebrity status.

It seems that book bloggers have emerged as important intermediaries in publishing, particularly in genres like crime, where they perform a valuable publicity role for authors and publishers alike, carrying reviews and author interviews on their websites. Popular authors may 'tour' blogs, contributing a series of articles across the sector rather in the style of a rock group performing at different venues over the course of a month. The scant academic literature on the phenomenon of book bloggers has arrived at strikingly different conclusions: Steiner's (2010) study of Swedish blogs, albeit an earlier one, argued their role was minimal, while Gijón (2014) believes they are beginning to challenge the literary field in general. A similar conclusion was reached by Allington (2016) in relation to online consumer reviews on sites like Amazon, although these arguably carry less weight within the publishing world than specialist blogs.

Most interestingly of all, book bloggers and authors exchanged mutual admiration in some tweets. In the following example, a blogger begins by enthusing over an author's book cover and receives thanks from the author, a typical celebrity/fan exchange. In the second exchange, the roles become blurred as the blogger praises the author's success ("you've come so far"), whereupon the author offers the blogger praise ("look what you've done, too"). These comments place the blogger almost on the same footing as the author (except that it is the blogger who has initiated the praise).

Book fan:	Look at this [*picture of Crime author's new book cover*]. How bloody gorgeous is this?
Crime author:	Thank you, [Book fan] x
Book fan:	I'm so pleased for you. Was reminiscing about the [publisher] launch, you've come so far [*emoji*]
Crime author:	A lot of water under the bridge. But good times. And look what you've done too!

The next exchange is similar, in that it is initiated by the blogger (who also closes it, with kisses), and her adulatory comment is reciprocated as in the previous example. On this occasion, it is even more emphatic ("loved you on line"), accompanied by a gushing hashtag reference that one would normally associate only with an infatuated fan.

Book fan:	Am in my element that I met you this evening [@crime author]. Adored [book titles] SO MUCH!
Crime author:	Feel I can rest easy now I've met you because I've loved you on line for so long! #justasgorgeousinreallife
Book fan:	xxx

Of course, there is no reason why the authors and bloggers in these cited examples might not have had previous relationships, as former friends or graduates of a writing class; clearly, the pair in the first example have seen their respective publishing careers develop in tandem. But this public dialogue positions the bloggers in a role that suggests they merit some degree of celebrity themselves, at least for the audience they and the authors perform to.

In this study of otherwise traditional celebrity on Twitter, such as musicians, actors, writers, do book bloggers constitute a new, digital genre of celebrity? For now, the spread of their audience keeps them in the micro-celebrity category, but there is no particular reason why, like other 'influencers' in fields like fashion and gaming, and these fledging crime authors themselves, they might not transcend the 'micro' boundary in time. I will return to these issues in chapter 8, where I consider book bloggers as a variant of the 'social media influencer' figure gaining prominence in fields such as travel, beauty, and fashion. In general, unlike media such as YouTube and Instagram that will be discussed in subsequent chapters, Twitter has *not* been a major source of new genres of celebrity and has acted more a soapbox for existing celebrities, from genres old and new, to articulate opinion, to promote their careers and, occasionally, to communicate with fans, fellow celebrities, and any one of the 300 million or so individuals in the world with a personal account.

PART III

NEW FORMS OF CELEBRITY

6

YOUTUBERS

One of the most striking features of twenty-first century celebrity is the diversity of domains in which individuals can now achieve fame. Fewer than two decades ago, it seemed remarkable that one could achieve overnight celebrity by appearing in a reality TV show, just by 'being yourself' and chatting with fellow contestants (Holmes, 2004). The Jade Goody path to celebrity, described in chapter 4, has been explained as part of a 'demotic turn' in media history that brought individuals into the public eye for their 'ordinariness' and high degree of identification on the part of the audience (Turner, 2010). Though such 'celetoids' (Rojek, 2001) enjoy relatively short-lived and fleeting fame, restricted largely to the TV-viewing audience for a particular channel, for a brief period they may even eclipse traditional celebrities from the entertainment and sporting worlds.

But if the success of reality TV brought about a demotic turn in celebrity, what has happened since has given it a 180-degree swivel: once social media allowed the consumers to get their hands on the means of production, so the control of media elites was surrendered to the fluctuating whims of the audience itself, the entire process was thrown into disarray. Who would have thought 10 years ago that, in 2018, one of the world's most celebrated individuals would be famous largely for playing video games while making obscene comments? PewDiePie, whose YouTube channel has now received no fewer than *16 billion* views, has attained a degree of exposure previously denied to all except the biggest Hollywood stars and popular recording artists.

The phenomenon of YouTube celebrity (as performers, the individuals are typically referred to as 'YouTubers') has fascinated the mainstream media for several years ever since it became apparent a new type of star was emerging through social media that displayed many of the characteristics of the demotic turn. Young, spectacularly 'ordinary', seemingly devoid of any 'talent' whatsoever, and lacking any *a prori* connection to the media industry (Turner, 2010), their success has baffled the traditional media. Notably, the phenomenon appears to have split the audience on generational lines. Almost exclusively, YouTubers are followed largely by younger audiences, but their influence in this demographic, on a global scale, is too great to be ignored.

In a survey for the US glossy lifestyle magazine *Variety* in 2014, the top five most popular celebrities among US teenagers were all YouTube stars rather than figures primarily working in broadcast media, the film industry and other traditional sources of celebrity. More recently, *Time* magazine (Time, 2016) included PewDiePie in its annual list of the 100 most influential people. As one online celebrity agent has claimed, this represents "a seismic shift in the way that generations consume media and celebrity" (Lowbridge, 2015). Nevertheless, for older generations, even the biggest YouTube stars remain utterly anonymous: when featured in traditional news media, the articles invariably begin: "KSI/PewDiePie/Zoella is *the most famous person you've never heard of*". Of course, the 'you' in these straplines refers not to the global YouTube audience but to the readers of national newspapers. At no point since rock 'n' roll have the generations been so divided by popular culture.

In the next two chapters, I aim to give the reader an overview of YouTube as a medium that affords a particular celebrity (and also grants their followers the kind of direct access afforded by other social media, such as Twitter). In this chapter, I discuss the emergence of YouTubers as a cultural phenomenon over the past decade, breaking it down into several distinctive celebrity genres. I argue that YouTubers are best understood as two broad generations of performers; again using 2010 as a general turning point, it is possible to see a transition from the types of performers who were celebrated for their amateurishness and novelty value to those with more generic styles of delivery and content. In chapter 7, I will go on to account for the popular appeal of YouTubers, examining the way that authenticity and ordinariness are constructed in their self-presentation (and responded to by the commenting audience).

The Emergence of YouTube as a Presentational Medium

Much writing about YouTube cites the tagline 'Broadcast Yourself' as embodying the site's "ideology" (Smith, 2014), opening the doors for a generation of digital stars. But the tagline was not YouTube's first. Back in 2005, prior to its big-money acquisition by Google, it offered users 'Your Digital Video Repository' (Burgess & Green, 2009), inviting them to use the technology to store home videos and share them with friends. In a classic example of the way that affordances only emerge through the interaction between individuals and their environment, YouTube's opportunities for fame and fortune took several years to be realised by more than a relatively small number of 'micro-celebrities'. Today, however, it is arguably the principal medium for generating twenty-first-century celebrity.

What sort of medium is YouTube? Its sheer scale is so overwhelming it would be almost impossible to capture its essence other than to say that it offers users the tools to upload video and to comment on existing videos. It still can be used as a digital video repository (it certainly saves on disk space), but as a mass medium, it has been described as "a kind of Internet nation-state" (Herrman, 2017), populated by a cast of characters whose numbers of subscribers exceed the total audiences of most national media outlets. Some critics have applied the term 'post-television' to YouTube (Lister et al, 2009) though this is loosely defined (and some authors even use it as a synonym for new media generally). Perhaps the most obvious contrast between YouTube and television is its global reach and consequent lack of (evident) agenda because, like Wikipedia, the content is provided by the users and, therefore, spills beyond traditional broadcast media's systems of censorship, quality control and scheduling. The most important distinction might be, as with Twitter, the presence and relevance of the *archive*, which – as I will go on to argue – has played a major role in the creation of YouTube celebrity. But, as Tolson (2010) reminds us, it is more than just a repository for user-created video because much of that archive consists of video (and audio) created originally in other media contexts: old television, cinema, musical, and radio recordings. As much as it shapes contemporary culture, YouTube is also a museum of electronic media's history.

For its earliest performers, celebrity arrived almost by accident. A 79-year-old English man delivering soliloquies straight to camera about his unremarkable life would seem a most unlikely candidate for celebrity status. But, in 2006, Peter Oakley was the first YouTuber to attract 25,000 subscribers to his channel (geriatric1927), making it the most heavily subscribed on the site. His only goal, as articulated in his debut video (the charmingly entitled *First try*[1]), was "just to bitch and grumble about life in general from the perspective of an old person who's been there and done that." Although Oakley initially shied away from the attention of the broadcast media, he did make some brief radio and television appearances in 2007, and reached the Top 30 of the UK singles charts with a version of The Who's 'My Generation' as a member of 'the world's oldest rock group': The Zimmers. 434 videos later, Oakley shocked his 40,000 remaining subscribers with the news that he had been diagnosed with an incurable cancer. On 12 February 2012, he posted his final video, a discussion of radar operation during the Second World War (Series 2: In conclusion[2]), signing off with the words "I would say my possibly final goodbye, so… goodbye."

Oakley is typical of what I would call the first generation of YouTube celebrities: those who set up their channels without any obvious fame-related or even career-related ambitions. Another example is Tay Zonday, a young graduate student from Minnesota called Adam Naymer who uploaded an original song called 'Chocolate Rain' (Burgess, 2014). Within months, it had gone viral, largely due to its circulation as an internet meme on the 4Chan image-sharing website, and Zonday was inundated with invitations to perform the song on various television and radio shows across the world. Nevertheless, it took him almost five years to make the song available via iTunes. Other first-generation figures might include the anarchic comedian Brooke Brodack, Scottish computing student James Provan who attracted world media attention for a video on making pancakes, guitar tutor Justin Sanderson (who offered 'FREE guitar lessons'), silent anime fan Magibon and prototype beauty vlogger Lauren Luke (Tolson, 2010).

Chief among the characteristics of this first generation is the amateurishness of the video production and performance itself. As one author describes it, "it is not surprising to find many first-time vloggers perplexed by the webcam, often reporting that they spent several hours transfixed in front of the lens, trying to decide what to say" (Wensch, 2009, cited in Smith, 2014). Even after launching her own cosmetic range, Lauren Luke's

---

[1] https://www.youtube.com/watch?v=p_YMigZmUuk
[2] https://www.youtube.com/watch?v=wegn36u75Cs

presentation style remained deliberately unpolished: "it is not just that the production is amateurish," wrote Tolson (2010, p. 281), "it is that she makes a transparent virtue of this."

This apparently authentic style of performance was part of the emerging artform that became universally known as the *vlog* and was successfully mimicked in 2006 by an amateur film production company responsible for the YouTube channel Lonelygirl15. This vlog, described as "a turning point in the history of YouTube" (Bakioğlu, 2016, p. 1), was delivered by an actress called Jessica Lee Rose in the character of a 16-year-old girl called Bree in which she ranted about her parents and other typically teenaged concerns. To heighten its verisimilitude, Bree had her own MySpace page where she interacted with fans, and her 'friends' also had their own YouTube channels, all of it carefully designed to resemble the vlogging style established on the site.

Over time, some fans became suspicious: the vlogs were, perhaps, a little too polished; the storyline, which involved the abduction of Bree's parents by a mysterious cult, was stretching their credulity. Finally, the truth emerged, and although Lonelygirl15 eventually ran to four series and retained a small but devoted following, the production team were widely denounced in the media for 'cheating' YouTubers into believing that Bree was a real teenage vlogger. It has since been argued that the producers never really got the credit they deserved for pioneering an innovative form of storytelling (Hall, 2014), and it is largely our fetishism for the real that leads us to label Bree 'inauthentic'. These issues will be discussed in more detail in chapter 7, but in the next section, I will discuss the personal vlog as a style of video production that has evolved into a distinctive performance genre.

The Second Generation of YouTube Celebrities

The transformation of YouTube from a repository of quirky videos to a star factory did not take place overnight, and the journey from Peter Oakley to a fully fledged celebrity culture is a gradual one. Clearly, economics has played an important role, as the owners have allowed advertising revenue to slowly trickle down to the individuals driving traffic to the site, as has the entrance of traditional star-makers like talent agencies and management moguls into what is still often perceived as 'DIY celebrity'.

But above all, contemporary YouTube celebrity is recognisable as a common culture, expressed in the layout and appearance of the channels and the content and delivery of the videos. Though second-generation YouTubers continue to embrace amateurism, at least when it comes to technical matters (Berryman & Kavka, 2017), the increased professionalization of vlogging has resulted in a certain degree of quality control and continuity across the community: "The sign-ons, sign-offs and key phrases [that] help to construct narrative unity, thematic cohesion, and a shared language that can be readily deployed by fan bases" (Betancourt, 2016).

Likewise, certain formats (such as tutorials and 'reaction' videos) recur across specific genres of vlog, being easily recognised by the huge audience for vloggers of all kinds. Perhaps the most noticeable feature of the contemporary vlogger is the custom thumbnail representing each uploaded video, typically displaying a startled or otherwise comedic expression on the vlogger's face and some eye-catching text in a stylish contemporary font. For example, Mexican beauty vlogger Yuya, currently the most heavily subscribed female on YouTube, advertises her videos with tantalising phrases, such as 'No lo vas a creer' (You're not going to believe it). Other creators use more descriptive text ('My dad does my makeup', 'ice bucket challenge', and so on).

Most second-generation YouTube celebrities establish their names initially within a clearly identifiable genre, such as gaming or beauty. (I will discuss genre in more detail shortly.) However, once subscriber numbers reach serious levels, the creators begin to diversify their output until a generic panoply of formats is available. PewDiePie, the most popular vlogger of them all, with a current subscription of over 62 million, established his channel in the 'Let's Play' format of gaming videos (Newman, 2016) but now offers a variety of comedy formats, confessionals, and even 'how to' tutorials, such as cooking Swedish meatballs. Though video games are still featured in his output they are outnumbered by other formats. One of the earliest 'beauty gurus' in the make-up tutorial tradition, Rachel Levin, offers few tutorials, her newer material consisting almost exclusively of the standard vlogger fare of pranks and challenges. The emphasis on comedy is something that seems to cut across vloggers from different linguistic and ethnic origins (Bevan, 2017; Peterson, 2016).

For a detailed example of how the second-generation YouTuber achieves celebrity, Maguire's (2015) analysis of the US comedian Jenna Marbles is a useful source. In common with many successful YouTubers,

Jenna Mourey's career was launched by a specific video that 'went viral': in her case, a parody of the make-up tutorial format, 'How to trick people into thinking you're good looking'[3], that she posted on her channel shortly after its creation in 2010. Like the standard make-up tutorial, the video begins with Mourey's unmade-up face, which is gradually transformed into "an exaggerated caricature of synthetic Hollywood beauty... while dispensing ironic and self-deprecating remarks about her appearance" (Maguire, 2015, pp. 75–76). Seven years later, the Jenna Marbles channel has 17 million subscribers and has received over two billion views of her uncompromisingly brash blend of comedy, pranks and challenges: applying make-up when drunk, eating soup with a fork, sharing her dogs' food, or impersonating Hillary Clinton and Sarah Palin.

By far the most extensive study of a specific YouTube celebrity to date is Garcia-Rapp's ethnographic work on the British-Chinese beauty vlogger Lindy Tsang, known as Bubz (Garcia-Rapp, 2016, 2017; Garcia-Rapp & Roca-Cuberes, 2017). Bubz is typical of the second-generation YouTuber in that she combines 'expert' videos (beauty tutorials) with personal/life-style vlogs (indeed she has separate channels for each). These are notably different in terms of presentation: the tutorials, which comprise over 60 per cent of her output, are more formal in style, focusing firmly on the make-up procedure itself, with voiceover and backing music; in her personal vlogs, Bubz addresses the camera directly, disclosing intimate details about her daily life. "Over the years she has included footage of intimate moments that one usually shares only with friends and family", says Garcia-Rapp (2017, p. 253), "such as her husband's proposal, her wedding and honey-moon, the moment she tells her husband that he is going to be a father, and the development of her pregnancy."

One of the most common features of contemporary vlogs is the inclusion of significant others. Boyfriends, girlfriends and spouses, mothers and fathers, and family pets are seamlessly incorporated into the most popular vlog-gers' material and come to function as celebrities in themselves: indeed many have their own channels although because YouTubers, like Hollywood stars, tend to date one another, these are often established before the relationship. It is common for dynasties of YouTubers to emerge around a single figure. Zoella (Zoe Sugg), the most popular British female vlogger (12 million

---

[3] https://www.youtube.com/watch?v=OYpwAtnywTk

subscribers) is the fulcrum of a cluster of vloggers that include her brother (ThatcherJoe), boyfriend (Alfie of 'PointlessBlog'), and various friends, many of whom have moved to Brighton on the English south coast, a location that has attracted other YouTubers such as PewDiePie and his partner Marzia Bisognin.

Coverage of YouTube celebrities in the traditional media invariably focuses on their earning potential (Deller & Murphy, 2016), and perhaps the biggest contrast between the two generations is the second's ability to generate income from various sources, notably a share of YouTube's overall advertising revenue. This is achieved through various 'monetization tools' such as rewardStyle, a program that links viewers to products visible in the videos (Berryman & Kavka, 2017). Externally, income flows in through various marketing deals with interested parties, particularly for gamers and beauty and fashion vloggers. Though most earn just enough to constitute a salary for vlogging, estimates of the most popular celebrities' incomes suggest that it is a very lucrative business. Zoe Sugg is claimed to earn £50,000 a month from her various income sources (Cliff, 2017), and US vlogger Connor Franta had an estimated net worth of 3 million dollars in 2015 (Lovelock, 2017). Even if some of these figures are wildly speculative, claims about the limited income and influence of YouTube celebrities (Marwick, 2016; Smith, 2014) appear somewhat dated.

Genres in YouTube Celebrity

I would like to say a little here about the variety of distinctive genres and formats that characterise contemporary YouTube celebrity. I use the term 'genre' here largely to distinguish thematic categories (e.g. fashion, beauty), and 'format' refers to particular styles of video. As mentioned previously, there is considerable overlap between genre and format, so a vlogger renowned largely for make-up tutorials may also produce videos in a variety of different formats. Indeed, few, if any, major YouTube celebrities (with well over a million subscribers) deviate significantly from the formats described below.

The Gaming Genre

Four of the seven most currently subscribed channels belong to vloggers whose principal claim to expertise lies in simultaneously playing, and commentating on, video games. This genre has almost a decade's standing in the YouTube community and has its roots in pre-social media gaming forums. The principal format used by gaming vloggers is the 'Let's Play' video, succinctly described by Newman (2016, p. 286) as "video captures of gameplay narrated by the player… [whose voice] is overdubbed onto the game's existing music and sound effects track… [and who] may also appear onscreen in an overlaid picture-in-picture window so that game-play, player, and the character they are performing with/as are simultaneously visible."

In addition to 'Let's Play' videos, popular gamer formats include 'live action' reports from conventions and 'unboxing' videos in which "gaming peripherals" are extracted from their packaging. None of these formats constitute game reviews as such (the players do not construct themselves as *critics* so much as expert consumers) although, given the top gamers' huge audience, they do have considerable influence on sales and subsequent game design (Newman, 2016). Rather than promoting themselves as experts, gaming vloggers aim primarily at entertainment. As Maloney, Roberts and Caruso (2017, p. 8) argue, the 'Let's Play' format can best be described as "improvisational comedic", and that the performers "are more interested in entertaining viewers through anarchic visual antics than in demonstrating their gameplay skills and achievements". Not surprisingly, therefore, most if not all of the celebrity gamers offer a full panoply of comedic formats on their channels, with pranks, challenges, and parodies being highly prevalent in this genre.

The Beauty Genre

Though the gaming genre may be popular, it is hard to imagine it is more extensive than the YouTube beauty genre, a vast community that comprises more than 180,000 'gurus' offering a hundred hours of content each day (Garcia-Rapp, 2017). The dominant format in the genre is the *tutorial*, a video with its roots in the 'free' guitar lessons of Justin Sanderson and other early YouTube pioneers of giving away expertise to a loyal following. These were formally categorised in the first generation under the 'How To & Style' banner, where figures such as Lauren Luke in Britain and Bethany Mota and Michelle Phan in the United States began to cultivate a substantial audience for their make-up tutorials, eventually landing contracts with leading cosmetic firms for their expertise, but more importantly, for their popularity with a youthful sector of the market. Though early 'gurus' advised on all manner of personal style, the beauty (make-up) category gradually began to predominate as its leading exponents grew into bona fide celebrities.

The tutorial format throws up an intriguing paradox in that it requires its creator to perform an 'expert' persona while remaining, in the You-Tube tradition, an 'ordinary' member of the public who happens to have access to a webcam. Despite the informal, conversational, unscripted, and even colloquial nature of the delivery, the performer is effectively dispensing advice via the kind of "pedagogical monologue that was rejected by broadcasters in the development of early radio" (Tolson, 2010, p. 282). Of course, a major difference here is that the audience has direct access to the creator through the comments function, and beauty gurus have long been highly interactive here, responding directly to specific questions in text or producing additional videos that specifically address subscribers' comments.

Berryman and Kavka (2017) have identified three further 'subgenres' of the beauty genre. (I prefer the term 'format' here because the distinction is based on the structure and style of the videos rather than their thematic content.) Along with the ubiquitous tutorial, these include 'first impressions', 'monthly favourites' and 'haul' videos. These three are variations on a similar theme, which is effectively the review of various commercial beauty products, often combined with clothing, and increasingly 'monetized' through clickable links to the products on show. Here, the beauty guru again occupies that liminal position between industry expert and ordinary consumer, which allows her to pass judgement on products while simultaneously playing the role of 'big sister' to her typically younger audience. The 'haul' video, probably the oldest format of the three, is particularly interesting here because it recreates the familiar moment when a shopper arrives home after an afternoon's spending and displays, one by one, the fruits of their labour. As with the 'first impressions' format, the appeal of haul videos derives from the same 'revelation' as in the makeover format of lifestyle television (Moseley, 2000).

Of course, there is a constant tension for vloggers as they rise in status, between preserving credibility with their loyal subscribers and fulfilling the requirements of their commercial ventures (Garcia-Rapp &

Roca-Cuberes, 2017). As Cocker and Cronin (2017) have argued, there is a risk to popular vloggers of losing the support of their long-term subscribers because they are perceived to have 'sold out' to sponsors. Though this is evident from some of the comments posted on the videos, gauging the overall impact on popularity is difficult; as Andò (2016, p.136) suggests, vloggers' "integration into a profit dynamic" does not seem to bother their young fans, and indeed, brands may even "provide a common language" that links creator and audience. This is an important point about contemporary celebrity-audience relations that I shall return to in chapter 8.

The Lifestyle Genre

With 'lifestyle' being a looser concept than the two genres described above, I am using it broadly to embrace any personal vlogs primarily organised around a specific way of life in terms of religion, sexuality, health (including mental health) or any theme that appeals to a recognisable, pre-existing audience. This includes the Islamic lifestyle vloggers described by Peterson (2016), LGBTQ vloggers like Tyler Oakley, Connor Franta, and Ingrid Nilsen (Lovelock, 2017), and those like Beckie Brown, whose videos are specifically organised around the hair-pulling compulsion known as trichotillomania. Many lifestyle vloggers resemble more the first generation of YouTubers, or what Marwick (2016) describes as "subcultural or niche celebrities", meaning that their potential audience is somewhat limited. But this depends entirely on the prevalence of the lifestyle and its wider appeal: Tyler Oakley, whose vlog has long revolved around gay issues, eating disorders and other mental health issues, has eight million subscribers.

The Parody

Somewhere between a genre and a format, the parody video is a YouTube mainstay. Most parodies are musical, and the genre/format is epitomised by Colleen Ballinger, creator of the MirandaSings channel, a performer whose act satirises amateur musical performers. In Marwick's (2016, p. 12) words, "she warbles popular songs off-key [and] gives questionable singing and dancing advice." Though this kind of parody might seem to challenge the amateur ethic (and aesthetic) that is at the core of YouTube's appeal, it is perhaps embraced as part of the more general culture of ludic irreverence that drives so many popular creators, whatever genre they have established themselves in, towards broadly comic content. The parody format incorporates all manner of satirical musical performance from lip-synching to popular songs, cover versions of songs with alternative lyrics, dramatic reconstructions, and 'mash-ups' of incongruous visuals and soundtracks. Other non-musical videos parody standard formats like the make-up tutorial (Maguire, 2015). Parodies are often the type of YouTube content that 'goes viral' across social media more generally, typically as 'memes' (see chapter 9), where they reflect the "fratboy humour" and mischief-making that still predominates in online entertainment more generally (Burgess, 2014).

The Prank Format

Largely the preserve of comedians (though highly popular with gamers and other vloggers who have branched out into comic content), pranks are performances firmly in the *Candid Camera* tradition where unsuspecting members of the public, though more often the vlogger's friends or family, are tricked into taking part in an activity with an unfortunate or surprising outcome. As with more gentle formats, like the beauty haul, the prank works in the same way as the 'revelations' of lifestyle television, chiefly as opportunities for authentic emotional display. (A vital element in the prank video, as in the television makeover, is the moment when the orchestrator of the prank reveals themselves and exposes the artifice of the situation.)

The Reaction Format

A format specifically devoted to the generation of spontaneous emotion, 'reaction' videos have become standard fare in most YouTube genres, pioneered by the Fine Brothers (Benny and Rafi), a comedy duo who have become a full online entertainment company and whose popularity is largely due to the creation of various channels devoted solely to reactions. The first, 'Kids React', in 2010, exploited the sector of the population most likely to provide authentic display; later channels featured teenagers, older adults, and well-known YouTubers reacting to all manner of content from video games, music, and general online content, typically of a 'viral' nature. Several versions of the format exist, some showing the original content on a small screen, though the guests constitute the main focus of the camera, others more like the 'Let's Play' format (usually where an individual is 'reacting') with the reactor(s) appearing in a small picture.

Some of the non-celebrities appearing in the Fine Brothers' videos became well-known simply for their contributions, and more generally in YouTube there is a tradition of fan reactions to music videos, usually within a specific genre such as K-pop, which can result in (micro)-celebrity for their creators (Oh, 2017). A popular sub-format is the 'reaction to old videos' in which popular YouTubers film themselves recoiling in mock-horror at archive footage from their own channel. There is also a 'reacting to reaction' sub-format which effectively doubles the amount of emotion on display.

The Challenge Format

A popular format among YouTubers of all stripes is the challenge, which has spawned several sub-formats of its own (the ice bucket challenge, condom challenge and so on), and gives them the opportunity to maximise their potential audience by enlisting the participation of fellow YouTubers. This is usually traditional slapstick entertainment that is particularly enjoyed by younger fans (Andò, 2016).

YouTubers as (Micro?)-celebrities

Having described the broad cultural environment of YouTube and its opportunities for new kinds of highly popular individual to emerge, I would now like to turn to the question of whether we can consider these individual celebrities in the traditional sense of the word (that is, in accordance with the definitions outlined in chapter 1) or whether they are better understood as an entirely new phenomenon. Is the concept of micro-celebrity sufficient to describe the likes of PewDiePie and Zoella with their vast global audiences, or do we need a unique concept to capture these emerging public figures?

The first issue to resolve is how we might best distinguish YouTube celebrities from other forms of celebrity, traditional and digital. A simple, but useful, definition is provided by Lovelock (2017, p. 90): "YouTube celebrity denotes an individual whose celebrity stems directly from their activities on the site." I would amend this slightly, replacing 'celebrity' with 'fame' because, though celebrity status may be somewhat in dispute (and some definitions of celebrity are based on representation in traditional media), there can be little disagreement with the claim that someone with 62 million subscribers is *famous*.

One interesting phenomenon to be considered is that YouTubers themselves, and particularly their fans, are not always comfortable with the term "celebrity". In a television interview with Sky News, Alfie Deyes claimed that his success was down to *not* being a celebrity: "I think what people love about vlogging is that we aren't celebrities, we're just normal... it's the normality that people love" (Nkadi, 2015). It is a sentiment echoed by (some of) his fans: "He's normal, not like celebrities", said one teenage girl at a Deyes book signing (Samadder, 2014) although another interviewee disputed this. The attractiveness of 'normality' has clear links with that of 'ordinariness', and inevitably, *authenticity*, which is explored in more depth in the next chapter.

A rare academic study that has collected interview data with vloggers and their adolescent audience is Andò (2016), in which the latter group was particularly dismissive of the term. Vloggers, according to one fan (Ibid, p. 133), "are not real celebrities... just simple girls who tell us about their lives. They don't want to be stars." Most fans stressed how similar the vloggers were to themselves ("they talk about their everyday life, their school and so on" and "the same things happen to me"); the age gap, rather than a distancing factor, was seen as a reason to trust their advice. Rather than explicitly rejecting the celebrity label, the vloggers themselves tended towards modesty, describing it instead as "this completely absurd experience on YouTube", as a temporary status that is "really nice", "beautiful", and so on.

If celebrity is a *practice*, as Marwick and boyd (2011) argue, then there is a contradiction here, as Andò (2016, p. 133) points out: "[the vloggers'] interviews recounting their experiences are not always consistent with their performances on YouTube." In these performances, typically, high subscriber numbers are celebrated, fans are given nicknames in the style of Lady Gaga (Cocker & Cronin, 2017), and celebrity itself is thoroughly dissected and debated to the point where Smith (2016) argues that they attain the position of 'meta-celebrity', continually reflecting on their status, even drawing on concepts from the academic literature like parasocial interaction. At best, then, vloggers are somewhat ambivalent about their relationship to the term.

How can Someone with 62 Million Followers be a Microcelebrity?

Since Senft (2008) first coined the word 'micro-celebrity' to describe the webcam girls of the pre-social media era, it has proved highly popular with academic authors in their search for a concept that captures the status of individuals whose fame extends beyond their immediate (or offline) social network without scaling the heights of traditional celebrity. Marwick (2013) refined the term to rethink it as a variant on the traditional practice of celebrity (only in this case, confined to digital contexts), and has subsequently refined it further, arguing that it describes a "mindset" rather than the scale of an individual's popularity (Marwick, 2016, p. 7), manifesting as "a set of practices drawn from celebrity culture that 'regular people' use in daily life to boost their online attention and popularity".

However, even this refinement runs into problems when applied to YouTubers like Zoella with massive global followings, paparazzi attention, bookshop mobbings and wax models in Madame Tussauds. Marwick's (2016) example of MirandaSings seems to fit a concept of micro-celebrity that successfully described the early 'niche' social media stars of tech companies and the first generation of YouTubers: a figure "who has garnered great online popularity but avoided the attention of mainstream media", and someone who has a desire for *attention* rather than a desire for fame as such. But how true is it of the vloggers described in this chapter who form the second generation? One specific attempt to apply 'micro-celebrity' to such figures is Jerslev's (2016) research on Zoella. For Jerslev, the distinction between "mainstream" celebrity and microcelebrity is a temporal one: the microcelebrity inhabits a different "media circuit" in which she is largely concerned with "permanent updating … immediacy … and instantaneity" (ibid, p. 5235). She illustrates the distinction by the increased distance between Zoella and fans at her book launch, where the rules of engagement are no longer set by the vlogger herself but by the publishing company (who, for instance, prevent fans from taking photos).

The emphasis on microcelebrity as a practice that involves a closer relationship with fans, and a more immediate sense of public visibility is clearly tied to medium. Traditional (or "mainstream") media are, or were, constrained by broadcast schedules, the strategic release of new product (like recorded music), and the interests of various gatekeepers, imposing quality control and censorship. YouTubers post videos when they like and how they like (within certain loose boundaries of acceptability), and they respond to which comments they choose to; these are all affordances of the particular medium in which they operate. Indeed, so attractive are these affordances to traditional celebrities that, as well as microcelebrities mimicking the practice of celebrity, traditional celebrities moving within online contexts have begun to mimic the practices of microcelebrity; Kim Kardashian, for example, has incorporated some of the 'self-branding' techniques of vloggers into her recent online marketing activities (Berryman & Kavka, 2017).

Put in that light, it seems that "microcelebrity" is not unlike "mainstream celebrity", a point Garcia-Rapp makes firmly (2017, p. 230) in her work on Bubzbeauty. "Even as 'just online celebrities', unknown to the public at large, [YouTube celebrities] appear to embody the same societal and cultural roles as mainstream celebrities. As a text, a site, and a sign of both symbolic and practical... values, they provide... opportunities... to discuss, learn, emulate, admire, and criticise." Garcia-Rapp uses Bubz as a modern illustration of Dyer's (1979) notion of the cinema star embodying both 'ordinary' and 'extraordinary' elements, drawing viewers in through her 'expert' beauty tutorials and building a loyal following through the personal disclosure of her vlogs, where visitors discover she is an 'ordinary' person like them, and "she has the role of an admired friend who supports them, who also shows herself as vulnerable and needing their support" (Garcia-Rapp, 2017, p. 238).

How can Someone so Ordinary be a Real Celebrity?

One of the reasons, I suspect, that the micro-celebrity concept has been difficult to shake off in recent years is that many academics, particularly those from the film studies discipline, continue to be troubled about what they perceive as the lack of cultural value in digital celebrity (the same is even more true of traditional media coverage of the phenomenon). Ironically, the same point has been made by authors in work on television fame (Bennett, 2011) where it is typically believed that performers in television (presenters and other figures) sit somewhere far below film actors in the celebrity hierarchy.

I do not wish to begin a cultural war by speculating about what it is exactly that Hollywood actors *do* to warrant such an elite position[4], but Bennett (2011) has laid out an excellent case for considering television performers as possessing three skills unique to their profession. He calls them *televisual skill*, *vocational skill*, and *vernacular skill*. Televisual skill concerns the individual's ability to exploit the conventions of television production to deliver a convincing and engaging performance, for example, as a chat show host; vocational skill refers to skills from beyond television that individuals incorporate into their performance (such as singing, or expert knowledge); vernacular skill is the ability to perform a credible authentic self that audiences can identify with. Clearly, the last of these skills is most important in vlogging although vocational skill is somewhat relevant, and for second-generation YouTubers, certain conventions of the medium have emerged that can be skilfully handled or botched depending on the performer's ability. For instance, one needs to be familiar with the structural and stylistic aspects of the various formats listed above to produce videos that are recognisable and credible in any given genre. So, instead of televisual skill, we might, for want of a snappier term, label this 'YouTube skill'.

The idea that *skill* might be involved in the production of vlogs takes second-generation YouTubers some way from the first although there remains a perception in some of the literature that vlogging is "easy DIY-style content creation" (Smith, 2014, p. 260), which is simply a matter of 'self-branding' and "the maintenance of celebrity status" (Andò, 2016, p. 127). There is undoubtedly a high degree of *labour* involved in generating sufficient content to keep the subscribers logging in; for example, the gamer Stampylongnose claims to upload a daily Minecraft video of between 20 and 30 minutes (Newman, 2016). Bevan (2017), in her study

---

[4] On this point, Dyer (1979) concludes his book by arguing that scholarly analysis of film stars cannot fully account for the 'beauty and pleasure' he experiences in contemplating his favourite actors: "when I see Marilyn Monroe I catch my breath; when I see Montgomery Clift I sigh over how beautiful he is", and the same argument is usually employed to claim legitimacy for academic fandom more generally. But owning one's fandom also generates an impartiality in film and media studies that leads authors to bang drums for their own specific enthusiasms, something that social scientists generally do not have to worry about. (We are impartial in other ways, I guess.)

of hairstyling tutorials, argues that an important aspect of vlogging is to make their labour visible: this is why the vloggers in her study deliberately include all the failed attempts to perfect a particular style. In this way, they manage to combine both 'YouTube skill', the ability to master and exploit their chosen medium, and vernacular skill, the art of appearing 'ordinary', or authentic. I will discuss this last quality in some length in chapter 7.

Isn't YouTube Merely a Springboard for Success in the Traditional Media?

Much of the extant writing about YouTube has either assumed, or explicitly argued that the site cannot be considered a celebrity goal in itself, citing stories about Justin Bieber and other traditional celebrities whose careers were launched not on YouTube as such, but after being 'discovered' through their videos. This was certainly the position of Burgess and Green (2009, pp. 23–24), who claimed that "the myth of DIY celebrity" – the idea that YouTube empowers anyone with a webcam to have an equal shot at stardom – was illusory because "the marker of success for these new forms [of celebrity] is measured not only by their online popularity but by their subsequent ability to pass through the gate-keeping mechanisms of old media – the recording contract, the film festival, the television pilot, the advertising deal".

Though this was arguably the case for YouTube's first generation of performers, similar claims continue to be made even in many latest studies of the phenomenon. Lovelock (2017, p. 92), for example, claims that "success is defined as the ability to travel beyond YouTube itself" irrespective of the size of vloggers' subscriber numbers, and undoubtedly, the media 'beyond' YouTube still has an irresistible attraction judging by the number of YouTubers who have released musical recordings (whatever their specialism), appeared on boring old television, and published books. Indeed, book publishing deals with YouTubers have almost cornered a section of the bookshop to themselves, with seemingly every vlogger with over a million subscribers appearing in hard copy print at some point. Most of the content, inevitably, is of dubious literary merit: even Zoella's first novel, the fastest selling debut in the United Kingdom since records began in 1998, was alleged to have been largely ghostwritten[5]. The appeal of book launches, financial considerations aside, may well derive from the prestige of 'being published': as one fan said of Alfie, "he has his own book… [you have to] admire… someone who has come THAT FAR" (Cocker & Cronin, 2017, p. 10).

If it has proved difficult to cross over from YouTube stardom into literary fame, the number of successful YouTubers migrating to traditional media like film, television, and music is notably low. It could be argued that they face the same hurdles as reality TV stars. As Bennett (2011) argues, skill from one medium does not necessarily carry over into others, citing the case of Craig Phillips, winner of the first UK *Big Brother*, who, despite further opportunities in television, was unable to convert his 'vernacular' skill into televisual skill. Certainly, reports of YouTubers venturing into television suggest that their performance style failed to meet the expectations of that medium, leaving the performers "uncomfortable" and deprived of the degree of control they are used to (Marwick, 2016; Tolson, 2010). Even Daniel Howell and Phil Lester, who broadcast a weekly show on BBC Radio 1 for 18 months that won an industry award, have disappeared from the airwaves. In their case, it seems that it was traditional radio that ultimately fluffed its lines, trying too hard to appeal to a younger demographic using material that is better suited to a younger medium; eventually they were replaced by a show drawing exclusively from university student radio.

What is also unclear is the extent to which YouTubers themselves aspire to these traditional markers of success. One of Andò's (2016) Italian

---

[5] While Zoe admitted that she had received 'help' in writing *Girl Online* (Penguin, 2014), other sources suggest the 'help' might have been rather substantial (Flood & Ellis-Petersen, 2014). Several sources describe an earlier blog post by Siobhan Curham in which the established YA novelist recounts having been commissioned to write an 80,000-word novel over a six-week period (the post in question was deleted around the time that suspicion arose over *Girl Online*'s authenticity). Fingers pointed in Curham's direction because the writer was credited in the book's acknowledgements for 'being with [Zoe] every step of the way' (Johnston, 2014). Remarkably, when the story broke, Curham received most of the online vitriol, mainly from Zoella fans seemingly projecting their disappointment on to the softer target. Zoe subsequently took pains to point out that her second novel was being written together with her 'editor' (Furness, 2015) although this and the third novel in the *Girl Online* trilogy have generated considerably less coverage in the traditional media despite enthusiastic consumer reviews.

vloggers suggests she might rather like ending up on television although there is scant evidence of YouTube acting as a mere vehicle for bringing its creators to the attention of these media. Yet clearly YouTube is not capable of generating celebrity solely by itself. Just as Hollywood and traditional broadcast media required the attention of the press to turn their performers into stars, the role of Twitter, Instagram, and other social media is crucial in helping build the vloggers' audience and cementing their reputation. In Zoella's case, Twitter acts as a way of consolidating a fan community (Berryman & Kavka, 2017). In this way, a coherent performance is spread across different media, creating a "composite cultural text" (Maguire, 2015), enhancing performers' authenticity for several overlapping audiences. A mere stand-alone website can function as a kind of backstage even for a medium such as YouTube. For instance, the Bubzbeauty fan page is a space "where I [Bubz] chill n catch up with you guys" (Garcia-Rapp & Roca-Cuberes, 2017).

The YouTube Audience and its Relationship with Vloggers

The psychological appeal of YouTubers is the subject of chapter 7, but here I shall say a little about the relationships that they enjoy with their subscribers. As Smith (2016) has argued, one of the central features of YouTube is that it breaks down the distinction between celebrity and fan although, as discussed in chapter 5, this point can be applied to most contemporary digital media.

Can subscribers to specific channels be described as fans (rather than friends or followers)? Many vloggers, whatever their claims to the contrary (Andò, 2016), certainly construct their audiences as being composed of Lady Gaga-type acolytes, according them their unique status as 'Burrbears' (subscribers to beauty vlogger Tanya Burr's channel), or 'Sprinklerinos' (subscribers to Louise Pentland's 'Sprinkleofglitter' channel) (Cocker & Cronin, 2017). Audiences can be strongly gendered: Zoella's is "an overtly feminine community" (Berryman & Kavka, 2017, p. 318); when she gets brother (Thatcher)Joe to apply her makeup, she is "excluding... the adolescent males he represents" while 'unifying' her own female audience by "strengthening gender norms about cosmetic use" (Ibid, p. 314). The gender of vloggers, however, is no guide to the nature of their audience: it is estimated that 88 per cent of identical twin brothers Jack and Finn Harries' audience for their JacksGap channel consists of teenage girls (Rainey, 2012).

The size, and global reach, of the most popular channels has long been a source of fascination for the traditional media. Even in the early years, performers like Peter Oakley and James Provan gained the attention of the world's press despite subscriber numbers that would be considered disappointing by an aspiring contemporary vlogger. Awareness of the global audience led some of the earlier YouTubers to trade on national characteristics and stereotypes to create their online persona, such as the British vlogger Charlie McDonnell, on whose 'charlieissocoollike' channel he instructed viewers in the art of making the perfect cup of tea (Smith, 2014). Today's astronomical viewing figures are a reminder of the potential audience. In 2013, YouTube announced it had one billion users a month though this figure did not specify by what route they arrived at the site; four years later, it was estimated that 1.5 billion people a month were watching content while logged in (Matney, 2017).

At the level of the individual vlogger, the various metrics need putting into context. Garcia-Rapp's (2017) analysis of the Bubzbeauty channel is instructive here. She makes the important distinction between the number of views a specific video receives and the number of subscribers to the channel that hosts it. Only the latter represents "sustained interest" in the performer; the former can be vastly inflated by 'viral' sharing (in which case viewers are often arriving via other media, such as Facebook, and not necessarily returning). Garcia-Rapp also identified a pattern of engagement whereby Bubz's beauty tutorials drew in viewers often through entering search terms related to their content, such as 'hair waves', and her more intimate vlogs were the ones that saw an increase in her subscriber numbers and generated large numbers of comments[6].

---

[6] Though I accept Garcia-Rapp's point that subscriber figures are more reliable a guide to a YouTuber's popularity than viewing figures for a single video, perhaps the best estimate of a performer's current popularity is the average number of views for videos posted over a recent time period. In late 2017, PewDiePie's videos typically receive 2 million views in their first 24 hours, gradually increasing to 3 or 4 million over the next fortnight. Zoella's respective figures are nearly half these, yet her subscribership is less than a quarter of PewDiePie's 57M. Charlie McDonnell, whose peak is arguably well past, still has over 2 million subscribers, but his videos struggle to attract 100K views within a month. Tay Zonday, very much of the first YouTuber generation, has over a million subscribers but some of his recent videos have taken months to hit 10,000 views. He is still largely trading on his 'Chocolate Rain' song, whose 10th anniversary video did pull in half a million. (As a YouTube user myself, I have subscribed to many channels which I have ignored for years. I suspect that most of us rarely cancel our subscriptions, however long it is since we have bothered to view the videos uploaded on those channels.)

The extent to which YouTubers engage with viewer comments varies widely. Though some respond directly to comments (typically ones requesting information, such as "what brand are your glasses?"), others read them out as part of a vlog (Peterson, 2016), and some use them as a way of generating material, like musical requests (Marwick, 2016). Others pay relatively little attention. Lovelock (2017) argues that the "dialogic asymmetry" between YouTubers and fans (or subscribers) is a defining criterion of celebrity on the medium although, as with Twitter, the sheer numbers involved make sustaining dialogic symmetry difficult, and it might be simpler to identify a subscriber cut-off figure to perform this function. Sheer numbers, however, do not by themselves explain why some YouTubers are more interactive than others.

YouTube Celebrity as 'Democratic' or Otherwise

Most academic studies of YouTube tend to take one of two positions. Either the medium is wholly subservient to the demands of the "neoliberal marketplace" (Lovelock, 2017) and offers limited opportunities for true emancipation, or it enables a vast range of different voices to achieve fame through circumventing traditional media routes (Cocker & Cronin, 2017). A third position is that the first-generation YouTubers had more opportunities to be radical and subversive, and the entrance of agents, advertisers and managers has now professionalised the medium to a degree that risks alienating vloggers and (some of) their audiences.

Nevertheless, the degree of subversion achievable through YouTube may depend on the relative opportunities offered by traditional media culture. One way in which it can be highly political is through challenging traditional roles and stereotypes. For example, the Islamic lifestyle vloggers studied by Peterson (2016, p. 5) have been able to use the medium "to shift what is considered attractive, beautiful and pleasurable" for young Muslim women and, as British citizens, to resist "being co-opted as icons of Western freedom or of Islamic piety." Likewise, Jenna Marbles can "[critique] the social order that objectifies, commoditises and sexualises girls" (Maguire, 2015, p. 82) because YouTube "[empowers her] to choose what to show, how she can regard her viewer… [and] shape how her image is read and consumed" (Ibid, p. 83).

The same kind of control and agency applies to gaming vloggers as much as to lifestyle ones, where the performance of celebrity contains an element of subversion. Newman (2016, p. 287) has argued that the video game industry has traditionally suppressed the creation of celebrity developers and other individuals by "actively [seeking] to hide the people who make the games" because it has preferred to focus its marketing strategy on technical innovation (special effects and so on). This has resulted, over the last decade, in hostility towards gaming vloggers around intellectual property issues. Newman makes the point that "the rise of the celebrity [gaming vlogger] was not planned by corporate executives, game designers or technologists at Sony, Microsoft or Nintendo". Then again, it is hard to see how the industry, at a broad level, has not profited massively from the vast exposure given to their products.

Ultimately, I do not think the issue is whether YouTube celebrity is 'democratic', simply because older forms of celebrity, such as cinema stardom, are assuredly not; indeed, they are as tightly tethered to the capitalist/neoliberal order. But for the creators as individuals, the comparative freedom of expression allows a more diverse range of identities to attain global recognition even if – like some of the hugely popular Latin American vloggers now clocking up over 20 million subscribers – it is little more than a worldwide platform for pranks, challenges and other schoolboyish larks. Perhaps this is, after all, the inevitable consequence of fully globalised entertainment.

7

THE POPULARITY AND APPEAL OF YOUTUBERS: 'AUTHENTICITY' AND 'ORDINARINESS'

Screaming obscenities while playing videogames would seem a strange way to acquire *celebrity*, and may be why vlogging fans and academics alike are reluctant to use the word to describe the likes of PewDiePie. But according to most definitions of celebrity (apart from those confining the phenomenon of celebrity to specific media cultures) they almost certainly *are*, and in this chapter, I am going to explore some of the factors that might account for their extraordinary popularity. Chief among these are the ubiquitous claims that YouTubers are more 'authentic' and 'ordinary' than traditional celebrities: so authentic and ordinary that, precisely for these reasons, the word 'celebrity' may be inappropriate.

A paradox is at work here. As Tolson (2001), Scannell (1996), Bennett (2011), and many other media scholars have argued, 'authenticity' and 'ordinariness' are integral components in the relationships audiences form with the stars of radio and television. Furthermore, authenticity and ordinariness are the very characteristics of reality TV stars that have led to what Turner (2010) refers to as the 'demotic turn' in the recent history of celebrity. Therefore, it is hardly surprising that a whole generation of *uber*-authentic celebrities has emerged in the age of social media. It is the latest step in a historic trend associated with technological developments, consumerism, and the cult of the individual.

I want to use this chapter partly to unpack these trumpeted virtues, largely because, as Moseley (2000) and others have argued, authenticity is more an element in *performance* than it is an inherent quality of the mediated individual. I will argue that YouTube stars are no more authentic than television stars or Hollywood icons, but they perform authenticity better. It is worth mentioning at this point that saying an individual 'performs' authenticity does not imply they are faking it, nor that it is a skill that can be learned (although, following Bennett (2011), we can attribute a certain 'vernacular' skill to its performer). Instead, in line with the discursive approach to celebrity taken more broadly in this book, we can think of authenticity emerging as a property of a performance that combines the reproduction of familiar tropes (such as vlog formats) that are understood by the audience, credible manner of speech and gesture, and the context in which the performance is nested. We can talk of performance here as something that extends across time (the video archive on each YouTube channel is significant here) and across different media. Perhaps the most fundamental requirement for authenticity is that the performance has to be consistent and coherent (Marwick, 2016).

Then there is the whole question of why media audiences should crave ordinariness in their celebrities and what it really means when a performer like Zoella, with her own wax likeness in Tussauds, is hailed as ordinary by her fans. Clearly it has something to do with her audience's *identification* with her as 'one of them' or at least, someone who resembles a familiar figure; a lot of commentators claim that Zoella represents a kind of 'big sister' figure to her younger fans (Berryman & Kavka, 2017). Evidently, a part of the vloggers' vernacular skill concerns their ability to inhabit these subject positions for their audiences. I will return to these issues shortly, but first I want to examine the concept of authenticity and how it has been applied to (traditional) media.

What is Authenticity?

Searching for a catch-all definition of authenticity is as difficult as nailing down concepts like 'media' and 'celebrity'. This is largely because it is tied to equally slippery constructs such as 'truth' and 'reality', so its meaning is ultimately defined by the context to which it is applied. There is, for example, much interest in consumer and marketing research in the extent to which consumers demand authentic brands and products (Beverland &

Farrelly, 2010), but this seems to refer to a different concept from the kind of authenticity discussed so far in this chapter. However, the authenticity of artifacts and the perceived authenticity of celebrities may be conceptually linked, as I will go on to argue.

The importance of authenticity in the art world is, of course, enormous. Huge sums of money rest on expert judgements of originality. Likewise, museums need to confer authentication upon their exhibits. In both cases, the authenticity of the object is linked to a conviction in the reality of the phenomenon; that the iron age fort really did exist in my back garden as believed; that the bone dug up by my dog belonged to a real dinosaur, and so on. The same concerns extend to other kinds of objects and memorabilia; a napkin that once belonged to a celebrity, or even my great-grandfather. This practice seems to have its roots in religion and the idea of the sacred (think of the relics of saints), whereby authentic objects are those believed to be 'contaminated' by material traces of a time, place, or person (Belk, 1990). The experience of sitting on a 'genuine antique' chair takes on a different sensation once it is revealed to be a recent imitation.

In the context of celebrity, authenticity becomes a matter of reconciling the performer with the performance. As Trilling (1972) has pointed out, a distinction exists between sincerity, which is the consistency of a performance with a commitment (e.g. acting in a prescribed role), and authenticity, which is the expression of innermost feelings and desires, meaning being 'true to oneself'. The latter concept, Trilling argues, emerged later in history and is inextricably bound up with the emergence of the individualised Romantic self, and then taken further by existential philosophers like Sartre and psychoanalytic thinkers like Winnicott (1971), who believed the 'real self' formed in childhood is constantly at risk from social obligations of being supplanted by a 'false', socially approving self. If truth is something tied to an inner essence (such as a real self), authenticity then becomes a property of persons as well as of sacred and other meaningful objects. So when we watch a vlog, we ask: is this person who they claim to be?

Tolson (2001) explored the notion of authentic selves in relation to the broad phenomenon of celebrity. He argued that "being yourself... is a type of public performance" (Ibid, p. 445), and it formed part of a "professional ideology" of media presentation. In the context of celebrity, authenticity is bound up with "[coming] across as a normal person" so the audience can "relate" to the performer, another variant on Dyer's (1979) ordinary/extraordinary paradox. Tolson argued that the best examples of this practice are the "pure personalities... without a definite talent or expertise" (Ibid, p. 447), such as Phillip Schofield and Terry Wogan on British television, performers who rely on their "televisual skill" (Bennett, 2011) for career success. That skill is tied up with the belief, on the part of the audience that those figures are 'being themselves', something which is largely derived from the coherence and consistency of their performances across different shows, alongside a diverse range of other performers.

In the next section I will explore how authenticity is understood in the literature on YouTube celebrity.

How YouTubers Construct the Authentic Self

Intimate Forms of Address

The first way in which YouTubers convince audiences of their authenticity is through the performance of *intimacy*. The vlog format has, since its inception, involved direct address through which performers employ a conversational style that invites the viewer to participate in a dialogue, irrespective of audience size (Frobenius, 2014). This is a contemporary update of the "fireside style" of radio presentation (Scannell, 1996), where the more didactic approach of early presenters was abandoned in favour of a mode of address that brought the performer into the listener's living room, enhancing the experience of parasocial interaction.

Along with the comments function in YouTube, parasocial relationships are enhanced by YouTubers' presence in other social media where, as discussed in chapter 5, direct contact is possible (Marwick, 2016). Even with millions of subscribers, the intimacy of YouTubers' address is maintained through their delivery. Almost all vloggers directly address the audience as "you", "you guys" or through some kind of identifiable fan name ("Sprinklerinos", etc.) though it is important not to make the viewer feel as though they are merely one of millions. Zoella, for example, addresses the camera as if chatting to "a few dozen, well-known friends" (Jerslev, 2016). PewDiePie has been quoted as saying that he records his 'Let's Play' videos as if he is "in a sports bar with a group of friends watching the game and cheering together" (Beers Fägersten, 2017, p. 8). The nature of the comments received by vloggers suggests this strategy is effective, with much personal disclosure, as though the dialogue opened up by the vlogger is continued by the individual viewer (Garcia-Rapp, 2017; Newman, 2016).

The parasocial relationship between YouTubers and fans is reinforced further by moments of vulnerability on the part of the celebrity, particularly in the form of *confession*. For Foucault (1993), the (Christian) practice of confession played a significant part in the development of the modern concept of self because it gave access to the inner truth (thereby allowing a priest to forgive sin). The confession has been instrumental in modern media, from the traditional celebrity interview (especially the one-to-one) to the video diaries of the camgirls (Senft, 2008). Perhaps its most spectacular manifestation is the 'diary room' format of *Big Brother* and similar forms of reality TV, where the audience is assumed to be hearing the 'inner truth' of the individual contestant, finally freed from the social constraints of the group context (Aslama & Pantti, 2006).

It is during these moments that viewers believe they have access to the inner reality of the celebrity, and we see the gap between vlogger and viewers narrowing. Jerslev (2016, pp. 5243–5244) describes a Zoella video entitled 'Sometimes It All Gets a Bit Too Much', in which she tearfully admits to "failing... I feel like I have to do videos that you will enjoy rather than ones I enjoy making... I don't know, I'm making no sense". Not only is she inviting viewers into her personal lifespace and relationships (her first video was '60 Things In My Bedroom'), she takes us further, along with various vlogs on her own difficulties with anxiety disorder, into the 'truth' of her private self. As with reaction videos and makeover television, emotional display plays a crucial part in this performance (Moseley, 2000; Oh, 2017). Notably, Zoella states at the outset of her tearful video, "I am not sure why I am filming this", and later, "I'll probably not even upload this". But significantly she does, in precisely the same way that lifestyle television producers leave the tears and awkward moments in their meticulously crafted final edits (Giles, 2002a).

Authenticity as a Product of "Liveness"

Another important element in the construction of authenticity is in the sense of 'liveness' that media can create for their audiences. As I mentioned in chapter 4, it is possible to regard reality TV not so much as a reflection of some external reality but as consistent with the reality of viewers' own lives: the sense of time unfolding in two parallel spaces, the medium as a backdrop to the audience's lived reality (Kavka & West, 2004). Of course, social media, with their continual sense of access to celebrities, contribute to and enhance this impression. But in addition, various features of vlogs, including their frequent production, help to consolidate the idea that the performers are living out their lives in tandem with our own.

Some of the ways liveness is achieved in media production are not immediately obvious. One such example is the action replay in sport, which should, on the face of it, detract from the live experience because it reminds viewers they are watching television and not watching the action in person (Marriott, 1996). However, as with other live events on television, the reality created is the viewers' own, allowing them to pursue their own lives while following the parallel reality of the game or ceremony[1]. A similar technique for creating liveness in YouTube is the *blooper*, which has spawned a format of its own (some vlogs are devoted solely to mistakes made during filming) as well as featuring regularly within formats like the tutorial. To keep bloopers in an edited tutorial, a video designed primarily to be instructional, seems counterintuitive, but they perform as important a function as Zoella's tears: as Bevan (2017, p. 768) puts it, such "moments of transparency" in hairstyle tutorials "legitimate their makers as genuine". In effect, bloopers remind the audience they are not watching a fake, glossy production with all the mistakes edited out, but a gritty, realistic slice of life. Although emphasising the amateur status of performers might seem to detract from the fluidity of the instructional tutorial, the blooper serves to narrow the gap between them and their audience.

Another way in which vlogs create a live experience for viewers is in their apparent *spontaneity*. One of the most important attractions of YouTubers cited by fans is the conversational nature of the vlog performance; as an interviewee of Andò's (2016, p. 130) puts it, they speak like "a normal person—it is like chattering". Again, we see the roots of this tradition in television, where the 'chat' form of talk has gradually invaded and interrupted the more formal modes, such as commentary (Tolson, 1991). Chat is important because it is seemingly unscripted and, therefore, provides audiences with another glimpse into the 'truth' of the celebrity self. However, the path to this truth takes a different route from that of the confessional. Like emotion, the spontaneity of chat offers glimpses of the

---

[1] Scannell (2001) points out the absurdity of a 'window on the world' belief that one is accessing "reality" when following a televised Grand Prix race from start to finish, which would be impossible for a spectator at the 'real thing'.

unguarded, even unconscious self, playing on the Freudian belief that slips and errors reveal the working of the unconscious and, therefore, authentic, mind. Like bloopers in tutorials and tears in confessionals, the mistakes are left in vlogs for all to see. Even the slicker editing of the second generation of YouTubers has not resulted in a cleaning-up process.

Threats to Authenticity: 1) Commercial Interest
One of the most oft-cited paradoxes in YouTube celebrity concerns the explicit relationship that exists between YouTubers and commercial brands. How can celebrities be 'true to themselves' when a large portion of their wealth derives from lucrative marketing contracts? The idea of authenticity seems under threat from the 'monetization' of vlogs, yet, "despite mentioning brand names over and over" (Jerslev, 2016, p. 5239), overt commercialism does not *seem* to damage performers' success unless they are found guilty of deception for profit[2].

The dilemma is usually resolved by seeing digital celebrity (or "micro-celebrity") as a unique form of "self-branding" (Marwick, 2013) that can be traced back to the legacy of webcam girls and early online celebrities such as Tila Tequila (Banet-Weiser, 2012). The theory of self-branding argues that all of us with online profiles are engaged in the cultural practice of self-branding, "sculpting" our personal brand through things like "taste performances" (Liu, 2007), and differentiating ourselves from rival brands through the cultivation of 'unique selling points'. Commercial interests are, therefore, seamlessly incorporated into the whole process of selling the celebrity persona (Genz, 2015), and authenticity becomes another marketing tool or even a brand of its own: "the authentic and commodity self are intertwined within brand culture, where authenticity itself is a brand" (Banet-Weiser, 2012, p. 14).[3]

---

[2] In a recent case, the gaming vlogger Trevor Martin (TMartn) was found guilty by a court in Florida of personally (co-)managing a gambling website that he lured his subscribers to by presenting himself as an impartial participant who happened to win a lot of gaming accessories (Dunkley, 2017).

[3] Potter (2010), in relation to marketing at least, calls authenticity a "hoax", a promise that can never be delivered, but Genz (2015) and Banet-Weiser (2012) both dismiss this position as it gives too much power to advertisers (and assumes that consumers are duped). I think it is more helpful for us to see it as a discursive phenomenon; something that is performed while constructing the celebrity persona (vernacular skill if you like).

If we are all self-branders now, product endorsement should be tolerated and even celebrated by the followers of YouTubers, who are just practising the same behaviours as the rest of us. This is more or less the conclusion that Andò (2016) reaches. The teenage vlogger fans she interviewed were unperturbed by the overt commercialism of haul videos and sponsorships; these elements of vlogging were seen as everyday cultural practices that constitute contemporary 'girlhood'. "The brands become symbolic material for vloggers' performances and a stimulus for interaction; they provide a common language and generate social ties and elements to share and recognize" (Ibid., p. 136).

However, not all YouTuber fans are so accepting of the inevitability of commercial interest. In their extensive analysis of comments relating to vlogs, Cocker and Cronin (2017) encountered considerable scepticism as to the motives underlying (some) YouTubers' commercial activities, and several were accused of 'selling out' their longer-term subscribers. "If I encounter another audio book advertisement in another YouTubers favourites I may in fact scream", wrote one Louise Pentland fan. "You have been doing so many sponsored videos lately", wrote a fan of beauty vlogger FleurDeForce. "Miss all of your honest videos!" "All of a sudden [Estée Lalonde] starts to sponsor all of these products without really saying anything about them to her viewers", wrote another beauty vlogger fan. "She has lost down to earth vibes from her older videos". These comments suggest that 'brand culture' is not so pervasive as to eradicate all personal integrity from the celebrity performance. How YouTubers manage the branding practice while preserving traditional notions of authenticity may partly determine their ability to hold on to their long-term subscribers. I will explore in detail how this is done later in the chapter.

Threats to Authenticity: 2) Acting and Censorship

The Lonelygirl15 controversy discussed in chapter 6 highlights a threat to authenticity pertinent to YouTube: suspicion that the performer might be reciting prepared lines: in other words, *acting*. As Smith (2014, p. 264) puts it, "lacking authenticity is anathema to the values of YouTube celebrity... the viewer finding out that the vlogger is inauthentic after the premise of the blog to be 'reality' is an insult to those same viewers who attribute fame and circulate the name". Not all commentators have interpreted the Lonelygirl15 production quite as negatively, arguing that some fans appreciated the contrivance and continued to follow the (fictional) story as it unfolded (Bakioğlu, 2016; Hall, 2014). However, Lonelygirl15 was a phenomenon anchored firmly within the first generation of YouTube celebrities, well before popular performers' subscriber numbers began to approach the millions, and is probably not a good yardstick by which to judge the medium's contemporary audience.

In relation to celebrity more generally, Tolson (2001, p. 445) argues that "being yourself" is "understood as a type of public...performance which, crucially, is not perceived as 'acting'" and is, therefore, located in performers' style of spoken delivery. Spontaneity is critical here, creating the impression that the performer is ad-libbing and not reciting memorised lines. This effect is achieved through the conventions of 'chat' and other techniques discussed earlier, where even if videos are tightly edited, they retain as many elements of "fresh talk" (Goffman, 1981) as possible, especially where suspicion of commercial interests might be at stake. I will explore these discursive aspects of authenticity in more detail in the case studies that follow this section.

Returning briefly to psychoanalytic theory (Winnicott, 1971) and existentialism (e.g. Sartre, Kierkegaard), we could argue that the problem with acting is that it is a performance of the 'false self' and, therefore, a self that is fashioned solely to gain social approval. Either this performance is a *role* scripted by an author (as in drama), or it is one that meets commercial or authoritarian obligations. In media contexts, authoritarian obligations might constrain the freedom of the performer in certain ways: the need to attract an audience, satisfy advertisers, maintain a certain standard of production and, perhaps, to meet certain ethical and moral standards. One of the great attractions of global digital media such as Twitter and YouTube is that they are seen to be free of these authoritarian obligations. Even the need to attract an audience and satisfy advertisers is non-obligatory: YouTube does not exclude or penalise vloggers for failing to build subscriber numbers.

The moral and ethical constraints imposed by traditional (broadcast) media are a different matter. Social media are charged repeatedly with claims that they lack moral responsibility by imposing so few constraints on users and performers, allowing all manner of abusive material through their generous filters in the name of free speech. Demands that these filters are tightened are generally met with indifference by social media companies, largely because they know their generosity is part of social media's attraction for performers and audiences alike. The lack of censorship on YouTube functions in the same way as Twitter (see chapter 5), to create the impression that performers are connecting with audiences directly, without the interference of gatekeepers, and 'bucking the system' in the process (Turner, 2014).

The attraction of bucking the system has long been appreciated by stage performers whose act is sufficiently controversial so as to require much modification for broadcast media. Stand-up comedians Bernard Manning and Buddy Hackett released recordings of stage shows in the 1980s proudly entitled, respectively, "ungagged" and "live and uncensored". The 'gag' and censors are those presumably imposed by traditional broadcast media, shackling the freedom of the comic to use obscene (and offensive) language, allowing audiences access to the true, authentic live performance rather than the watered-down substitute seen on TV. Though some authoritarian obligations are associated with the sale of recordings (Manning and Hackett released their live videos through major companies), they are more relaxed than those of television and radio.

Though YouTubers do not proclaim their videos are 'uncensored', the nature of the medium assumes they have the full range of expression needed for audiences to enjoy their true, authentic performance. An abundance of obscene language often reinforces this, particularly in comedy videos, such as pranks and reactions, where unconstrained swearing plays the same role as emotional display. A notable exponent of such material is PewDiePie, whose career will be discussed shortly. As Beers Fägersten (2017) argues, the swearing in PewDiePie's commentaries strengthens the bond between him and his (mostly adolescent male) audience: "[his] use of swearwords is casual and care-free, and without any indication of inhibition, which further serves to index the intimacy and informality of the parasocial relationship" (Ibid, p. 9). This way, swearing and other informal language, alongside the chat, bloopers, and emotions, builds the YouTube celebrity performance as authentic: a window on the normal, everyday behaviour of the vloggers.

Case studies of YouTube Celebrities and the Construction of 'Authenticity'

In this section, I want to examine how YouTubers perform authenticity in greater detail by focusing specifically on language and discourse. The approach I take follows in the tradition of earlier studies of 'broadcast talk' (Scannell, 1996), which studied the delivery of radio and television performers in terms of its connection with the imagined audience.

Researchers in this tradition have identified a number of forms of "authentic talk" that performers use to engage with the broadcast audience (Montgomery, 2001, pp. 403–404; Van Leeuwen, 2001), drawing on Goffman's (1981) notion of "fresh talk" (Goffman, 1981): spontaneous, conversational, ad lib, typical of radio presenters. As suggested earlier, such talk may be scripted, but convincingly acted out, as in the case of Bree/Lonelygirl15, so performers need to incorporate as many techniques as they can to demonstrate this is not the case.

In order to perform authenticity, celebrities need to convince their audience they are normal and ordinary, qualities fans value highly (Andò, 2016). As discussed earlier, the vlogger persona requires audiences to identify with the performers so they can trust their accounts of their life and their opinions on the products they review. Any suggestion the performers are following some hidden agenda (of a sponsor or manipulator of some sort) threatens their authenticity. The audience has to believe they are, essentially, one of them – or at least a close associate (in the guise of a 'big sister', or friend).

Therefore, "doing being ordinary" (Sacks, 1984) is an important task for YouTubers to accomplish. For Sacks, "being ordinary" functions as a conversational strategy for persuading the audience that an account is valid. 'At first, I thought... but then I realized' builds up a more convincing account because of the speaker's initial 'ordinary' reaction (Jefferson, 2004). Much of the time, YouTubers are not trying to convince us they or their experiences are extraordinary, but they do need to make a claim on our attention to attract subscribers and build their 'brand', whether as expert consumers, entertainers, or lifestyle advocates.

Constructing the 'Expert Consumer': Bubzbeauty Product Reviews

I mentioned earlier in the chapter that vloggers need to manage personal integrity while being heavily 'monetized' through their relationship with various commercial bodies (sponsorships, marketing deals, and so on). Vloggers like Bubz and Zoella, whose performances are saturated with commercial produce, need to tread a fine line between being seen as 'experts' (when it comes to all things beauty) and ordinary people with the same needs and motives as their followers. Garcia-Rapp and Roca-Cuberes (2017, pp. 7–8) cite comments on the Bubzbeauty channel where Bubz is hailed as "true", "real", and "not selling out by pushing products onto us". To see how she achieves this, let's look at a recent product review.

The video in question, posted on January 17, 2017, is called 'CLEAN & DRY Brushes in seconds?' and consists of a review of a make-up brush cleaner (8'23" in total). At the time of writing, it had received 245,243 views, making it one of her more popular videos (typically 100–150K). Bubz is positioned throughout in her kitchen (the dishrack is visible on her left, and photos are attached to what is presumably a fridge door on the right). She addresses the camera for the most part, occasionally looking away to gather relevant items that she is about to present to the viewer. Various jump cuts occur, though not excessively (some vlogs have these every few seconds), and occasionally white text appears onscreen in a friendly modern font, in some instances accompanying a brief cutaway close-up of a piece of equipment. Bubz is in full flow throughout.

It is worth noting at this point that the same brush cleaner has been reviewed by many other YouTubers; the more successful the performer, it seems, the more sceptical they are about the product. Some of the more effusive reviews begin with half-hearted attempts to ward off viewers' suspicions, usually by announcing, early in the piece, that "this is not a sponsored video or anything", before unleashing superlatives like "amazing", "incredible", and "revelation". One video even attracted a gushing appreciation from the manufacturers in the comments thread. Several videos attracted critical comments about "sponsorship" even when denied by the performer, perhaps indicating that he or she had failed sufficiently to persuade the audience of his or her authenticity. Even in a 'brand culture', it seems, brand affiliation is distrusted by (many) consumers.

Bubz signals her (apparent) lack of brand affiliation through a series of much more subtle moves. The following extract begins at 1'12".

1	so we shall see [.] I don't know why but I expected it to come in a bigger box,
2	but as you can see it's quite small [*holds box in palm of one hand and gives it a*
3	*rather disdainful look*]. It wasn't cheap either [*text onscreen:* £50 NOT
4	INCLUDING THE CLEANING SOLUTION], so let's see if it's worth the [.]
	hype because I saw it on Facebook and [*jump cut*] part of me was wondering if
5	it'll be a gimmick but it's something that I thought, OK it's something that I
6	will have to try [*text:* FAB or FAD? *Removes product from box*]

The overall review is structured as a kind of experiment in which the claims of the manufacturer are tested in an appropriate setting, with teasers ("we shall see", "let's see", "fab or fad?") building up the promise of some eventual revelation. This is in direct contrast to those videos that begin by proclaiming the wonders of the product, with one or two even having claims like "amazing!" in their titles.

One of the most common rhetorical figures identified by discursive psychologists is *stake inoculation*, the way speakers position themselves as neutral, objective and unbiased, so as to deflect any accusation that their accounts are insincere (i.e. designed for an ulterior motive) (Potter, 1996). Issuing a disclaimer (such as "I'm not racist, but" or "this video is not sponsored") is not usually the most effective way of doing this. By contrast, Bubz distances herself from any accusations of complicity through a series of remarks that construct grounds for scepticism. She begins in lines 1–2 by commenting about the unimpressive size of the box. "I don't know why but" (line 1) is a variant of a common construction in stake management (see Abell and Stokoe's (2001) analysis of Princess Diana's use of "I dunno") to convince the hearer the idea is spontaneous rather than premeditated[4]. She then expresses scepticism about the price, which is reinforced by the appearance of text that supplies the requisite information (and furthermore, the £50 does "not [include] the cleansing solution"). Further stake inoculation is achieved in lines 4–6 where she makes a case for ordering the product based on casual grounds: she "saw it on Facebook" (line 4), "[wondered]" about the claims made for it (line 5) and finally decided she would "have to try" it out (line 6). The use of the words "hype" in line 4, "gimmick" in line 5 and "FAD" in the text in line 6 alerts the audience to the possibility that the product is merely a piece of clever marketing, a claim that will be finally settled once the trial is complete.

This preamble, conducted as Bubz is gradually unboxing the cleaning product itself, serves two rhetorical purposes. It is classic stake management of the kind that clever advertisers might build into their own scripts, but as Edwards (1997, p. 123) points out, it is "not an abnormally strategic or Machiavellian process restricted to advertisers, lawyers, politicians and propagandists" but "a pervasive... feature of mundane talk". It is made to seem natural because Bubz has the vernacular skill, developed over years

---

[4] Whether the idea really *is* spontaneous is not the point. One tradition in discursive psychology (probably deriving from conversation analysis) is not to speculate on such private, internal matters because they are fundamentally unknowable. The focus should be on the talk per se and the effect it produces on its audience (in this case, gleaned from things like user comments and subscription numbers/video views).

of vlogging, to pull it off. Not only does she manage to distance herself from the product and manufacturer (and the possibility that she is being paid to say positive things about it), but this sequence also serves to build up viewers' curiosity around what is going to transpire in the remaining six minutes of video.

The next extract (starting at 2'19") provides a nice example of the blend of instruction and amateurishness, unique to YouTube videos, that characterises beauty tutorials in particular (Bevan, 2017). It is a reminder that the product review (sub)format has evolved out of the tutorial format and retains a mildly pedagogical tone, while 'bloopers' and other flaws are deliberately incorporated for the important work they do to accomplish 'ordinariness'.

7	[*shot of instructions leaflet; text*: THE WATER SHOULD NOT TOUCH THE
8	BRUSH FARRELL] Let's give it a <u>go</u> [.] According to the instructions it tells
9	you not to pass the farrell [.] and the farrell is basically the metal part of your
10	brush [*camera pans to display of brushes, finger pointing to a copper farrell*].
11	Which <u>one</u> [*Bubz tries inserting brush into different rubber collars*] I think this
12	one is too big [.] hmm [.] will have to be this one [*jump cut; sound of stylus*
13	*scratching vinyl; Bubz pulls brush from collar without handle attached; affects*
14	*mock-glum expression with bottom lip protruding*] I guess I can easily fix it [.] be
	careful when you fit these in the [.] rubber collars [*while looking at instructions,*
	taps collar in didactic fashion]

This sequence comprises part of Bubz's preparation for the brush cleaning trial, where the user has to insert the brush into the rubber collar that attaches to the hand-held motor. Instructional features, typical of the tutorial, are present from the start (the onscreen text in line 7), although these are deferred to 'the instructions' (line 8). Bubz's index finger performs the didactic work in the sequence, pointing to the 'farrell' of the brush in line 9 to indicate this feature (which is presumably informative for the viewer; it was for me), and then tapping the rubber collar in line 14 to accompany the warning "be careful" (line 13). These may be minor features in the sequence as a whole, but they serve to maintain Bubz's expert status as beauty vlogger who is instructing her audience in the art of cosmetic use as well as reviewing a commercial product (more generally, there is also an instructional element in the sense that viewers are taught to fully evaluate a product before splashing out £50).

Bubz's ability to be simultaneously expert and ordinary is accomplished by the 'blooper' that takes place in lines 10–13. Earlier in the video, she introduces a nest of eight rubber collars that are seemingly designed to fit various differently sized brushes. The onscreen text, maintaining the sceptical mood, reads CLAIMS TO FIT ANY BRUSH SIZE. In the current sequence, she selects a brush and pushes it into a couple of collars before its handle becomes stuck and is left behind when she pulls the brush out. This is accompanied by a sound effect intended to indicate a mistake and an exaggerated facial expression of disappointment. One might expect a slick, professional film or TV company to delete such a sequence from the finished broadcast, but its inclusion here reinforces Bubz's status as amateur, whose inability to master the technology on show puts her on a level footing with the audience (and further distances herself from the product).

The trial (with brushes successfully fitted) proceeds in experimental fashion, with varying quantities of cleaning solution and different types of brush, yielding mixed results which Bubz conveys in an engaging fashion by effectively deciding on an open verdict which, as the text summary beneath the video puts it, leaves it up to the audience ("you guys decide"). Several comments express dismay at the price of the product although some critique Bubz's method (don't add water, start off with cleaner brushes). Most comments, however, complement Bubz on the "hilarious" thumbnail tile she used to represent the video, in which she contorts her face in mock disgust as the spinning brush showers her with eyeshadow residue: another blooper[5] that clearly connects with her audience and invites them to view the video.

The Making of the Authentic Self: PewDiePie

In this second case study I want to illustrate the role of "fresh talk" in the construction of a popular YouTube persona. I have chosen to focus on PewDiePie in order to observe the discursive elements that helped attract such a huge audience to his channels. Some of this work has already been

---

[5] Not only is this blooper deliberately retained in the finished product but, I suspect, partly staged. Bubz does not need to hold the brush so close to her face to check its operation, and the disgust expression forms almost the moment she turns the device on. Faces contorted in mock amazement, disgust, or terror are typical thumbnail vlog images and are often, presumably, contrived for this purpose.

done (Beers Fägersten, 2017), particularly around the use of swearing in game commentaries, but here I want to focus in particular on the construction of authenticity through dysfluent, disorganised talk that serves the same role as the 'bloopers' in Bubz's product review.

One might not automatically think of video game commentary as a vehicle for fame and stardom, yet this is one of the ways in which YouTube has afforded a genre of celebrity which could not have been created in any other medium to date. Sports commentary, in radio and television, has produced its share of stars over the years, but most of the time, the figure behind the microphone is hidden from view: audiences develop parasocial relationships with the voice alone, while the real stars are the performers on the pitch. But YouTube's gamers are commentators *and* performers: their commentary is inseparable from their performance. PewDiePie's verbal commentary alone has not brought 62 million subscribers to his channel. Just as Bubz draws viewers to her videos by highlighting exaggerated facial displays, PewDiePie's face as he reacts to events taking place in the game he is playing communicates a continuous sequence of emotional expressions from surprise to hilarity to disgust.

PewDiePie's horror game commentaries provide Beers Fägersten (2017) with most of her data, and an early video in this genre ('Scariest moment in Amnesia... /w LIVE Commentary part 1'[6] uploaded on 25 December 2010) provides a typical example of commentary that is sufficiently fragmented to be convincingly authentic. The video is a 2'10" playthrough of a game in which the player negotiates the dimly lit corridors of a mediaeval castle; several exits are blocked, until he enters one chamber and is confronted by a white figure looming out of the darkness. We hear a strangled scream followed by a stifled laugh, and, accompanied by nothing but a darkened screen displaying the menu options to exit the game, he sobs: "I don't wanna play this game any more". This is followed by the following commentary from 1'09":

15	Oh oh oh [.] oh my gaahd [.] oh my gaaahd [.] oh my god [*strangled laugh*] holy
16	fuck [.] that was [.] aaaarghh [.] hhh [.] Jesus fucking Christ [.] oh my gaahd [.] oh
17	my fucking god...oh my g--- [.] jesus, jesus [.] oh my [.] aargh [.] holy holy fuck [.]
	this game [.] is going to give me a heart attack

Beers Fägersten (2017) raises the query of whether PewDiePie stages outbursts of terror solely for entertainment, yet cites research which suggests that such vocal reactions are typical for the players of such games, and it seems therefore that his performance genuinely reflects the experiences of his audience. This whole sequence, which occupies nearly 40 seconds, takes place after the brief manifestation of the white figure, by which time the play has finished and the screen displays nothing but the menu options. This then is an example of cathartic, "recovery" swearing that ironically establishes the setting as "relaxed and comfortable", and enables PewDie-Pie to engage and entertain his subscribers (Beers Fägersten, 2017, p. 8). Its duration and intensity convinces the viewer that he has been genuinely affected by the game and, as with Bubz's occasional mishaps in the make-up process, places him on an equal footing with his audience.

By February 2011. PewDiePie can be found celebrating his channel's 2,500th subscription, and another dimension to his performance unfolds as we see, for the first time, his face in the corner of the 'Let's Play' screen, allowing the emotional performance on the soundtrack to be supplemented by corresponding facial expressions. This format is first used in 'Crysis 2: Video Commentary / Vlog – Partnership? Livestream? BlackPlague?:)' (26 March 2011)[7]. He begins by addressing his audience with a nervous laugh as though still rather self-conscious about speaking direct to camera: "All right [.] hh [.] how's it going everyone? PewDiePie here", followed by his trademark stylised rendering of his name: "p↑e::wdie↓pie". Throughout this video, a playthrough is on the main screen though it is largely ignored throughout the whole six minutes.

He signals a change of format by saying, "I kind of feel like these aren't commentaries any more—they're more like vlogs" and explains that the current game (Crysis) is merely a demo version because he couldn't afford a copy of the actual game. At one point, he breaks into a tuneless snatch of Harnick and Bock's 'If I Were a Rich Man' to underline the point although he sings "maybe I'm a rich guy" before, in typically self-effacing style, apologising for not knowing the words. Then he announces his Facebook page (link underneath video) and discusses his nascent fan following (1'05–28"):

---

[7] https://www.youtube.com/watch?v=JnLLZchh5lU

18	Some of you ha- [.] er [.] well a lot of you actually huh [.] have been saying hi and
19	stuff already [.] and it's it's a lot of fun to erm [.] I dunno [.] get the chance to see
20	your face and not just some [*shrugs shoulders*] random [.] made-up wor- [.] <u>name</u>
21	[.] or whatever [.] it's fun to see who watch my videos [.] and stuff [.] and [.] so
22	yeah [.] if you want to go there and say hi [.] and like it [.] or whatever you wanna do that's fine

Throughout this speech, PewDiePie keeps one eye on the screen, and his gaze flickers back and forth between the screen and the webcam. In fact, he probably spends more time looking directly at the webcam, thus strengthening the intimacy with the viewer. This sequence is a laboured process of working up to his invitation in line 21 for viewers to 'like' his videos and so it is important here to do the stake inoculation work that makes this blatant appeal for endorsement seem natural and uncontrived. By self-repairing from "some of you" to "a lot of you" in line 18 he seeks to maximise his appeal while at the same time employing distancing devices like "I dunno" (line 19), along with much hedging, and shrugging of shoulders.

In the same way that beauty vloggers have to skilfully negotiate the dilemma of being 'expert' while also being 'ordinary', so PewDiePie needs to do more than scream and swear. Though the comments beneath his videos make it clear that PewDiePie's subscribers are largely drawn to his commentaries for their entertainment value, the manner in which gaming advice is delivered is also a key element in PewDiePie's appeal as the next sequence of commentary (1'29–48") seems to indicate:

23	I think in this gameplay I actually figured out how to use the killsticks for the first
24	time [.] it's kinda different [.] you have to walk over the [.] you have to walk over
25	the >oh look at this (nadefell?)< hhh you have to walk over the [.] er [.] guy you
26	killed to get the killstick and [.] it took me FOREVER to figure that out [.] so there you go [.] if you haven't played it already and you're about to

The 'advice' is presented here, like the playthrough itself, as largely tangential to the primary purpose of introducing himself to his audience. This particular sequence follows immediately from the previous extract without any reference to the specific action onscreen, as if the idea suddenly formed itself, and is typical of the work he is doing to align himself with the audience footing as an *enthusiast* rather than a technical gaming expert. Whereas an expert might be expected to swiftly grasp the use of "killsticks" in this game, PewDiePie has taken "FOREVER to figure that out" (lines 25–26). The comment at the end of line 26 seems, by contrast, to be thrown in as if he has just remembered his audience might be there for technical advice; this is a delicate balancing act.

In those 'Let's Play' videos where the focus is squarely on the game-play itself, PewDiePie's presentation style is equally dysfluent. In 'Nightmare House 2: Playthrough Part 8 - RODRIGUEZ IS SEXEH'[8], uploaded 30 May 2011, the viewer is pitched straight into the middle of a game accompanied by commentary that only makes partial sense when seen in conjunction with the onscreen action.

27	All right, welcome- [.] >I need to go offline< [*menu options onscreen*] erm [*return*
28	*to action*] wel<u>come</u> back to::[.] er [.] what is this game called [.] hello ladies [.]
29	>they keep following me it's so weird< right honestly I haven't played this so long I
	don't remember where I left off [.] oh shit

Whereas a professional sport commentary, or even a traditional home movie maker, would open with a clear, formal introduction explaining the context of the playthrough (here, that it is part 8 of an ongoing series of videos featuring the same game), PewDiePie begins with a brief welcome before breaking off to adjust his controls. When he repeats his welcome (line 28), he is then seemingly unable to recall the game's name and (in line 29) confesses that he cannot recall where he "left off", presumably at the end of part 7[9]. Furthermore, he allows his introduction to be broken, instantaneously, by in-game activity. His deviation from a script is taken to the limit so he reacts spontaneously to the images onscreen: his comment "Hello ladies" and the following aside (bracketed in the transcript by hair-pins to illustrate a change in register) is typical of the kind of utterance a game player might make to a close companion but not to a watching audience by now numbering several thousand.

---

[8] https://www.youtube.com/watch?v=3Smj53EL904
[9] Although part 7 is still available on YouTube, from a fansite called 'Pewdie ScaryGames' (https://m.youtube.com/watch?t=78s&v= 3sYtRyRf45c), this and other videos were, according to the comments, removed from PewdiePie's official channel because they feature co-commentary from an ex-girlfriend. I am unable, therefore, to ascertain the original date of the video.

Even from its relatively early days, the YouTube style of production differed markedly from that of the traditional home movie maker, who in the above instance would have quickly pressed the 'stop' button on the camera and begun the action afresh (for a discussion of the difference between these styles of production, see Strangelove, 2010). The home movie maker would have undoubtedly *rehearsed* the introduction to begin with. But the home movie maker, though unashamedly amateur, must not to appear *amateurish*. For YouTubers, cultivating huge global audiences and lucrative commercial deals (PewDiePie was being courted by game companies at this stage), the reverse is true. The complete (or deliberate) absence of any evident rehearsal, or any commitment to a formal, scripted introduction consolidates PewDiePie's growing reputation as an enthusiastic amateur rather than a professional expert, and it is clear from the comment threads that this style is appreciated by his fans.

Four years later, with subscriber numbers approaching 40 million, we can see a change in production style. The audio and visual quality of the videos is superior to those from 2011. His commentary is punchier, still with occasional digressions and asides, but with more sense of scriptedness (either there *is* a script, or he has become more confident in front of the camera). The introductions are more polished, with many variations on the p↑e:::wdie↓pie motif, including human beatbox/rap interjections, playful and ironic visual and musical effects, many references to "bros" (his fans) and frequent 'brofist' gestures (a non-aggressive salute with the fist thrust forward).

'Maya's Big Date' (25 June 2015)[10] is an example of this change in presentation. His onscreen presence is now foregrounded; only the visual presence of a microphone acts as a boundary between his contribution and the playthrough. At specific points in the video his image is enlarged so he occupies a large part of the screen (sometimes the entire screen): this maintains his close relationship with the audience, but at the same time, this clear evidence of tight editing sacrifices some of the spontaneity of the earlier videos. It is also perhaps noteworthy that PewDiePie does not face the viewer in his new position, thereby losing a degree of intimacy (by placing himself at a 45° angle, he does not need to keep switching his gaze between the camera and the screen, but the result is that he only occasionally

---

[10] https://www.youtube.com/watch?v=zpsiIMx36kQ

directs his gaze outwards and the viewer is potentially less involved in the broadcast). Thematically, his material has become considerably more diverse (which is true of most YouTubers, who rarely remain specialists). He still uploads 'Let's Plays', but includes a much wider variety of games. The playthrough featured in this video is a comedy pet-dating game, into which he incorporates one of his own two pugs (the other, Edgar, is also an occasional guest star).

The evolution of PewDiePie's commentary style can best be seen in a later playthrough, 'Anime AF' (18 October 2015)[11]. This extract begins around 18 seconds after a relaxed introduction where he explains that "one of you bros" recommended this game in the comments to a previous video.

30	It looks [.] it's supposed to be like [.] not [.] apparently not a lot of people know about
31	it [.] it's a free game and it looks really cool [.] so we're going to check it out [.] OK
32	[.] let's go [.] play [.] solo [*frantic music begins*] oh my god [.] oh my god what is
33	happening [.] aaa:::::::hhh [*voiceover, cut to still frame advertising game*] ah [.] I don't
34	[*images swarm across the screen*] >oh my god I have to collect all the salad< [.]
35	woo::::oo [*PewDiePie starts sliding across bottom of the screen*] ahahaha [.] THIS IS FRUIT NOT SALAD but whatever

The (very basic) description of the game is delivered in the dysfluent manner of his earlier playthroughs, but once the playthrough is underway, PewDiePie's responses feel a good deal less spontaneous, and more contrived than in the 2010–2011 videos. The trademark "oh my god"s in line 32 begin almost the moment the game's soundtrack kicks in, and create the impression that he is responding in a manner his audience expects, without anything particularly noteworthy having taken place in the game. Likewise, the two elongated howls in lines 32 and 34 lack the ring of authenticity of the terrified reaction in the 2011 extract. The game itself is seemingly devoid of any elements that might provoke such a response in a seasoned gamer like PewDiePie, as reflected in the many derisive comments below that later viewers have posted about his performance.

The stylised effects also detract from the sense of immediacy in this video. Several humorous insertions and other gimmicks, such as the sliding

---

[11] https://www.youtube.com/watch?v=8XRMMR4XU5s

image in line 34, create the impression the film has been skillfully edited while maintaining the 'madcap' commentary style that has helped build his audience. This is still clearly not scripted, allowing him to retain some spontaneity, such as the salad/fruit error in line 34, but by shouting the correction in the following line, he seems to be trying a little too hard to draw attention to the fact that, despite all the whizzy effects, this is still live[12]. Perhaps the most surprising thing about this video is that, unlike the 'Crysis 2' example from 2011, the game is the central feature. Instead of the playthrough being used as a vehicle for general vlog-style chat, it has reverted to its generic function. Plenty of other formats allow him to develop the other sides of his persona.

Does all this mean that PewDiePie has become *less* authentic as his global fame has increased? I have argued throughout this chapter that authenticity is something that celebrities perform, and (at least on this isolated evidence) there seems to be less obviously performed authenticity in his 2015 work than in his early videos. Whether or not fans perceive his 2015 persona to be less authentic is another matter. Though some comments posted later on his early videos have a nostalgic tone (e.g. "I miss the old Pewds"), these are massively outweighed by positive ones. Even if he has lost some fans along the way, their number is a mere drop in the ocean.[13]

Conclusion

The two case studies here illustrate the ways in which YouTube celebrities negotiate the seemingly opposing roles of expert and novice in constructing an authentic vlogger persona. It is clear from viewers' comments and other data that authenticity is an important quality for YouTubers to be seen to

---

[12] In the summaries of many of his early videos, PewDiePie mentions the fact that his commentary is live.

[13] Whether this continues to be the case may depend on the increasing frustration on behalf of his supporters with publicity surrounding his use of offensive language and gestures. A particularly unpleasant recent story concerned a video which featured a banner reading 'Death to all Jews', and Disney terminated his contract after discovering nine unacceptable instances of such material in his work (Mahdavi, 2017). PewDiePie himself defended these on the grounds that they were essentially ironic, used for shock value alone, and understood by viewers in this context. Thus far, there has been no obvious exodus of subscribers or drop in viewing figures.

possess, and their perception as normal or ordinary leads some fans to claim that the term 'celebrity' is inappropriate. However, where they are successful and can claim global audiences of many thousands or millions of subscribers, it is hard to see how they can avoid the trappings of traditional celebrity. Certainly, the income available from brand sponsorship imposes additional demands on the need to remain ordinary, and it is perhaps a matter of vernacular skill that enables some to do this more convincingly than others.

8

INSTAGRAM AND THE RISE OF THE SOCIAL MEDIA 'INFLUENCER'
(with Lucy Edwards[1])

For some years now, big business has been devising increasingly surreptitious ways of marketing products to consumers. While the jury is still out on whether or not 'subliminal advertising' actually works, there is broad consensus that the recommendation of trusted friends represents the most effective tool in marketing. In the first decade of the current century, more and more companies were experimenting with "stealth marketing" (Osterhout, 2010), by which 'ordinary' consumers were paid to promote new products to unsuspecting passers-by, or contracted to become 'brand pushers' whose targets were their unsuspecting friends. Most of this work took place through word of mouth, in public spaces, through e-mail, or early social media. But by the 2010s, a new marketing phenomenon was emerging: the *influencer*. This was an individual with a significant personal audience but who, like the YouTubers discussed in the two previous chapters, was perceived as sufficiently 'ordinary' to act as a trusted source of advice. Someone who did 'being ordinary' well enough to disguise the fact they were being paid to promote products. Or maybe, as Banet-Weiser (2012) might argue, whose audience was so saturated in brand culture that they did not mind.

---

[1] Lucy Edwards graduated from the University of Winchester with a 2.1 in Psychology in 2017. Her final year project studied the impact of 'haul videos', created by YouTubers, on their audiences. After graduation Lucy worked as a Research Assistant at the University where she was investigating the phenomenon of micro-celebrity.

In this chapter, I am going to discuss the influencer as a uniquely twenty-first-century genre of celebrity like the YouTuber. There is, of course, considerable overlap between the two: beauty vloggers like Bubz and Zoella are unquestionably influencers whose primary medium is YouTube. But the popular figure of the influencer is someone whose "brand" transcends any specific medium, who curates accounts on numerous social media, but whose "hub" is a stand-alone blog or personal website (Pedroni, 2016). This sounds rather like a plain old celebrity, where the star effectively operates outside media as such, but as I have argued in earlier chapters, this was never really the case, and it is no coincidence that the figure of the influencer has emerged alongside developments in social media that have afforded new and specific forms of famous individual. Chief among these is the rise of Instagram, launched (as an app) in 2010 and sold to Facebook in 2012. While envisaged as a social network rather than a promotional tool as such, Instagram's visual focus is thought to have contributed to the popularity of the 'selfie' and the use of images in general that favour certain types of self-presentation (Marwick, 2015).

So, while this chapter is primarily about the figure of the influencer *per se*, I will argue that the affordances of Instagram in particular have helped privilege certain genres of new celebrity that fall into this diverse category, from bloggers in travel and fashion to digital visual artists, food, and health bloggers, and 'ordinary' models whose vocation seems to be little more than product promotion.

What Kinds of Influence?

The *social media influencer* is a relatively new concept even though variants can be traced back to the last century. The term, as understood in popular discourse, probably originated around 2015–2016 as illustrated in an article on the British *Independent* news website called 'Meet the Influencers' (Saul, 2016). The individuals discussed in this article are explicitly referred to as a new genre of celebrity that appeals to "generations Y and Z" and comprises such subcategories as models, bloggers, and 'trainers' (the last being a further subcategory of lifestyle bloggers). Subsequent media stories broaden the definition to include reality TV stars and beauty bloggers (at least those active on Instagram) (Marsh, 2017), writers and general "Instagrammers" (Wedgwood, 2017).

The academic literature stretches the net wider, identifying 'family influencers' (Abidin, 2017), food and wellness bloggers (Khamis, Ang, & Welling, 2017), and online celebrities exerting influence in specific locations, such as Italian fashion bloggers (Pedroni, 2016) and 'Singaporean influencers' (Abidin, 2016). A rather earlier paper (Freberg, Graham, McGaughey, & Freberg, 2011) identified four figures who were primarily writers (some had authored books) and tech 'analysts' – essentially digital media entrepreneurs, not unlike the first wave of popular Twitter users that Marwick (2013) identified as 'micro-celebrities'. Even under contemporary definitions, these figures would still qualify as influencers, being essentially bloggers with an identity that does not rely on association with a specific medium, although the popular image of the influencer derives largely from the same criteria as the YouTubers discussed in the previous chapters: 'ordinary' consumers, typically under the age of 30 and active on Instagram in particular, albeit with accounts on most social media.

One of the areas in which social media influencers have had the most impact is the world of fashion media. Pedroni (2016) explains the rise of the fashion blogger-cum-influencer in terms of Bourdieu's (1993) theory of the cultural field. Particularly in Italy, fashion bloggers (i.e., writers who manage a personal website alongside several social media accounts) have accumulated sufficient cultural, economic, and social capital to enable them to occupy dominant positions in the fashion world. Sometimes literally: one blogger claims that "[traditional] journalists have been ousted from the thrones which they occupied for years, from the front row at fashion shows" (Pedroni, 2016, p. 332). While several print magazines have gone out of business over the last decade, fashion blogging has emerged as an important sub-field and their creators have acquired celebrity status, courted by designers and agents, and have earned legitimacy in the fashion field as a whole.

Abidin (2016) describes a quite different set of figures in her work on Singaporean influencers. These appear to be largely young, good-looking social media users (some of whom have, at some stage at least, authored blogs), who have been signed up by companies for the sole purpose of advertising products on social media. Central to their performance is the 'selfie', through which they are able to promote products and services in 'advertorials' (the social media appropriation of the long-established journalistic practice of embedding advertisements in what appear to be feature articles). The social media advertorial is simply a picture – typically on Instagram – that advertises a product and commands a fee from the manufacturer. These types of influencers, then, are essentially *models*: Abidin credits them with a measure of skill, though this is largely in the service of engineering the best angle, lighting and ambience to showcase their own photos.[2] Through their association with the products they sell – and, presumably, their physical attractiveness – they are able to command influence in the marketing world, live a celebrity lifestyle, and accumulate yet more followers on social media, even to the point of being able to charge for personal appearances in publicity events.

The overt link between commerce and media performance is ultimately what marks the distinction between social media influencers and the YouTubers discussed in chapters 6 and 7, including the beauty vloggers with multiple links to product pages. While many of the latter stars have extensive management and sponsorship ties, these are largely kept under wraps in order to develop the 'authentic' side of their performance. While many influencers might derive their popularity through crafting an image of an 'ordinary', independent agent, there is no attempt to disguise the fact that they are acting on behalf of multiple brands. Some even make a virtue of their business acumen: the travel blogger Kiersten Rich ('The Blonde Abroad') has articulated her marketing strategy in terms of "multiple income streams", "product lines", "diversification", and "campaign analytics". "I have my own capital to be my own investor", she says (Halpern, 2017). This is 'self-branding' *par excellence*.

This tightrope act, balancing social media content with advertising revenue, may yet result in some painful falls. Already the Advertising Standards Authority, the UK's regulatory body, has upheld complaints over 'advertising breaches' where influencers' 'advertorials' did not make their commercial nature sufficiently clear (Marsh, 2017). Technically, UK influencers are supposed to indicate such posts by using the hashtag #ad, though ultimately, the watchdog's pursuit of offenders is driven by customer complaints, and requires compliance from media companies like Instagram themselves for any serious action other than the removal of the post in question.

----

[2] I will discuss selfies later in the chapter, but from Abidin's (2016) and others' writing on the subject, there is no great differentiation between the modern practice of snapping oneself while holding a mobile device and being photographed by a professional in the traditional model/celebrity sense: In this literature, the term 'selfie' largely refers to the presentation of one's own image in social media.

While much of this material just sounds like old-fashioned capitalism dressed in shiny digital garb, the relationship between marketing and social media influence has opened up some opportunities for new genres of celebrity to emerge that are more than just digitized versions of former genres (e.g., fashion bloggers replacing old-style fashion journalists). One such area is rock climbing, an unlikely source of fame (as distinct from, say, mountaineering), but one which has seen influential individuals cultivate a substantial following on social media through the sponsorship of climbing activities and the blog posts, Instagram pictures and YouTube videos that accompany it (Dumont, 2017).

Whereas fashion blogging simply transforms the career opportunities for people working around the fashion industry itself, professional climbing, driven by the visibility afforded by social media, has transformed what it means to be a successful climber. Long-standing climbers bemoan the shift from competition (where performers were evaluated in terms of their skill in negotiating difficult climbs) to brand allegiance, with companies demanding that their climbers hit monthly targets of social media content. Some of the most influential figures in this new domain deliberately eschew those trickier challenges in favour of novel climbing trips that allow them to "bring back funny and interesting contents and stories with beautiful pictures" (Dumont, 2017, p. 112) which, along with intimate pictures (family and so on) and 'mundane' details, ensure a greater number of 'likes'. This is really travel blogging rather than adventure sport, but the profile identity is that of an athlete rather than an aesthete.

The same concerns voiced by old-time rock climbers are being made in relation to the popularity of influencers in other fields. There is a general anxiety around the usurpation of expert status by people who cultivate a large audience for claims that are not informed by traditional sources of knowledge or supported by traditional forms of evidence, such as lifestyle bloggers with little or no education or training promoting diets and health treatments. Of course, fears about online 'disinformation' have been prevalent ever since the mass uptake of the Internet in the late 1990s, usually in the form of finger-wagging warnings from medical professionals (see Gallagher, 2017, for a recent story of the NHS allegedly trying to steer the public away from 'Dr Google').

Much of this stems from the 'digital dualism' discussed in chapter 2 (the belief that the online and offline constitute discrete social worlds, the former a poor simulacrum of the latter), whereby 'the Internet' *per se* is distrusted, even though it holds much of the information (diagnostic manuals and so on) that doctors themselves rely on. Nevertheless, the fear that influential yet poorly informed individuals are circulating dangerously inaccurate information is given credence by cases such as the Australian food and health bloggers Belle Gibson and Jess Anscough, who built up large social media followings by claiming to have discovered dietary cures for cancer (Khamis et al., 2017). Although these two particular figures really pre-date the contemporary 'influencer' figure, their level of online success reflects populist discourses that are hostile towards traditional 'experts', and promise to swiftly resolve problems through homespun methods (Molyneaux & Osborne, 2017).

This is a contentious issue that feeds into many contemporary debates around knowledge, culture, legitimacy, and representation, and takes us back eventually to the book bloggers discussed in chapter 6 – themselves increasingly influential in their own literary fields, and whose relationship with publishers and authors is quite different from that of the traditional critic. Does the increasing significance of these intermediary figures herald a 'legitimation crisis' in the critical reception of literature? This is not really an argument that a book on celebrity could do justice to. For the present, it is simplest to think of book bloggers as classic examples of micro-celebrities, lacking the large-scale audience and influence of traditional celebrities like Oprah Winfrey (whose Book Club occupied a similar position within populist critical discourse, but had significant commercial impact on the publishing industry). I will now turn to the relationship between social media influencers more generally and the concept of micro-celebrity.

Celebrities, Micro-celebrities or *Meso*-celebrities?

Pedroni's (2016) work on Italian fashion bloggers introduces a novel concept: the "*meso*-celebrity" – somebody who has "passed through the status of micro-celebrity" but still lacks the large-scale fame associated with traditional celebrity. The category of meso-celebrity is needed, he argues, because there is currently a "shortcoming in the literature" (Pedroni, 2016, p. 108) that fails to capture the 'intermediate' cultural position that many successful social media influencers occupy. Pedroni compares Chiara Ferragni, listed by Forbes magazine as the current number one fashion influencer for her blog 'Blonde Salad' and her 10.9 million Instagram followers, with up-and-coming influencers Alessandro Magni and Arianna Chieli.

These last two still have "thousands" of followers and are gaining influence in the Italian fashion world, but currently lack Ferragni's global stardom.

These concerns reflect the ambiguity in the literature around micro-celebrity that I outlined in chapter 4. Much of the time, the criteria required to define someone as a micro-celebrity are not met by the individuals described in the research. For example, Abidin (2016) applies Marwick's (2013, p. 114) definition to the Singaporean influencers that she has studied, notably that micro-celebrity "is a state of being famous to a niche group of people". However, we are later told that some of the influencers boast in excess of 200,000 followers (a similar problem occurs in Mavroudis and Milne's (2016) study of micro-celebrity practices). Further, most original definitions of micro-celebrity require that such figures sit outside mainstream media and lack financial success (Marwick & boyd, 2011; Senft, 2008), yet Abidin's influencers make television appearances and are sponsored extensively by manufacturing companies. Their entire vocation is predicated on making money through their celebrity.

To some extent, the micro-celebrity concept is dated because it ultimately derives from Henry Jenkins's work in fan studies and "convergence culture" (Jenkins, 1992, 2006) – writing that was ground-breaking at its time but essentially describes a media world that has changed beyond all recognition (think of web 1.0 morphing into web 2.0). The micro-celebrity in this tradition is one who occupies a liminal position between fan and celebrity: one who is in continuous communication with their audience, who is simultaneously producer and consumer of media (or "produser" – Bruns, 2008). This version of micro-celebrity has been picked up and developed within Persona Studies (see chapter 10), for example in the article on travel bloggers by McRae (2017), in which micro-celebrity is described as a continuum, with celebrity itself at the extreme pole. This re-definition has the advantage of being flexible, but (just like, for example, the autism spectrum) it risks simply ironing out all the variations within the construct, leading one to differentiate cases solely on the basis of a single metric. One person is simply more or less of a (micro-)celebrity than another; not, then, so different from the original idea of celebrity itself.

It could be argued that Pedroni's (2016) "intermediate" category of meso-celebrity is effectively another variant of the continuum idea. The basic distinction between micro-celebrity, meso-celebrity, and celebrity is largely the number of followers each category of person attracts (hundreds, thousands, and millions respectively). Meso-celebrity, then, is essentially a temporary state – a limbo between relative obscurity and global fame – that people pass through on their way to celebrity. Micro-celebrities are said to 'aspire' to collaboration with meso-celebrities (Pedroni, 2016, p. 115), although going by Marwick and Senft's earlier definitions, micro-celebrity has never really been thought of as a transition phase, and its original practitioners were not actively seeking celebrity in the traditional sense.

In Marwick (2015, p. 138), micro-celebrity gives way to "Instafame" – a variety whereby micro-celebrity "exists on a particular platform". Because Instagram is a "photographic" medium, it affords a different kind of micro-celebrity to Twitter and other primarily text-based networks. Instafame depends on "the ability to emulate the visual iconography of mainstream celebrity culture" (Ibid, p. 139), privileging conventional good looks and 'cool industries', such as modelling and tattoo artistry. But Instagram is not a vehicle for fame by itself: like Twitter, it serves, through micro-celebrity practices, "to amplify fame found in another medium" (p. 146). In other words, it acts as a promotional tool for those who are already achieving in some other domain – bloggers, for example.

Strangely enough, none of the three case studies that Marwick presents in her paper actually meet this description. One of them, Cayla Friez, is a high school student who maintains a mysterious aloofness, but at the time of the research had inspired a number of fan pages celebrating her good looks, along with a fair amount of abuse for her unresponsiveness. Marwick notes that this marks a departure from the micro-celebrities she has studied thus far, suggesting that Friesz's appeal derives from a "studied unaffectedness" (p. 150). A couple of years on, however, her Instafame seems to have dried up altogether. A second case study is a friend of the singer Rihanna – a fairly typical case of fame by association; a third is the son of a Singaporean billionaire with an Imelda Marcos-like shoe collection whom Marwick describes as a "luxury enthusiast". None of the three seems to have had any pre-existing fame for Instagram to "amplify"; any fame they have can be attributed solely to the photographic affordances of this particular medium.

Ultimately, Pedroni (2016) is right: the term micro-celebrity, and certainly the various ways it is defined in the literature, does not quite capture those YouTubers and influencers who have built audiences in the tens (never mind hundreds) of thousands who are not quite global superstars but enjoy celebrity lifestyles and wield considerable commercial influence. Nor do I think it resolves the problem by recasting it as a set of practices for self-branding, since all celebrities are, in the digital era, required to follow the same practices (and indeed many of the practices are explicitly modelled on pre-digital celebrity anyway). I will return to this issue for one final time in chapter 10 when I develop this idea in relation to the emerging field of persona studies.

The Unique Affordances of Instagram

As Marwick (2015) argues, Instafame's glamorous nature derives from its visual, or photographic, focus. But it is more than just a photographic medium, since its visuals are accompanied by texts and these can be replied to by other members (and reciprocated by the account owner). Admittedly, most of the verbal interaction is minimal, consisting of short phrases at best ("You look gorgeous"), and often just a single word or a few emoticons. Unlike Twitter, though, there is no restriction on the amount of text a user can post, and some accounts feature more extended discussion than can be found on that particular medium. And like on Twitter, the hashtag has an important communicative function – not just thematic (grouping together pictures on a similar topic) but rhetorical, inviting certain interpretations.

But Instagram's most enduring contribution to contemporary culture is probably the selfie, a unique style of presenting the self, made possible by a combination of portable media devices (doubling as cameras) and a visually-orientated social network. Selfie culture is at the medium's heart: 92 per cent of teenagers have uploaded one (Marwick, 2015), and the idea that you do not have to organize a professional shoot in order to load your own image on to your social media account has led long-standing celebrities to supplement their publicity material with their own on-the-go footage that heightens the sense of realism and fans' consequent engagement. Selfies are certainly popular with followers. One actor-cum-artist studied by Mavroukis and Milne (2016) complains that his "shirtless selfies" get twice as many likes as pictures of his paintings (a quick browse through his Instagram account seems to bear this out).

There are selfies, however, and photographs of the self, and the distinction between the two is not always clear from the literature. Abidin's (2016) Singaporean influencers, whose income depends on having the sponsoring brand represented in the best light, take great pains to create the "most professional and stylized selfies with thoughtful captions" (p. 6), often in communal sessions, to the point where the person holding the camera need not actually be the person pictured in the image. The archetypical selfie is one that bears witness to the subject's actual location; hence the trade in 'selfie sticks' at popular tourist destinations, and the use of selfies to accompany eyewitness reports in news media (Koliska & Roberts, 2015).

Instagram's association with the selfie is not mere historical coincidence. In another example of how media affordances evolve over time out of the interaction between users and technological functions, the meaning of the selfie determines its use within any given context. For the Singaporean influencers, it is the "stylized" image that ends up on Instagram because it is through this medium that professional business is conducted. Twitter is reserved for images that are "less serious in terms of photography aesthetic", and those that depict their subjects "goofing around behind the scenes" are more likely to end up on Snapchat, where they disappear after 24 hours and so evade any "long-term consequences" of misrepresentation (Abidin, 2016).

One study that has explicitly addressed the role of medium in shaping the nature of content is Duguay's (2016) analysis of the LGTBQ model Ruby Rose. The author's focus here are the "platform mediators" – the *intended* affordances of technology – that, she argues, determine the possibilities different media have for challenging dominant social constructions, or discourses. Directly comparing Instagram with Vine, Duguay argues that the former medium affords a conservative self-presentation because its instructions to users, and restrictions on content, favour a passive, consumerist mentality ("see the world through someone else's eyes"); while Vine encourages creativity ("people have an entirely new medium to express themselves"). Correspondingly, Ruby Rose's Instagram pictures promote normative standards of beauty and the glorification of celebrity, while her six-second videos ('Vines') allow her to challenge and subvert these same discourses. Ultimately, this is a technological deterministic position since it suggests that users have no scope to adapt each medium's functions to their preferred use.[3] It may also be the case that, as a model, Instagram's

---

[3] There is also the problem that Instagram does now allow its members to post short videos although, like the extended tweet limit in Twitter, these additional 'intended affordances' differ from those affordances that emerge over time through people's actual use of the medium, and the single snapshot is still the defining feature of Instagram culture.

affordances for Ruby Rose are rather predictable (pictures of shopping in Beverly Hills and so on).

A rather different type of Instafame, and one that could not be predicted from studying the intended affordances of the medium, concerns a new generation of poets known as *Instapoets* (Qureshi, 2015). By framing a few lines of verse in a picture, these writers, completely unknown prior to Instagram, have grown audiences, signed publishing deals, and, in some cases, released best-selling volumes of poetry far outstripping anything produced in the conventional literary field. Probably the leading light of this generation is Rupi Kaur, a young Canadian woman of Indian heritage, whose first collection *Milk and Honey* (Andrews McMeel, 2014) has sold in excess of a million copies. Another is Tyler Knott Gregson, who has combined his interests in poetry and photography in order to upload a daily haiku over several years (and further best-selling hard copy books). Rupi Kaur's creativity also extends to other artforms, notably performance art; she attracted much publicity by apparently being censored by Instagram for posting a picture of her menstrual blood staining her trousers and bedsheet. While the company claimed that it had deleted the post in error, Kaur welcomed its restoration as a victory for sexist taboos around menstruation (Saul, 2015).

Instagram and Authenticity

In late 2015, before the term 'social media influencer' had become common currency, an Australian teenager Essena O'Neill made headlines across the mainstream media for turning her back on her 600,000+ Instagram followers, deleting many of her 'advertorial' selfies in the process, and loudly proclaiming that she was "[quitting] all social media [in order to] focus on real life projects" (Hunt, 2015). Leaving aside the obvious irony that this announcement was made on her YouTube vlog, her online vanishing act seems to have been successful; no trace of her can be found in the two years since closing down her personal website in late 2015. O'Neill's charge against social media, and Instagram in particular, was essentially that of *inauthenticity*. She relabelled those pictures she had not actually deleted, unpacking the stories behind them (how long it had taken her to get made up, what health risks were posed by the food she was eating), and denouncing the whole influencer lifestyle as purposeless consumerism.

There is a certain acknowledgement, even by those committed to the medium, that the images posted to Instagram are not a 'true' reflection of the self. For example, among the influencers interviewed by Mavroudis and Milne (2016), one argues that Instagram is "not in any way a true portrayal of who I am"; one takes care to avoid posting certain images such as "party pictures" that might create an unflattering profile; while another prefers to have a "stupid face" in his selfies to create the impression that he is "not taking himself too seriously". In each case, this suggests that conscious control is exerted to enable the medium to present them in a particular light that is not necessarily the whole story. As discussed earlier, Abidin's (2016) Singaporean influencers use different media to present different sides of the self, and this is also the case with the same author's family influencers (Abidin, 2017), who document different sides of family life on Instagram (more formal) and Twitter ('backstage' moments). Other influencers employ the same division of images on public and private Instagram accounts respectively: as one fashion blogger says, her private account contains "real moments", such as "a personal selfie with my boyfriend", while her public account features "an idealized reality" (Wedgwood, 2017).

In chapter 5, I discussed the frontstage/backstage analogy of Goffman (1959) and how the distinction has become increasingly blurred in Twitter content. The same argument has been made in relation to selfies by Collings (2014), specifically in relation to Twitter, although the issues are arguably more pertinent still with regard to Instagram. Collings (2014) argues that many celebrity selfies are actually frontstage affairs, even if they promise their audience a glimpse of the backstage, since they are all part of the celebrity performance, "catering to viewer expectations" (p. 513). In the case of the "ironic selfie", epitomized by rapper Cazwell's use of the format (detailed in his song *No Selfie Control*), Collings argues that "inauthenticity [has] an authenticity of its own". We could extend this argument further still by suggesting that *any* celebrity selfie is intrinsically ironic by the very fact of it mimicking a non-celebrity activity. Marwick (2015) highlights the paradox that, while micro-celebrities strive for glamour by framing themselves as celebrities, once behind the camera (as it were), celebrities largely post "mundane pictures of meals and cats". Of course, as the distinction between celebrity and micro-celebrity becomes itself more blurred, this paradox ultimately resolves itself: the mundane pictures acquire a glamour of their own.

"Questions of *what* authenticity looks like, and *who* has the authority to decide, cannot be fully resolved", writes McRae (2017, p. 25) in relation to travel bloggers. Her research on the topic throws up a number of thorny issues, not least the fundamental distinction between authentic travel experiences and professional travel blogging/writing, which echoes the concerns in the rock climbing field about commercially-orientated climbers crowding out the achievement-orientated (and arguably 'more authentic') climbers of old (Dumont, 2017). These tensions are most fully realized in the online community *Get Off My Internets* (henceforth GOMI) from where most of McRae's data are taken. GOMI[4], now a decade old, is described by McRae as an "anti-fan forum", although it is framed more as a kind of quality control watchdog where members systematically and repeatedly berate lifestyle, food, and health bloggers for poor advice, self-aggrandisement, excessive mysticism, or absurdly optimistic cant. Van Syckle's (2016) description of it as "the peanut gallery" is about right, and as with a crowd of persistent hecklers, there is often a fine line between deserved criticism and bullying. Travel bloggers get a sub-forum to themselves, and it is not hard to see why, since they embody the very worst excesses of mass tourism dressed up as self-actualization. But much of the abuse levelled at them centres around their lack of "authenticity", which makes them a valuable case study for the phenomenon.

As McRae argues, the main charge of travel bloggers' inauthenticity stems from the very work that they put in to demonstrate otherwise. Kate McCulley (101,000 followers on Instagram – "the perfect level of internet famous" as she claims in her Twitter profile) calls her blog, much to the derision of the GOMI community, *Adventurous Kate*. "I promise to show you reality", she writes in the introduction, "with honesty and humour". However, her detractors beg to disagree, finding her blog "full of humble brags and first world problems" (McRae, 2017, p. 20). Fundamentally, it is argued, nobody who claims to travel the world for a living can lay claim to showing "reality", since it is so obviously a position of privilege available to very few individuals across the world. This suggests, of course, that authenticity is somehow bound up with social status, though while YouTubers can do 'being ordinary' through their modest domestic interiors and mundane everyday content around relationships and pets, travel bloggers have no such material to turn to. Liz Carlson (*Young Adventuress* – "a normal girl living her... dreams"; 193,000 Instagram followers) deals

---

4 https://gomiblog.com/forums/

with this problem by focusing on 'misadventures' in the section of her blog headed "where I screwed up big time". This is the equivalent of the vloggers' deliberately highlighted 'bloopers'; strategic reminders that they are not quite as slick and professional as their performance might suggest.

The threat to authenticity is greatest when travel bloggers try to tackle it head on. Liz Carlson does this by devoting a whole section of *Young Adventuress* to the various critiques and abuse she has received, year by year. Particular criticism on GOMI is directed at her attempt to ward off claims of inauthenticity by contrasting herself favourably with other travel bloggers, who are "anything but authentic because they all take the exact same photos" (cited in McRae, 2017, p. 21), or fail to be "in the moment" (i.e., staging photographs). Another strategy is to counter the implication that their activities represent the fruits of inherited wealth by emphasizing the labour and hardships involved in travel blogging. On *Adventurous Kate*, McCulley describes her work as "extraordinarily difficult... it requires an immense amount of time, work, and networking". In reply to a question about her career, Kiersten Rich claims that "the struggle was definitely real... I hustled like crazy" and that the hardest part of her job is that "it's every day, all day long". Another blogger is pilloried by the GOMI community for a post entitled "Travel Blogging isn't for the Faint of Heart".

Why are travel bloggers so keen to avoid the taint of privilege? Even Kane Lim, the billionaire's son whose luxury clothing displays have brought him thousands of Instagram followers, claims his collections are the product of "hard work" rather than inherited wealth (Marwick, 2015). It seems that, for critics and bloggers alike, online celebrity should be something that is earned; a reflection, perhaps, of the moral discourse around celebrity more generally (and discussed at some length in chapter 4 in relation to reality TV). Ultimately, the charge against the travel bloggers is not so much a matter of authenticity – at least in Trilling's (1972) terms, – as one of *sincerity*.[5] When they say their life is hard, they are simply not believed.

---

[5] There is also the important caveat that travel blogging is *not* authentic travel as constructed by the GOMI critics, in the way that televised Formula One racing never claims to provide viewers with the experience of being at the side of the race track, where they would only glimpse a tiny part of the onscreen action (Scannell, 2001). The same point is lost on some bloggers themselves, of course, when they criticise others for not being 'in the moment'. It is not, after all, the blogger's job to *be* in the moment.

Instagram: Conservative or Empowering?

The contrasting studies of Rupi Kaur and Ruby Rose prompt us to ask the same question of Instagram celebrity as of YouTube: is it a fundamentally conservative medium, rewarding only those who reproduce dominant discourses, or does it allow members to critique and challenge social norms? Marwick's (2015) analysis tends to the former view: as a photographic medium, it inevitably favours those "with the ability to emulate the visual iconography of mainstream celebrity culture" (p. 139); that is, "thin but buxom bodies, sports cars and designer clothes" (p. 153). This is pretty much in line with Duguay's (2016) conclusion. In each case, their critique is based on what the authors see as Instagram's (technological) affordances. Marwick suggests that the prominence of visual representation means that Instagram (at least) can scarcely be considered part of Turner's (2010) "demotic turn" – it does not open up celebrity to 'ordinary' people unless they have the requisite physical apparatus.

However, there are a number of counterarguments to this position, largely from the celebrities themselves. One influencer (described as a "feminist sex writer and model") claims that Instagram allows her a platform for "a certain message… that feminism is cool" and enables like-minded users "to see how other people are standing up for certain things – seeing the women's march, seeing people getting together" (Wedgwood, 2017). Others claim that it provides them with the chance to act as role models for disadvantaged ethnic groups or sexual minorities. Chawansky (2016) argues that the mere visibility of Black lesbian basketball star Brittney Griner provides the online audience with a positive role model. While she acknowledges this is not by itself equivalent to political change, it can nevertheless act as a counter-discourse to restricted representations in mainstream media.

As with YouTube, Instagram also gives its members the opportunity to bypass some of the entry criteria for traditional forms of celebrity. Saul (2016) argues that it has "overturned the conventions that once determined whether a person could become a commercially successful model", citing the example of Iskra Lawrence (3.8 million Instagram followers), who was rejected by modelling agencies as a teenager on the basis of her hip size, and who was compelled to brand herself as a "plus size" model before establishing her own fashion site *Runway Riot!* that challenges prejudice in the modelling industry (Chan, 2015). So while Instagram's technological (or intended) affordances might seem to favour archetypally photogenic models, its social (or emergent) affordances – specifically, the absence of entry criteria into celebrity culture – enable its users to challenge some of the conventions of traditional celebrity.

Case Study: Interview with an Instagram Fashion Influencer

Nadia Anya Walker (*nadiaanya_*) is a clear example of how you can develop and build your online presence, with the future intention of having a full-time career in blogging, YouTube, and Instagram. Nadia started using Instagram in 2012, but it wasn't until the start of 2017 that she decided to tailor her page towards fashion blogging, from then she started her own blog (nadiaanya. blogspot.com) and towards the end of 2017 created her own YouTube channel, where she shares videos surrounding how she creates her makeup look, her hair, and a variety of hauls. At the age of 21, after a year of focussing on her social media platforms, she has gained a following of over 50,000 on her Instagram account, and gets asked weekly by brands to promote their products.

Nadia typifies the fashion blogger on Instagram, due to her keen eye for aesthetic appeal, the consistent engagement between her and her followers, and also her diverse fashion sense that includes both luxury and high-street brands – which therefore attracts a wide audience. An interview was carried out in order to capture the thoughts and aspirations behind a typical female fashion blogger. Engagement and interaction with followers was a consistent finding when building an online presence, and Nadia thinks these two aspects have given her the continuously growing following that she has.

When did you first join Instagram?
I first joined Instagram about 4 years ago, but only started focusing it around fashion, and trying to build an audience around 9 months ago.

How did you first start to increase your following – did you use techniques like 'followforfollow'?
When I started to try build a following I used hashtags such as #fashion #blogger #ukfashionblogger etc, and with each outfit I would tailor the hashtags specifically, such as brands, style etc. I also tagged lots of accounts in my photos, in order to get reposted onto fashion accounts and therefore spread my pictures across the platform as much as possible, and the final thing I did was liking LOTS of accounts, and pictures on the discovery page – again to increase interaction and get other accounts to notice me.

I think the more you put out, and the more consistent you are, the more people are going to notice your page.

When did your page really start to take off with followers?

I built a steady following from the get go really, but it really took off when I went to Greece in May-loads of summer/fashion accounts with 1 million+ followers were reposting my pics and tagging me in them, as well as Missguided reposting my image, so in the space of about 3 weeks I gained about 4k more, and from thereon it has just snowballed (about 1.5k a week)

Assuming your first followers were friends/acquaintances... do they now get crowded out by all the new followers?

When I decided to focus my Instagram on fashion, I made my account a lot less personal, so people who don't know me too well (but followed me because they had met me a few times) then unfollowed me, and vice versa – I think I unfollowed around 1k people, so now the only people I follow are close family and very close friends (around 10 people). So although yes, they get crowded out, I only have about 15 people on there that I am interested in on a personal level, which makes it easy to keep up to date with them!

Do you prioritize your early followers more than your newer followers? This can be in ways of interacting: reply to their comments, like their photos more...?

I wouldn't say I do, but I have a few girls on my Insta who I don't personally know, but we have this little unspoken support system I guess – so when they comment I make sure to reply to them, and comment on their pictures. There's so many bloggers and influencers on Insta, so it's hard to support everyone but there are a handful of people I resonate with and gel with and make sure to prioritise them. I also make sure to reply to all my DMs [direct messages] as the job I'm doing is only possible because of my followers, so I want to be as helpful and friendly as possible to all of them!

What do your early followers think of your new-found 'instafame'?

They all are so supportive and happy for me – I've had so many girls message me and congratulate me – it's so lovely, but I wouldn't say 'instafame' about myself, as I think you're constantly reaching milestones and then wanting to reach the next. 8 months ago, 10k was unimaginable, and now I'm almost at 30k, but it feels like so many other people are on 100k etc, and therefore I'm like 'I'm not on that many followers'. but when I stumble across accounts I used to follow of girls who I would think 'wow they have so many followers' and now I have double – that's when I realise that yeah, I'm growing pretty quickly and its so exciting (don't know how to answer that without sounding cocky hahaha – hope it doesn't come off as that!!!) xx

Why do you think you have so many followers? What are you doing that has gained thousands of followers?

I think engagement is key. Making sure to build personal relationships with your followers is a huge part of it, answering to comments and reply- ing to DM's adds to just the 'picture' aspect of Instagram. I also think creating consistent and different content is a huge part of it, I try to post at least once a day, and keep an aesthetic theme going as this will attract followers initially.

Would you consider yourself as a micro-celebrity, or something else for that matter?

Definitely not a microcelebrity – but I would say 'influencer' – I think this job or hobby is about showcasing your own style in such a way that people are interested enough to stay and see your journey – giving inspira- tion and inspiring people. I wouldn't class myself as instafamous or any- thing along those lines at all – not until I hit maybe 100k (if that ever happens!!)

What do you see for your future on Instagram?

I would hope for it to continue to grow – social media and fashion are two things I'm seriously passionate about, so if I am able to really work at it and make it my sole income I would be over the moon!

What sorts of people do you follow on Instagram? Friends, family, role models?

I follow lots of other bloggers, and influencers, as well as brands (high and low end) and anything that I feel is similar to me and I can get inspira- tion from. I only follow immediate family, and close friends!

What attracts you to following these people?

Definitely their style, and their Instagram aesthetic. I'm quite selective about who I follow and I don't want to scroll through my feed and only like every other picture, I want to scroll through my feed and love every picture, and be inspired by a lot of it, so I try to only follow people who I think are similar to me – that being influencers, and brands who offer items I love

Do you have a role model that has gained "instafame" too? Someone you aspire too?

Lydia Elise Millen is my absolute number one idol – I'm so obsessed with her style, aesthetic, blog and everything she produces.

In terms of other social media sites (Facebook, Twitter, Tumblr) do you use these as much as Instagram?

I only have Facebook and Snapchat – I use snapchat a lot, but Facebook I keep very personal (I only have about 300 friends on there). Apart from that I have my blog, which I love but haven't been using as much as of lately due to life being so hectic but will get onto that properly soon!

Do you have a large following on these sites as well?

My blog is reasonable... around 4k views per post. Snapchat I get around 800 views per snap, but Instagram is definitely my main platform.

9

"WHAT ELSE DOES HE DO?" MEME CELEBRITIES

In *The Selfish Gene*, celebrity biologist Richard Dawkins invented a new concept, the meme. A meme is a piece of cultural material that replicates itself, like a gene, by being imitated in some way; examples are "tunes, ideas, catch-phrases, clothes fashions, ways of making pots or of building arches" (Dawkins, 1976/1989, p. 192). Dawkins then argues that memes are represented in the brain, which causes a problem given the sheer variety of cultural phenomena lumped together under the concept. If a meme is a *cognitive* representation rather than a merely cultural one, then an "idea" needs very careful definition. What bits of an "idea" are beyond language?

It is of course ironic that the idea of the meme is itself a meme, and, as Dawkins claims in the second edition of his book, a rather successful one. Initially, at least, its usage was consistent with Dawkins's rather loose definition (e.g., Blackmore, 1999), but then along came the Internet and, in Dawkins's own words, "hijacked" the original concept by applying it to very specific pieces of digital culture that are deliberately altered rather than replicating through random mutation and selection (Solon, 2013). Up to a point, this particular mutation of the meme idea is an improvement. Without speculating about brains and ideas, the replication of JPEGs, MPEGs, and so on, uploaded, altered, circulated, downloaded countless times, passing from one Internet user to another, is a much more robust and tangible phenomenon. Certainly this usage of the meme concept has proved even more popular than the original, and, given the pervasive nature of digital culture, seems to have usurped the original concept.

Mention 'meme' in 2018 and Richard Dawkins is probably not the first association that springs to mind.

While many (most?) Internet memes are purely textual, or feature animate, or inanimate non-human subjects, there are a substantial number that feature individual people who become widely recognized as the content of the meme. In the majority of cases, the individuals are not complicit with the creation of the meme itself. Their visual representation is effectively kidnapped by a creator who grafts other material (text, music, dialogue) on to the original piece of digital information, leaving the individual as a symbol, typically representing some generic phenomenon ('Overly Attached Girlfriend', for example). Sometimes, the meme is so unflattering that the original subject becomes a magnet for mockery and even abuse, both on- and off-line. In several cases the mental health of the individual has even been affected.

Some meme celebrities have attempted to profit from the publicity, though with decidedly mixed success. Unlike YouTubers with multi-million subscriptions, the fame of these individuals has something of a mayfly existence. Hardly micro-celebrities because of the sheer numbers and degree of mainstream media exposure involved (and lacking any evidence of micro-celebrity *practice* in most cases), these individuals attract the kind of press attention that Hollywood stars and musical performers would pose naked for, but it does not last: the meme eventually dies out, and their celebrity wilts and dies along with it. Like the first generation of YouTube celebrities, most meme celebrities do not generally set out to be famous beyond their immediate social media network. Fame catches them unawares, and they are rarely equipped with the ability to maintain it.

In this chapter, I discuss the phenomenon of meme celebrities with reference to both general theories of celebrity as well as the unique aspects of twenty-first-century celebrity that I have considered in the book so far. But the first task, as ever, involves disentangling just what is meant by the "hijacked" concept of the Internet (or digital) meme.

NAILING DOWN THE CONCEPT OF THE MEME

As with the various other concepts discussed in the book, the (Internet) meme is new, yet massively popular in terms of its usage. Like micro-celebrity, it is often applied uncritically to all digital phenomena whether they accord with its original definition or not. The confusion pervades the small but growing academic literature. For Shifman (2012), Xu, Park, Kim, and Park (2016) and others, the archetypal meme is a YouTube video, or excerpt ('clip') from a video. Perhaps the best example of such a meme is the 'Gangnam Style' videos that proliferated on the Web in late 2012. Although the original video by K-pop artist Psy has itself generated enormous success, recently passing 3 billion views (the third highest in YouTube history), it was the intensity and rapidity with which the parody videos circulated, and the level of mainstream media exposure they received, which demonstrate the mimetic quality of the phenomenon. It could be argued the actual meme here is not Psy's original video but the elements of that video that have been reproduced in the parody/tribute versions; the 'horse dance', performed by a significant number of people (including 'flash mobs' of several thousands), and its spontaneity (typically erupting out of a static tableau).

Of course, YouTube, with its colossal reach, is an ideal vehicle for meme replication. Such was the speed with which memes spread in its early days, the term 'viral video' was preferred by some. Burgess (2014, p. 87) saw the meme itself as largely a "faddish joke or practice" that, contrary to Dawkins's claim about the Internet hijacking his concept, "[appears] to spread and mutate via distributed networks in ways that the original producers cannot determine and control". An example of this type of meme might be the lolcat craze of 2007, which consisted of pictures of cats accompanied by orthographically or grammatically incorrect text (originally 'I can has cheezburger'). Lolcats spread rapidly during this period across various online platforms and media; no doubt, they still have their devotees. The 'image macro' format that acted as the typical lolcat vehicle has since become ubiquitous online, where a photograph is accompanied by (usually) white (usually) upper case text (most readers will be familiar with the format).

Wiggins and Bowers (2015) have attempted to refine the meme concept further, by differentiating video memes (such as Gangnam Style[1]) from image macro memes, arguing that the fundamental process in each case is

---

[1] Ironically, Wiggins and Bowers dismiss 'Gangnam Style' as a viral video, using it as an example of what a meme is not. I cannot see their point here at all because the whole point of Gangnam Style is its reproducibility beyond the original video. Alongside the many useful insights in their article, they make other strange distinctions, such as the meme having greater 'staying power' than the viral video because of sites like memegenerator.net allowing for their storage. It is almost as if the authors have never visited YouTube.

recognizability. Their work comes closest of all to identifying the elements of a meme, boiling down cultural material into its constituents; in other words, what is the actual *unit* of reproduction that makes a meme resemble a gene. They argue (Wiggins & Bowers, 2015, p. 1902) that successful memes "contain *the rules and resources* [my italics] necessary for further remix", or the elements that need to be recognized to constitute a meme. One such element is what Wiggins and Bowers term the "phrasal template" (p. 1901) carried by an image macro, which in most cases consists of a two-part phrase.

The example they use to illustrate this is *The Most Interesting Man in the World*, an image macro based on a still from a TV beer advert featuring a "self-aggrandising" character played by Jonathan Goldsmith. The advert featured the phrase "I don't always drink beer, but when I do, I prefer Dos Equis" (a cracking example of stake inoculation – see chapter 8), and image macros reproducing this meme use the same still but with ever more absurd variants on the 'I don't always X, but when I do, Y' template. While such macros have a necessarily short life as mass circulation memes, there is sufficient cultural infrastructure to ensure their survival; websites, such as knowyourmeme.com and memegenerator.net have long archived the cream of the genre.

SOME EXAMPLES OF MEME CELEBRITIES

'Bus Uncle'

It is probably fair to say that the best-known meme celebrity was a 55-year-old Hong Kong restaurant chain PR worker named Roger Chan Yuet-Tung. One spring evening in 2006, he was on a bus, feeling depressed after breaking up with his partner, and was in the midst of an emotional call to a suicide hotline when a young man sitting behind, Elvis Ho, tapped him on the shoulder and asked him to keep his voice down. What followed was a six-minute finger-wagging rant, delivered from over the back of his seat to the hapless Mr Ho behind, which has now been viewed over 4 million times on YouTube after it was surreptitiously filmed by a nearby student. It turned out to be YouTube's most watched video that May, and turned Roger Chan, dubbed 'Bus Uncle',[2] into a media sensation in Hong Kong

---

[2] The 'Uncle' part derives from a Cantonese term for a generic older male. It is not disrespectful. The original video can be seen at the following URL: https://m.youtube.com/watch?v=H20dhY01Xjk.

as well as further afield (several video copies with English and Mandarin subtitles have also clocked up over a million views).

While 'Bus Uncle' itself is probably better categorized as a viral video, it is arguably the creative output surrounding the video, and the prolific reproduction of its memetic elements, that brought the individuals to the attention of the mainstream media. Chief among these are Chan's phrases "I've got pressure! You've got pressure!" and "Unsolved! Unsolved! Unsolved!" (the latter in response to Ho's claim that their dispute had been settled with an apology[3]). T-shirts bearing these phrases were sported in Hong Kong, and they were even used as greetings for a short while (Chu, 2009). The meme endured for longer owing to the plethora of 'mash-up' videos blending clips of the original with other material from music, cinema, TV, news footage, and video game footage. There were even mash-ups of mash-ups.

News reporters tracked down and interviewed the two individuals, and the story entered global media (ending up in the *The Wall Street Journal* and *The Washington Post*). While Elvis Ho shied away from media attention after the initial flurry of interest (shooing away reporters who had tried to engineer a reunion between the two[4]), Chan seems to have been less reticent, allegedly using the publicity to influence regional politics, although he is likely to have been deterred for milking the story further after he was attacked at work and badly beaten by masked intruders a few weeks after the story broke. Apart from a one-off story about him looking for romance on Facebook a couple of years later, the brief celebrity of 'Bus Uncle' flared and died faster than that of most reality TV contestants.

Fenton: A Celebrity Dog

A 'Bus Uncle' for the Twitter generation, Fenton was a black Labrador (and former guide dog) who was filmed chasing several dozen deer in London's Richmond Park one afternoon in 2011. The incident would not have been anything remarkable were it not for the reaction of Fenton's owner Max

---

[3] Apart from initially declining to shake Chan's hand, Ho behaves impeccably throughout, despite Chan threatening, among other things, to attach his penis to Ho's mother (a rather literal translation of the Cantonese, I suspect).

[4] The media coverage of the 'Bus Uncle' story has become something of a *cause célèbre* of intrusive journalistic practice in the Chinese media (as well as the ethics of using online footage as news).

Findlay, which generated a media frenzy a day or so later, prompting over half a million views on YouTube. The video was uploaded by a local teen-ager who had been walking in the park with his father when he decided to film the large herd of deer that had gathered nearby.[5] After a few seconds, the film skips to the first appearance of Fenton, and the panicked reaction of the deer, after which the peaceful autumnal scene is shattered by Findlay's yelling "Fenton!" several times with a rapid crescendo, followed by a desperate "Jesus Christ!" The next moment Findlay himself appears, sprinting across the park in pursuit.

In the six or so years since, we have become so used to 'trending topics' on Twitter that the popularity of this undeniably comic clip already seems surprising. But, in the same way that 'Bus Uncle' opened up affordances for the mass circulation of user-generated content on YouTube, the speed with which Twitter users – many of them fairly high-profile British celebrities – shared and commented on the Fenton video link was the first time the British public really came to appreciate the power of Internet memes. The trivial nature of the content only added to, rather than detracting from, its newsworthiness. Before long, the usual range of creative responses was in full flow: spoof videos, customized ringtones, T-shirts and the inevitable pop record, as well as inspiring several Twitter accounts purporting to be the real Fenton: regular accompaniments to the phenomenon of animal celebrity (Giles, 2013a). As for Fenton and Findlay, anything remotely approaching celebrity *practice* was negligible in this case; a former barrister, the human in question was more concerned about the legal repercussions of failing to control his pet (Telegraph, 2011).

Gary Brolsma: 'The Numa Numa Guy'

Another example of a video meme, from a time before social media, is 19-year-old American Gary Brolsma's lip-synched performance of a 2003 song by Moldovan boy band O-Zone (*Dragostea Din Tei*). Uploaded to video-sharing site newsgrounds.com in 2004, the clip was watched two million times over a short period and went on to become the most-watched viral video of all time until Psy's 'Gangnam Style'. What generated the mass circulation of the video, however, was the creative editing of the original,

---

[5] https://m.youtube.com/watch?v=3GRSbr0EYYU.

reducing it to a brief snatch of the song – typically the 'nu ma nu ma iei'[6] hook accompanied by Brolsma's arm-waving and facial gesticulations. As Wiggins and Bowers (2015) argue, it is this particular snippet that constitutes the meme.

When you are famous for waving your arms in the air while lip-synching a pop hook, that initial burst of attention is not necessarily a life-enhancing experience. One of the problems of becoming a celebrity through a meme that other people have copied and shared is that, much of the time, the attention is not flattering. In Brolsma's case, the appeal of Numa Numa video was evidently related to the incongruence between his physical appearance and the energy and dynamism of the music. Rather missing the point at the time, *The New York Times* (describing Brolsma as "a pudgy guy from Saddle Brook") labelled the video "earnest but painful" (Feuer & George, 2005), and claimed that Brolsma had gone into hiding, "distraught" and "embarrassed" and unable to cope with the "flood of media attention" the video had attracted. When reporters showed the Numa Numa video to a class at Brolsma's former school, one child asked, "What else does he do?"

Where Brolsma differs from 'Bus Uncle' and Fenton is that he was the willing subject of his own original video, and after apparently recovering from his initial embarrassment, he has not shied away altogether from capitalizing on his fame. He has continued to make YouTube videos as well as regularly releasing original music on sites like SoundCloud. He is appropriately modest about his own claim to fame ("I've gotten the opportunity to do so many cool things because of this silly little video I made" he says on his personal website garybrolsma.com), although his audience figures alone would place him firmly in the micro-celebrity category. But he is not really a micro-celebrity, because he has a permanent place in Internet history as 'that Numa Numa guy'.

Ghyslain Raza

Gary Brolsma may have only suffered at the hands of the media, but for some meme celebrities the unwanted attention brought about by instant fame through unsolicited file-sharing has a high price. Ghyslain Raza was a Québec schoolboy in 2002 when he unwisely made a home video of

---

[6] Romanian for 'you don't want, don't want to take me' as reported in Wiggins and Bowers (2015).

himself enacting a *Star Wars* routine with a golf ball retriever. It fell some-how into the hands of a fellow student who digitized it and uploaded it, whereupon, thanks to the kind of pre-social media interactivity that made stars out of Webcam girls, it was viewed and passed on by over a million people in less than a year, enough to spark the interest of mainstream press and television.

Like Brolsma, Raza's body shape plays a significant role in both the pos-itive and negative attention his performance received. Again *The New York Times* provides the euphemism; he is "heavy-set" (Harmon, 2003), and his lumbering performance is either inspirational or derisory depending on your level of empathy. While *Star Wars* fans defended his enthusiasm, classmates and anonymous others bullied him mercilessly, recommending suicide (and even claiming, later, that he had carried it out). Raza dropped out of school and reportedly received psychiatric treatment for a period; a decade later, fresh out of law school, he offered his services to anti-cyberbullying campaigns (Hawkes, 2016).

Laina Morris ('Overly Attached Girlfriend')

A happier story this one, largely (I suspect) because the individual in ques-tion happens to be conventionally good-looking, but also because the meme was prompted by her own creative work and consistent with the character she portrayed. It stemmed from a contest initiated by Justin Bie-ber, who asked fans to post their own versions of his 'Girlfriend' single; Morris, then a college student in Texas, responded with a humorous song from the perspective of an obsessively jealous partner, with wild staring eyes and creepy expressions. The video, posted to Reddit, was an immedi-ate success and received a million views within hours (Oppenheim, 2016).

However, it was not the video itself that eventually catapulted Mor-ris to fame but an image macro designed using an appropriately crazed still and posted on memegenerator.net. The 'phrasal template' element of the meme consists, like most image macro memes, of two clauses with the punchline in the second (appearing at the foot of the image). Example phrases include: "I sewed my name on your shirts/In case you forget you're taken" and "I tell everyone you're bad at sex/So nobody tries to steal you away from me", so the image itself and the basic concept underpinning the phrasal template constitute the memetic elements. The image macro was viewed 300,000 times within 12 hours and generated 175 other image macros, leading to television and other media appearances for Morris.

Like Gary Brolsma, once the initial attention had died down (and the inevitable quest to reveal her identity), Morris capitalized on her sudden fame by producing a series of YouTube videos developing the Overly Attached Girlfriend persona, adding other spoof recordings, introducing a boyfriend persona, and gradually forging a career as a YouTuber. Currently, she has 1.2 million subscribers to her channel and continues to release vlog-style material.

THE CELETOID COMES OF AGE

Given the brief and fragile nature of meme celebrity, we might regard it as the ultimate example of the "celetoid". Rojek's original (2001, p. 20) concept was formulated with short-lived fame in mind ("compressed, concentrated, and attributed celebrity") and seemed to reach its apogee shortly after its coining with the stars of reality TV shows like *Big Brother*, where typically contestants enjoy several weeks or months of sudden, excessive fame, followed by a rapid decline. It is 'in the nature' of celetoids, argued Rojek (2001), "...to receive their moment of fame and then to disappear from public consciousness" (p. 21), listing various "one-hit wonders" and "have-a-go heroes" as examples. A related concept is that of *accidental fame*, listed as one of the four types of fame in my own typology (Giles, 2000) and also discussed by Turner (2004), who cites Princess Diana's butler Paul Burrell as an example; another is Amanda Knox, the (now formally cleared) suspect in the Meredith Kercher murder enquiry (Clifford, 2014). In both cases it was an unproven criminal charge that brought them initially to the attention of the media, and both figures have, to a greater or lesser extent, made the most of the publicity in carving out modest careers on the fringes of mainstream celebrity.

The distinction between Rojek's original definition of the celetoid and the category of 'accidental fame' is that the former does not specify any kind of agency or motive behind the individual's rise to fame other than the claim that it is 'attributed' celebrity as compared with 'achieved'. The distinction might seem arbitrary, but in later work, Rojek has stretched the concept to encompass two forms: short-life celetoid and long-life celetoid. While the former is consistent with the original definition, the latter denotes an individual "…devoid of perceptible talents and disciplined accomplishments" (Rojek, 2012, p. 165). As Driessens (2015, p. 379) points out, this is a "contradiction in terms" since the 'long-life celetoid' could be better described as a celetoid who has since attained common-or-garden celebrity. It also suggests that there is an element of moral evaluation in the concept of celetoid, that somehow those people are unworthy of their fame compared to 'achieved' celebrities who are rewarded for their innate skills. As discussed at several points in this book, the distinction between these categories is subjective and arbitrary to say the least.

While meme celebrities fit with the original definition of celetoid, it is also fair to say that, whatever their original intentions, they are almost all famous by accident. It is also true that the celetoid concept pre-dates the era of social media and that digital archives allow memes to immortalize their subjects in a manner not available to traditional media. So while Gary Brolsma's period in the glare of mainstream media was probably restricted to a matter of weeks, his fame as a meme persists as long as there is sufficient interest in digital culture.

WHAT MAKES MEMES SO APPEALING?

One of the factors behind the success of 'Bus Uncle', it is claimed (Chu, 2009), is that the memetic phrases echoed concerns in Hong Kong during that period, when lots of residents felt under "pressure" and partially identified with the pent-up frustration expressed in Roger Chan's outburst. Many macro image themes, meanwhile, seem to reflect the 'fratboy humour' (Burgess, 2014) of much online entertainment; one suspects that many of them are the work of adolescent North American males and are principally enjoyed by that particular demographic. In other words, memes capture popular discourses and preoccupations within the population through which they are circulated.

Sometimes they can be used to advance an particular ideological agenda. In 2014, a travel blogger named Helene Sula posted a tear-streaked selfie following an unfortunate visit to a hair salon. The image was picked up and turned into a macro by a right-wing website carrying phrases that poked fun at then-US president Barack Obama's healthcare policy ('Obamacare'). Sula, a supporter of Obama, caused more trouble for herself by attempting to have the image removed from Facebook, where it had been reproduced several thousand times, and received a further shedload of abuse, much of a sexist nature (Broderick, 2014). Sula had the last laugh, her blog (*Helene in Between*) receiving plenty of unanticipated publicity in the process; now she has 134,000 followers on Instagram.

In many ways, meme celebrities fulfill the same public function as the early reality TV stars, whose fame was similarly unplanned. While bloggers and wannabe YouTubers may generate the material from which image macros and memetic clips are sourced, they have no control over the level and nature of attention the memes eventually attract. But whereas reality stars are now seen as shameless careerists already drawing up plans for their future nightspots and clothing brands, meme celebrities still retain that precious ordinariness on which other digital celebrities expend so much effort. Like animal celebrities, their lack of agency in the fame process gives them an undeniable authenticity (Giles, 2013a). As Chu (2009, p. 349) puts it, "the spicy and abusive speech of "Bus Uncle" was not scripted. Everything recorded was spontaneous. It was completely genuine".

One of the phenomena that accompanies the initial surge of media coverage of meme celebrities is a desperate scramble by traditional media and social media alike to 'find' the individual behind the meme. In this respect, the meme celebrity is a perfect example of Marshall's (1997, p. xi) claim that authentic celebrity is always predicated on the assumption that a "real person" lies behind the "celebrity sign". We are not satisfied with a depersonalized image.

When, in another example of a fat-shaming meme, a video clip of Liverpudlian 'Dancing Man' Sean O'Brien attracted online mockery and abuse, a gaggle of international celebrities teamed up to try and track him down. The hashtag #finddancingman trended on Twitter, and eventually the unwitting subject of the meme was wined and dined in Los Angeles by showbiz stars (Khomami, 2015). While O'Brien, like Ghyslain Raza, was held up as a happy resolution to 'cyberbullying', there is nonetheless a requirement for the victims to be good sports and allow themselves to be 'found' and occupy the subject position demanded by the mainstream media. Very few meme celebrities manage to avoid the glare of the spotlight; at least 'Annoying Facebook Girl' remains, admirably, unidentified.

PART IV

THE FUTURE OF CELEBRITY

10

SNAPCHAT, PERSONA STUDIES, AND TWENTY-FIRST CENTURY POLITICAL CELEBRITY

I want to use this final chapter to tie up a few loose ends and to cast an eye towards the future. In the first few pages, I explore the unlikely phenomenon of Snapchat celebrity. Unlikely because, among the diverse forms of social media, one would not really expect a communication platform whose material archives disappear within 24 hours to be a medium that afforded enduring fame. Yet Snapchat, the app whose appeal is largely based on the fact that messages leave no permanent trace, has nonetheless proved to be fertile ground for celebrity of a certain kind. I then move on to the emerging field of Persona Studies, an outgrowth of Celebrity Studies pioneered by P. David Marshall and colleagues in Australia, that takes a somewhat different route to that navigated in this book, but from the same basic assumption that social media have heralded a fundamental sea-change in terms of the nature of celebrity. However, Persona Studies is less concerned with documenting new genres of celebrity than analysing the extent to which 'presentational media' have inducted all of their users into the practices of (micro)-celebrity. Some of the most convincing work in this field has been around political persona, and I end the chapter by discussing the ways that social media have facilitated new forms of 'populism' that have seen celebrities from non-political fields emerging as serious contenders for public office. Donald Trump is the obvious example, but he is far from a single case. As social media infiltrate all human activities, we are starting to see important changes in the way that politics gets done; and, one way or another, celebrity is very much at the heart of this process.

THE PECULIAR PHENOMENON OF SNAPCHAT CELEBRITY

The celebrity affordances of Snapchat squarely address many of the issues covered in this book. The first is the way that affordances are more than just technological features, more than just the possibilities foreseen (and encouraged) by the creators and owners of media. The second is that celebrity is rarely granted by one medium in isolation; it requires the interaction of at least two, whether they are cinema and magazines, television, and the written press in general, or YouTube and Twitter. Snapchat by itself would not deliver fame to the creative artists discussed in this chapter. It is a vehicle, like Instagram, through which the latest work of artists and photographers is circulated, briefly but intensively, before they are preserved for posterity in more permanent online archives.

So unusual is the phenomenon of Snapchat celebrity that it had not been touched upon within academic literature at the time of writing. The few studies that mention Snapchat at all explore its use among adolescents and young adults and work from the premise that its appeal is based on its transience, or 'ephemerality', thus avoiding some of the pitfalls of social media like Facebook that allow users to archive large collections of images, and Twitter and Instagram whose textual content, depending on members' activity levels, remains visible for months or even years. Snapchat is, therefore, a safer medium in that it allows users to make mistakes and not have them preserved for posterity, though there is nonetheless a high degree of suspicion by young people who worry about the fate of the apparently disappearing information (Waddell, 2016).

While Snapchat may lend itself to rather more trivial content than other media ("it's raining", "I got a new haircut", etc.), its short-lived nature (images decay in ten seconds once they are accessed by the user) encourages greater vigilance by users. As one of Bayer, Ellison, Schoenebeck, and Falk's (2016, p. 969) interviewees put it, "you take in as much as you can in however many seconds it gives you". Of course, ten seconds allows plenty of time for copying and storing information, or shifting it to another, more permanent location. Handyside and Ringrose (2017) talk about teenagers using screenshot captures of Snaps on other social media, such as incriminating photographs sent to significant others, as "relationship currency".

However, the 'Snapchat Stories' feature allows users to generate photo-narratives that, in the short timeframe, have a theatrical impact; as McRoberts, Ma, Hall, and Yarosh (2017) have argued, this acts as "experimental studio space" for creative individuals to pilot artistic projects. If unsuccessful, they vanish into thin air and the process can start anew. If successful, they can be screenshotted and stored elsewhere.

This is precisely what has happened in the case of the handful of creative artists who have used Snapchat in order to deliver a degree of celebrity. Cyrene Quiamco, a Philippines-born US designer, has been dubbed the 'Queen of Snapchat' (Stampler, 2014) for her Disney-themed images and celebrity portraits. Her trademark is a selfie in which she is partnered by a graphic image of a famous figure; she has also done a series of celebrity interviews using the Snapchat Stories facility. She has also earned herself lucrative contracts with Burger King and Disney and can reportedly earn up to $10,000 for a single Snap (Rudulph, 2015).

Although Snapchat has the facility (through its ten-second video stories) to promote its own stars – for a while, radio presenter Mark Kaye produced a regular interview show 'Talkin' Snap' – the best way to archive the work of creative visual artists is to store it in a suitably visible location elsewhere on the Web. Cyrene Quiamco did this by setting up www.the11thsecond. com to showcase the work of the most-followed Snapchatters. Though it has rather succumbed to an overt 'monetizing' ethic over the last year or so, it remains a useful hub for promoting the unique work of film-makers and graphic artists exploiting the affordances of short video clips and ephemeral image creation. These include Shaun McBride, known as Shonduras, another Disney-orientated artist; Jerome Jarre, a French prankster; and Chris Carmichael, a comic book artist who also uses Twitter to disseminate his work.

While Snapchat clearly lacks so many of the features that afford celebrity in media like YouTube and Instagram, its different timeframe generates a sense of urgency and immediacy that acts as a super-fast form of publicity, rather like radio. At the same time, there is little that Snapchatters actually create that could not be created using other social media, and tech commentators have been sounding the death-knell for the medium for some time now (Snapchat still has fewer than 200 million users; they should have sold it to Facebook when it offered; Instagram has aped its Story feature with greater success). It is possible that, while still relatively trendy as a source for certain types of celebrity, it may not have enough fuel in its tank to last the distance.

If it is the specific affordances of a medium that generates celebrity, what happens to those celebrities when the medium ceases to exist? In Snapchat's case, the best-known artists would presumably invest their energy in YouTube or Instagram, whose affordances still allow them to do what they do on Snapchat, only at a rather more leisurely pace. They would no longer be big fishes in a relatively small pond. Some would adapt and prosper; others might have to settle for mere micro-celebrity.

PERSONA STUDIES: ARE WE ALL CELEBRITIES NOW?

P. David Marshall made his name writing about the semiotics and "affective power" of celebrity (Marshall, 1997). His case studies were grounded in global superstardom – Hollywood, television, the pop music industry – but the emergence of digital culture has prompted him and his colleagues[1] to rethink the whole celebrity phenomenon and re-orientate his thinking towards the impact of 'presentational' media on society more generally. For Marshall (2014, p. 153), celebrity research is now "a subset of a wider study of how the self and public intersect". His fundamental unit of interest is no longer the celebrity sign as such, but its digital manifestation, the *persona*: a construction that represents the public interface of all individuals with any kind of online presence and which is rooted in "the celebrity discourse of the self" (Marshall, 2010, p. 35).

Persona Studies has been mapped out on a number of different levels from the historical and political through to the sociological and psychological, but in Marshall (2014), three "key frameworks" are identified that work together to explain contemporary culture. The first is the changing nature of labour, where the individual as agent has more purchase than in traditional societies, leading to the kind of "self-branding" discussed in chapter 8 of this book. The second is the "reorganisation of society" produced by social media (or 'networks') that puts the individual in charge of constructing their outward-facing selves through "presentational media". Finally, the affective power traditionally associated with celebrity is now channelled through this presentation so that each individual builds his or her own "micropublic" of friends or followers whose relation to that individual mirrors the emotional bonds that connect celebrities with their fans.

---

[1] Collectively represented as the Persona, Celebrity, Publics research group at Deakin University in Victoria, Australia.

The contemporary persona is a logical extension of the individualisation of Western society that has increased over time, reflecting the influence of psychoanalytic and therapeutic culture and confessional media from the twentieth century (Marshall, 2014). We can see this influence most strongly in the 'celebrification' of individuals from politicians to the perpetrators of high-profile crimes (Driessens, 2013a). By casting the individual as the active agent of their own media (re)presentation, networks like Facebook and Twitter lock us all, potentially, into position as micro-celebrities: "the fundamental premise [of persona studies] is that all personas are embedded with strategy and intention... [persona studies] is fundamentally a study of agency" (Marshall, Moore, & Barbour, 2015, p. 290).

At the psychological level, the concept of persona draws from Jung's distinction between the outward-facing "mask" that an individual presents to the outside world and the "real", unconscious self[2] that can only be accessed through therapy (Jung, 1953). Marshall has adapted this distinction through the lens of Goffman's performative theory to understand contemporary persona as a kind of "script" through which we interact with the world in any number of digital contexts (Barbour, Marshall, & Moore, 2014). While the creation of this script may be an act of individual agency, once the script is let loose in digital culture, it interacts with the world "on our behalf" and leaves behind "...traces... scattered across digital networks" (Barbour et al., 2014). In some ways, this is a twenty-first century continuation of the work of social constructionist authors like Rom Harré (1983) and Kenneth Gergen (1991), whose respective concepts of 'file self'

---

[2] My own understanding of the rationale behind Persona Studies is that, from a psychological perspective, it currently lacks theoretical cohesion. If persona is indeed a 'mask' (or 'script') then we still need to explain what the individual's 'true nature' (Jung, 1953) might consist of. Marshall et al. (2015) attempt to resolve this problem with the aid of phenomenology, drawing on Martin Heidegger's hermeneutics (the science of interpretation). Personally, I think this is the wrong path to go down because Jung's basic idea of 'persona' (and arguably most psychoanalytic theory) suggests that the individual is more than simply a text to be interpreted and that there is a 'true' or 'core self' that the analyst needs to be able to access at some, typically unconscious, level. If, as social constructionist writers have argued, the true self is a fiction, and subjective experience merely a narrative we construct in order to create meaning in our lives (Potter, 1996), then the 'mask' metaphor is inappropriate. There is no 'true self' to disguise. If the persona is a series of masks (my Facebook profile, my Twitter profile, and so on), this still leaves the question of what unifies the individual (a stand-alone blog, perhaps?). I am not saying that either position is right or wrong, but in choosing 'persona' as the unit of interest, sooner or later, they will have to arrive at some theoretical compromise.

and 'saturated self' theorised similarly the way that media extend the traditional, unitary concept of 'self' (and these ideas are not entirely inconsistent with Marshall McLuhan's work).

Speaking of McLuhan, what seems to be missing from Persona Studies at this point is some sense of how *media* fit into the overall social context. In a special issue of the *Persona Studies* journal on the topic of political persona, Marshall and Henderson (2016) make an important distinction between what they term 'legacy media'[3] (in this book, I have largely referred to 'broadcast media' or 'traditional media') and social media. This distinction is important politically because, until the present century, the power of politicians was hidden in the 'black box' of press, radio, and television, which allowed them to operate invisibly (as far as the audiences for those media were concerned). Social media, however, force them out from this cosy hideaway and bring them into direct contact with the voting public, necessitating a new strategic approach.

Marshall and Henderson (2016) illustrate this distinction by comparing the rival campaigns of Donald Trump and Hillary Clinton in the 2016 US elections. Clinton represented the traditional, 'legacy media' operation of politics – "a persona with the quintessential embodiment of elite thinking and action" (p. 13), while Trump, "[crossing] the lines of public and social etiquette repeatedly and with a force never seen in public political performance" represented the 'hybrid' model, railing against the political establishment and the 'fake news' of legacy media, emphasising his outsider status as a non-politician, and at the same time providing 'clickbait' that was nonetheless irresistible to the headline-writers in the traditional press. Whether or not this contrast had any bearing on Trump's victory, it mirrors the success of several non-traditional political candidates across the world who have used social media in similar ways to position their opponents as stuffy, elitist, and outdated (Olczyk & Wasilewski, 2016).

---

[3] I have avoided the term 'legacy media' in the book because it seems to suggest that the ideological effects of those media are somehow separate from their affordances (and that, by implication, social media are liberating and democratic, an interpretation that is strongly contested by most people in media and cultural studies). My point throughout is that broadcast media (and the hard copy press) generated affordances that are quite different to those of digital media and resulted in different forms of celebrity. At the moment, it is true, we are in something of a 'hybrid' situation, with broadcasters having digitised, and digital media still drawing on broadcast conventions (the idea of a 'show' on YouTube or even Snapchat, for example).

What implications does Persona Studies have for the continuing study of celebrity? In some respects, its approach is similar to that taken in this book. Marshall and Henderson (2016, p. 1) are uncompromising in their assertion that "the changed media environment we now inhabit is producing a new, unstable political environment". Replace 'political' with 'celebrity', and you have the essential argument that I have outlined here. The authors do concede that their position might be seen as "technologically determinist", but it is impossible to ignore the impact of digital culture on society generally. At present, I think concepts like 'micropublics' risk the same redundancy as 'micro-celebrity' as does the suggestion that (re)presentation on all social media is equivalent (YouTube seems less comfortable a fit with the 'persona' construct than, say, Twitter). But these are risks that are run by any academic researcher attempting to capture and explain the rapid changes of digital culture while they are still taking place.

Where I think Persona Studies has most to contribute to celebrity studies is in the way that personae in general reflect the affordances of digital media. This is seen most clearly in the political examples, so I want to conclude this chapter with a brief discussion of the way that twenty-first century politics intersects with the changes in celebrity culture outlined in the book so far.

POLITICAL CELEBRITIES OR CELEBRITY POLITICS?

In chapter 1, I suggested that there was nothing particularly paradoxical about the idea of politician as celebrity, and that historically, the two identities are much closer in nature than is often assumed. People who have made their name in some non-political field have always entered politics, particularly in unstable or 'young' nations. One of the early Prime Ministers of the Polish Republic after World War I was the pianist and composer Ignacy Jan Paderewski.[4] More recently, of course, Hollywood actors from Ronald Reagan to Arnold Schwarzenegger have used their affective power to attain prominent positions in American political life. There is travel in the opposite direction too, of course, with political figures using their public visibility to pursue their own celebrity ambitions – whether as a best-selling novelist like the former Conservative MP Jeffrey Archer, or as contestants in reality TV shows (examples too numerous to be worth mentioning).

---

[4] A successful, if short-lived, tenure, largely arising out of Paderewski's diplomatic skills (he spoke seven languages fluently).

The distinction between politics and celebrity is perhaps best understood with reference to Bourdieu's (1993) theory of the cultural field. From this perspective, politics constitutes a discrete cultural field with its own system of social rules and relationships. In order to enter the political field an individual usually needs to have accumulated sufficient capital in a neighbouring field (such as journalism) to acquire the legitimacy required for success in politics – standing for (and winning) an election, or being offered a high-ranking party position. Driessens (2013b) has argued that celebrities accumulate their own special kind of capital (*celebrity capital*) by which their "recognisability" allows them to cross field boundaries more easily than would otherwise be the case. For a non-celebrity to cross into the political field from a not-obviously-neighbouring field such as literature (say, a minor literary agent), they would need to demonstrate a high level of political knowledge, considerable experience (e.g., in public speaking), and possibly some other form of capital (economic or social). In short, they would need friends in high places. Celebrities can bypass these requirements simply by being recognizable (and trailing an army of fans behind them).

One example of a celebrity attempting to hurdle the fence between fields is British comedian Russell Brand (Arthurs & Shaw, 2016). In the run-up to the 2015 UK general election, Brand appeared to be carving out a niche for himself within the political field, delivering a vehement anti-capitalist rhetoric and advising young people not to vote in the election because of the conservative, elitist nature of the dominant parties. His outspoken stance saw him invited into media roles usually preserved for agents from the political field, editing the *New Statesman* magazine, appearing on the BBC shows *Question Time* and *Newsnight*, where in the latter he was subjected to a grilling by Jeremy Paxman, renowned scourge of political interviewees. When he eventually turned tail and threw his support behind the Labour Party, it was only after their leader, Ed Milliband, had deigned to appear on Brand's YouTube channel. Although there was to be no happy ending for either of them,[5] the whole affair showed how far celebrity capital can get you even in the hallowed spaces of political media.

---

[5] Milliband was trounced in the election by David Cameron, who a year later launched the disastrous referendum that saw a small majority electing to leave the European Union. Since his equally disastrous U-turn on the ethics of voting, Brand has seemingly (and wisely) dropped out of political debate altogether.

In some cases, it has taken celebrities further than that. Donald Trump is the obvious example, though his financial clout and social capital have given him far more leverage than Brand was able to muster. He also chose to represent an established political party. More impressive still are the achievements of Beppe Grillo, another comedian, who founded a new Italian party (*Cinque Stelle* or Five Star) who have enjoyed considerable success in regional elections across Italy in recent years; and Polish rock singer Pawel Kukiz, who polled 20 per cent of the vote in the 2015 election on an independent ticket.

Whatever their many differences, Brand, Trump, Grillo and Kukiz all represent the current wave of populism that has mounted such a serious challenge to establishment politics in the present century. Populism, according to Molyneux and Osborne (2017, p. 3), is characterised by "…the notion that the people… have a moral sovereignty that it is the duty of representative politics to express as directly as possible" and is far from a new phenomenon, having been central to Latin American politics in the twentieth century and evident even in Ancient Greece. However, there are distinctive features of twenty-first century populism that unite the aforementioned figures and others: a general dismissal of 'elites' of all kinds, irrespective of ideology; a preference for informal language and direct communication; and liberal use of social media (Engesser, Fawzi, & Larson, 2017).

Populism, Social Media, and the Figure of the (Political) Outsider

In their analysis of Pawel Kukiz's 2015 election campaign, Olczyk and Wasilewski (2016) identify a number of stylistic features of Kukiz's online communication that differed sharply from his rival presidential candidates. First was the use of emotive style, such as multiple punctuation marks (also noted by Marshall and Henderson as characteristic of Trump's campaign tweets). Second was his tendency to address individuals directly in his comments, often by name. He was also highly responsive to direct tweets, and on other occasions retweeted posts from his supporters. Above all, his profile and communication style resembled those of an 'ordinary' social media user, in contrast to the highly polished, professional presentation of the established party candidates.

Engesser et al. (2017) have argued that the primacy of social media in populist movements is no coincidence because digital culture is fundamentally suited to the basic tenets of populism challenging elites (represented by the 'legacy media') and representing 'the people'. These points echo several of the claims made in this book about social media allowing their users to seemingly bypass censors and other gatekeepers and communicate directly with their followers, creating a very different cultural landscape than one shaped by broadcast media and national newspapers with their strict entry criteria and tight editorial control. Furthermore, as Engesser et al. argue, social media suits the style of populists: the reduction of complex issues to convenient soundbites (Trump's campaign and presidency are full of 'simple' solutions to historically and ideologically sensitive problems), and emotive and emotional discourse, particularly generating anger and fear and a sense of negativity.[6]

It is also not surprising that one should find comedians at the forefront of contemporary populist movements because they embody many of the qualities that characterise populist leaders. They have long enjoyed a reputation for direct communication with the people, illustrated by the success of 'uncensored' recordings of 'live' (stage) shows, that carry the suggestion that they are 'gagged' by gatekeepers when broadcast on radio and television. The comic persona, deriving historically from court jesters and Shakespearean 'fools' is that of the social outsider delivering an ingenuous 'truth' that cuts through the formalities of the established order (notably, Jung saw the masks of persona as something that were essential for social accomplishment, since to tell the truth is to betray the self – one only has to think of figures such as Dostoyevsky's Prince Myshkin in this context, albeit without the comic timing).

Getting votes and maintaining power are two rather different challenges, however. In Kukiz's case, the latter has proved rather more difficult. Poland operates a semi-presidential system (like that of France) in which the successful candidate in the presidential elections then has to assemble a parliament, and select a Prime Minister, on the basis of a second election. Between the two elections in 2015, Kukiz's share of the vote dropped by over half (to seven per cent in the parliamentaries). What went wrong? Olczyk and Wasilewski (2016, p. 65) argue that, once in office, Kukiz's outsider status was severely compromised: he began acting like a politician.

---

[6] It isn't clear from Engesser et al's argument why emotional language should generate negativity, or why either should be uniquely suited to the online context. One could argue that these things are *de rigueur* for political candidates in opposition, especially those standing on an anti-establishment platform.

Despite campaigning alongside "an arsenal of semantic markers" that referenced his previous identity as a rock star, his new affiliations with established politicians and courting of traditional ('legacy') media made his movement look, to use his own derogative terminology, "like yet another political party from the realm of 'particracy'".

The figure of the outsider giving it straight to the people is part of what Manning, Penfold-Mounce, Loader, Vromen, and Xenos (2017) have identified as the *informalisation* of contemporary politics, a trend not only found among politically-aspiring celebrities but also among the established parties themselves. Perhaps the most obvious example of this is the British Conservative politician Boris Johnson. Former Lord Mayor of London, then Foreign Minister in Theresa May's post-referendum cabinet, Johnson would appear, on the face of it, to be the least qualified 'outsider' in British politics. Right out of the upper echelons of the British class system, educated at Eton and Oxford, up to his neck in social and economic capital, and only slightly to the left of Donald Trump, Johnson is nonetheless a celebrity by any definition of the term. Recognised throughout the world for his "upper class twit" persona demonstrated by various gaffes and other seemingly unrehearsed and controversial statements, Johnson revels in his "charming knack of not taking life too seriously" (Ruddock, 2006).

Wood, Corbett, and Flinders (2016) have argued that Johnson represents a blend of two different types of celebrity politician: the superstar and the everyday. In doing so, he resembles Dyer's (1979) paradox of stardom, where (film) stars represent the ordinary person plucked out of obscurity on account of their extraordinary talent (or, in most cases, beauty, charisma, and so on). They suggest that, in Johnson's case, the paradox is largely strategic. While his various media activities resemble those of the superstar politician, his adoption of an informal register at certain points enables him to establish "…an emotive connection with the audience, appealing to norms of fallibility and imperfection" (Wood et al., 2016, p. 593). In an analysis of Johnson's letters from supporters (in the pre-social media era), Ruddock (2006) found that many resembled those of fans, asking Johnson about personal details even though they were writing to him on a specific issue.

Ultimately, the appeal of the outsider and the use of informal registers bring us back to the old matter of authenticity. Johnson is, despite his unpromising credentials, seen as someone who plays himself rather than a professionally circumscribed role – just like the populist agitators who are "untainted by power" (Engesser et al., 2017). By stepping beyond the borders of how politicians are meant to talk and behave, outsiders like Kukiz appear "reliable and authentic" (Olczyk & Wasilewski, 2016). It could be argued that established politicians take a huge risk in doing so: indeed Manning et al. (2017) suggest that there is a fine line between public affection for politicians who share personal disclosure on social media and disrespect for those who seem to be abandoning their more serious responsibilities by wasting time in courting voters (at worst, informalisation is seen as nothing more than a publicity stunt). And, as Van Zoonen (2005) has argued, there are other prejudices brought into play when female politicians invite the media into their private lives.

Is Politics Changing?

If social media have been largely instrumental in bringing about changes to the face of celebrity more generally, have they also succeeded in shifting the parameters of what is considered political? Marshall (2014) argues that the significance accorded to celebrity has, over time, changed the face of news media by shifting the focus towards the personal lives of politicians and away from more impersonal matters like policy and ideology. Moreover, the emergence of celebrities as activists for specific causes – from African drought to Third World debt – has begun to challenge the very notion of what should be considered *political*; "the moving constellation of what constitutes politics and who can be thought of as a political persona" (Marshall & Henderson, 2016, p. 3).

One way of thinking about this is through the concept of celebrity capital. As Driessens (2013b, p. 555) argues, the conversion of celebrity capital into other kinds of capital (economic, cultural), "can disrupt the relative value of the different kinds of capital and the corresponding power dynamics within social fields". Historically, this has tended to result in what Habermas (1973) termed "legitimation crisis", whereby the public loses confidence in politics: if mere celebrities can gain office just by being visible and popular, how can we respect the democratic system as a whole? The same problem can arise when established political figures begin to court celebrity, as Manning et al. (2017) have found in their research on informalisation.

However, the cultural changes being brought about through social media may be creating longer-lasting disruption to the operation of capital in the political field, as politicians are increasingly forced to enter into direct dialogue with their constituents. Of course, this has always taken place (in Britain, at least) within the formal constraints of 'surgeries' where MPs hold meetings on local issues, but media like Twitter afford open discussion on national or even international affairs. This has led to some very strange exchanges indeed, such as the one in late 2017 between UK Health Secretary Jeremy Hunt and comedy actor Ralf Little (Parkinson, 2017). Hunt had claimed, during a television interview, that his government had invested more in health than any other country in Europe. Little tweeted a direct challenge to Hunt's claims, and when Hunt responded in kind, he produced a string of 40 separate tweets providing counter-evidence. Having already waded into the debate feet first, Hunt felt obliged to retaliate, sending Little 26 tweets of his own.

Naturally, the irony of this extensive extra-curricular activity was not lost on Twitter users, with hundreds of tweets expressing dismay at Hunt's alleged refusal to meet with health professionals while being content to spend time on a slanging match with a minor celebrity. But it echoes developments elsewhere in the political system that have seen social media used not only as tools for courting voters but as legitimate channels for information and communication. Indeed, the Trump administration's first year or so has been played out on Twitter, where he continues to cast aspersions about 'fake news' in mainstream media, implying that the medium operates as a backdoor to what is really going on in the White House. This has led to repeated accusations of "politics by Twitter", although it could be equally well argued that it is the mainstream media that allow Trump's tweets to attain the legitimacy that they have, by scrutinizing and reporting them so intensively and enthusiastically. As Marshall and Henderson (2016) point out, 'clickbait' is not something only casual browsers of the Internet are seduced by.

POSTSCRIPT: CONCLUSIONS AND REFLECTIONS

By the time you are reading these words, the history of twenty-first century celebrity may have turned out to be completely different from the way I have presented it in this book. Such are the hazards of media research in these rapidly-changing times. As I write, there is something of a backlash going on against what has become known as 'Big Tech' – the domination of digital culture by a handful of West Coast US billionaires and their phenomenally successful media. Much of this backlash has been promulgated by traditional media, particularly those news outlets most threatened by upstart online competitors, although their concerns are not merely self-serving, and raise serious questions about globalisation and the future of democracy itself. There is no space in this book to deal with these issues, and in any case it seems that sociology and cultural studies in particular have tended to follow this line of enquiry in much of their recent literature on matters digital. However it is worth reflecting on the possibility that the digital free-for-all described here actually represents a relatively small slice of time before things change again in ways that are impossible to foresee even for the custodians of Big Tech themselves.

It is with these prospects in mind that media scholars and other social scientists often say that they have steered clear of burrowing too deeply into the mysteries of Twitter or YouTube in case they suddenly disappear and an entire line of research goes up in smoke overnight. This is clearly not a problem for researchers in computing/digital fields of inquiry, where yesterday's tech continues to resonate as part of the historical lineage of the field. It is rather harder, however, for a psychologist or sociologist to convince a funding panel to part with money for several years of research that goes nowhere because its object of study is a fleeting phenomenon that, however culturally important at the time of application, can be sold and transformed into something different before the first phase of data collection gets underway. For this reason (and many others), the book is a better home for any research that carries the risk of redundancy.

But would the material in this book become redundant if Big Tech and other greedy people conspired to sabotage the present culture? I prefer to think of it along the same lines as 'microcelebrity'. I have, at various points, written slightly disparagingly of the concept of microcelebrity and its shifting definitions, but I am convinced that the original work of Terri Senft and Alice Marwick has been hugely valuable in charting the history of digital culture and its impact on celebrity. That some of the original criteria that defined microcelebrity were no longer relevant ten years on is not the fault of Senft and Marwick. That some media scholars have clung to the term despite its redundancy is not Senft and Marwick's fault either (nor does it mean that those media scholars' work is redundant; far from it in many cases). Media scholars are academics like any others, constrained by the same professional requirements around publication, funding and dissemination of research. Academic research is historically a slow process (compared to, say, journalism) and there is simply not the infrastructure to enable us to move any faster.

So, in 2028, it may be that PewDiePie and Zoella have gone the way of Tay Zonday and Lauren Luke. They may be no more than a footnote to some kind of digital history that assumes a form as yet unrecognizable. They may have been completely forgotten by all apart from their nearest and dearest. I think, however, that there are substantial differences between those two figures and their digital predecessors. First is the sheer global reach of YouTube circa 2018. Already Zoella (and Alfie) have their images immortalized in Tussauds. There are wax figures from bygone eras, it is true, which museum visitors hurry past without any sign of recognition, but not many who have entirely vanished from the pages of some cultural history. Even pop stars whose brief string of hits anchor them to a specific era are still fondly remembered by those who bought their records and even those who just saw them on *Top of the Pops*.

While I think PewDiePie and Zoella, and many others of their ilk, are *bona fide* celebrities, I am a bit cautious about stretching the category boundary too wide. Some of the travel bloggers and other 'influencers' in chapter 8 may indeed disappear from the face of the inhabited world without comment. Maybe their level of celebrity is not as perfect as some of them seem to think. But fame is a multi-layered phenomenon. As I wrote in *Illusions of Immortality* (Giles, 2000), it is not all or nothing. We cannot just draw a line between the famous and the not-famous. In the domains of travel blogging or rock climbing, fame may simply not be enough for that influential figure to attain recognition in the wider world without them doing something truly remarkable, or branching out into a different, more celebrated, field. More than vloggers, influencers are very much of their time. Once their 'influence' fades, who will pay attention to them?

One of the reasons, I suspect, that more media scholars have not turned their attention to the kind of celebrities documented in these pages is that they simply prefer to write about other people – film stars, pop stars, TV personalities; the traditional roll-call of celebrity. They want to research people they think are worth researching. Psychologists like me have never been in this game to write about people we like. Do I like PewDiePie? No. Do I like Zoella? Not particularly. I like both of them more than I like the travel bloggers. But other people like these people, and I respect their opinions. More importantly, I believe they are worth taking seriously, for better or for worse, and not necessarily because I fear their 'influence' will be harmful. I am not here to wag a finger on behalf of the social science community.

In some respects I see my role rather like that of the original Cultural Studies scholars, to defend cultural material that is devalued by others, partly because it is enjoyed by a sector of society not deemed to be worthy (young people, in the digital example). Maybe I can afford to take this stance because I am now too far away from the vlogger/influencer audience to ever be accused of partiality. Maybe, alienated as I am from contemporary popular culture generally, I cannot see any serious difference in merit between the new genres of celebrity and the current generation of film and pop stars, most of whom seem to be grinding out endless permutations of artforms that are long past their peak. This makes me different from most celebrity researchers, but I like to think it allows me to take a broad overview that is not weighted in favour of any particular celebrity field.

This brings us back full circle to where we started at the beginning of chapter 1 and the forever floating negotiation of meaning. Whether it all adds up to 'celebrity' will depend entirely on your own definition of the word.

REFERENCES

Abell, J., & Stokoe, E. (2001). Broadcasting the royal role: Constructing culturally situated identities in the Princess Diana *Panorama* interview. *British Journal of Social Psychology*, 40(3), 417–435.

Abidin, C. (2016). 'Aren't these just rich, young women doing vain things online?' Influencer selfies as subversive frivolity. *Social Media + Society*, 2(2), 1–17. Retrieved from http://sms.sagepub.com/content/2/2/2056305116641342.full.pdf+html

Abidin, C. (2017). #familygoals: Family influencers, calibrated amaterusim, and justifying young digital labour. *Social Media + Society*, 3(1), 1–15. Retrieved from http://journals.sagepub.com/doi/abs/10.1177/20563 05117707191#articleCitationDownloadContainer

Adams, R. L. (2016) '10 impressive Instagram profiles to follow', *Forbes*. Retrieved from https://www.forbes.com/sites/robertadams/2016/04/14/the-top-10-instagram-influencers/2/#64b327014bbd

Alberoni, F. (1972). The powerless "elite": Theory and sociological research on the phenomenon of the stars. In D. McQuail (Ed.), *Sociology of Mass Communication* (pp. 75–98). Harmondsworth: Penguin.

Allen, M. (2012). What was Web 2.0? Versions as the dominant mode of internet history. *New Media & Society*, 15(2), 260–275.

Allington, D. (2016). 'Power to the reader' or 'degradation of literary taste'? Professional critics and Amazon customers as reviewers of the inheritance of loss. *Language and Literature*, 25(3), 254–278.

Anderson, D. R., Huston, A. C., Schmitt, K. L., Linebarger, D. L., & Wright, J. C. (2001). Early childhood television viewing and adolescent behavior: The recontact study. *Monographs of the Society for Research in Child Development*, 66(1), vii–147.

Andò, R. (2016). The ordinary celebrity: Italian young vloggers and the definition of girlhood. *Film, Fashion & Consumption, 5*(1), 123–139.

Arthur, C. (2008, October 16). Andy Murray v Stephen Fry serves up a surprise winner. *The Guardian.* Retrieved from https://www.theguardian. com/technology/2008/oct/16/blogging-stephen-fry-andy-murray

Arthurs, J., & Shaw, S. (2016). Celebrity capital in the political field: Russell Brand's migration from stand-up comedy to *Newsnight. Media, Culture & Society, 38*(8), 1136–1152.

Ashe, D. D., Maltby, J., & McCutcheon, L. E. (2005). Are celebrity worshippers more prone to narcissism? A brief report. *North American Journal of Psychology, 7*(2), 239–246.

Asia Pacific News. (2006, June 8). Hong Kong's 'Bus Uncle' beaten up by three men. Retrieved from http://www.channelnewsasia.com/stories/eastasia/view/212671/1/.html

Aslama, M., & Pantti, M. (2006). Talking alone: Reality TV, emotions and authenticity. *European Journal of Cultural Studies, 9*(2), 167–184.

Attrill, A. (2016). *The manipulation of online self-presentation: Create, edit, re-edit and present.* Basingstoke: Palgrave.

Ault, S. (2014, August 5). YouTube stars are more popular than mainstream celebrities among US teens. *Variety.* Retrieved from http://variety. com/2014/digital/news/survey-youtube-stars-more-popular-than-mainstream-celebs-among-u-s-teens-1201275245/

Bakioğlu, B. S. (2016). Exposing convergence: YouTube, fan labour, and anxiety of cultural production of Lonelygirl15. *Convergence.* Retrieved from http://journals.sagepub.com/doi/full/10.1177/1354856516655527. Accessed on August 19, 2016.

Banet-Weiser, S. (2012). *Authentic™: The politics of ambivalence in a brand culture.* New York, NY: New York University Press.

Barbour, K., Marshall, P. D., & Moore, C. (2014). Persona to persona studies. *M/C Journal, 17*(3). Retrieved from http://journal.media-culture. org.au/index.php/mcjournal/issue/view/persona

Barker, M., & Petley, J. (Eds.). (2001). *Ill effects: The media/violence debate.* London: Routledge.

Bayer, J. B., Ellison, N. B., Schoenebeck, S., & Falk, E. B. (2016). Sharing the small moments: Ephemeral social interaction on Snapchat. *Information, Communication & Society*, *17*(7), 956–977.

Baxter, L. A. (2004). Relationships as dialogues. *Personal Relationships*, *11*(1), 1–22.

Beer, D. (2008). Making friends with Jarvis Cocker: Music culture in the context of Web 2.0. *Cultural Sociology*, *2*(2), 222–241.

Beer, D., & Penfold-Mounce, R. (2010). Researching glossy topics: The case of the academic study of celebrity. *Celebrity Studies*, *1*(3), 360–365.

Beers Fägersten, K. (2017). The role of swearing in creating an online persona: The case of PewdiePie. *Discourse, Context & Media*, *18*, 1–10.

Belk, R. W. (1990). The role of possessions in constructing and maintaining a sense of past. *Advances in Consumer Research*, *17*(1), 669–676.

Benjamin, W. (1963). *Das kunstwerk im zeitalter seiner technischen reproduzierbarkeit*. Frankfurt: Suhrkamp.

Bennett, J. (2008). The television personality system: Televisual stardom revisited after film theory. *Screen*, *49*(1), 32–50.

Bennett, J. (2011). *Television personalities: Stardom and the small screen*. London: Routledge.

Bennett, L., & Holmes, S. (2010). The 'place' of television in celebrity studies. *Celebrity Studies*, *1*(1), 65–80.

Bennett, J., & Strange, N. (Eds.). (2011). *Television as digital media*. Durham, NC: Duke University Press.

Bennett, J., & Thomas, S. (2014). Tweet celebrity. *Celebrity Studies*, *5*(4), 501–503.

Bennett, L. (2014). 'If we stick together we can do anything': Lady Gaga fandom, philanthropy and activism through social media. *Celebrity Studies*, *5*(1–2), 138–152.

Berryman, R., & Kavka, M. (2017). 'I guess a lot of people see me as a big sister or a friend': The role of intimacy in the celebrification of beauty vloggers. *Journal of Gender Studies*, *26*(3), 307–320.

Betancourt, R. (2016). Genre as medium on YouTube: The work of Grace Helbig. *Journal of Popular Culture*, *49*(1), 196–223.

Bevan, A. (2017). How to make victory rolls: Gender, memory and the counterarchive in YouTube pinup hair tutorials. *Feminist Media Studies*, *17*(5), 755–773.

Beverland, M. L., & Farrelly, F. J. (2010). The quest for authenticity in consumption: Consumers' purposive choice of authentic cues to shape experienced outcomes. *Journal of Consumer Research*, *36*(5), 838–856.

Biocca, F. A. (1988). Opposing conceptions of the audience: The active and passive hemispheres of mass communication theory. *Communication Yearbook*, *11*, 51–80.

Bird, S. E. (2011). Are we all produsers now? Convergence and media audience practices. *Cultural Studies*, *25* (4–5), 502–516.

Bonner, F. (2013). Celebrity, work and the reality-talent show: Strictly come dancing/dancing with the stars. *Celebrity Studies*, *4*(2), 169–181.

Boorstin, D. (1961). *The image: A guide to pseudo-events in America*. New York, NY: Harper and Row.

Bourdieu, P. (1993). *The field of cultural production: Essays on art and literature*. Cambridge: Polity.

Boyd, D. (2010). Social network sites as networked publics: Affordances, dynamics and implications. In Z. Papacharissi (Ed.), *A networked self: Identity, community and culture on social networking sites* (pp. 39–58). New York, NY: Routledge.

Boyd, M. (2000). *Bach*. Oxford: Oxford University Press.

Brady, T. (2013, December 4). 'If you're famous and on Twitter, you're a moron': Clooney on his 'Zen-like' approach to celebrity, being tougher than Clark Gable and how he longs to stroll in Central Park. *Mail Online*. Retrieved from http://www.dailymail.co.uk/news/article-2517989/George-Clooney-says-famous-Twitter-moron.html

Braithwaite, D. O., Bach, B. W., Baxter, L. A., DiVerssniero, R., Hammonds, J. R., Hosek, A. M., …Wolf, B. M. (2010). Constructing family: A typology of voluntary kin. *Journal of Social and Personal Relationships*, *27*(3), 388–407.

Braudy, L. (1986). *The frenzy of renown: Fame and its history*. Oxford: Oxford University Press.

Braun, R., & Spiers, E. (2016). Introduction: Re-viewing literary celebrity. *Celebrity Studies*, 7(4), 449–456.

Brecht, B. (1932/1979). Radio as a means of communication: A talk on the function of radio. *Screen*, 20(3–4), 24–28.

Broderick, M. (2014, March 28). A blogger discovered the picture she took at the hair salon was turned into a viral anti-Obamacare meme. *Buzzfeed*. Retrieved from https://www.buzzfeed.com/ryanhatesthis/a-blogger-discovered-the-selfie-she-took-at-the-hair-salon-w?utm_term=.vkWRBEloo#.qpMYxQKzz

Brügger, N. (2015). A brief history of Facebook as a media text: The development of an empty structure. *First Monday*, 20(5).

Bruns, A. (2008). *Blogs, Wikipedia, second life and beyond: From production to produsage*. New York, NY: Peter Lang.

Bryant, J., & Zillmann, D. (1994). *Media effects: Advances in theory and research*. Hillsdale, NJ: Lawrence Erlbaum.

Burgess, J. (2014). 'All your chocolate rain are belong to us?' Viral video, YouTube, and the dynamics of participation culture. In N. Papastergiadis & V. Lynn (Eds.), *Art in the global present* (pp. 86–96). Sydney: UTS ePRESS.

Burgess, J., & Green, J. (2009). *YouTube: Online video and participatory culture*. Cambridge: Polity.

Burgin, V. (2000). Jenni's room: Exhibition and solitude. *Critical Inquiry*, 27(1), 87–99.

Butler, J. G. (1991). 'I'm not a doctor, but I play one on TV'. *Cinema Journal*, 30(4), 74–89.

Cavicchi, D. (2007). Loving music: Listeners, entertainments, and the origins of music fandom in nineteenth-century America. In J. Gray, C. L. Harrington & C. Sandvoss (Eds.), *Fandom: Identities and communities in a mediated world* (pp. 235–249). New York, NY: New York University Press.

Chan, L. (2015, November 13). Meet Iskra Lawrence, plus-size fashion's newest It Girl turned fashion editor. *Glamour*. Retrieved from https://www.glamour.com/story/meet-iskra-lawrence-the-next-b

Chawansky, M. (2016). Be who you are and be proud: Brittney Griner, intersectional invisibility and digital possibilities for lesbian sporting celebrity. *Leisure Studies, 35*(6), 771–782.

Chu, D. (2009). Collective behaviour in YouTube: A case study of 'Bus Uncle' online videos. *Asian Journal of Communication, 19*(3), 337–353.

Click, M. A., Lee, H., & Holladay, H. W. (2013). Making monsters: Lady Gaga, fan identification and social media. *Popular Music & Society, 36*(3), 360–379.

Cliff, M. (2017, June 13). Superstar vlogger Zoella and her partner Alfie Deyes swap their £1million home for an even MORE luxurious Brighton mansion (complete with trendy neon wall art, a log burner and a VERY expansive garden). *Mail Online*. Retrieved from http://www.dailymail.co.uk/femail/article-4599218/Zoella-moves-luxurious-Brighton-mansion.html

Clifford, K. (2014) Amanda Knox: A picture of innocence. *Celebrity Studies, 5*(4), 504–507.

Cocker, H. L., & Cronin, J. (2017). Charismatic authority and the YouTuber: Unpacking the new cults of personality. *Marketing Theory, 17*(4), 455–472.

Colapinto, C., & Benecchi, E. (2014). The presentation of celebrity personas in everyday twittering: Managing online reputations throughout a communication crisis. *Media Culture & Society, 36*(2), 219–233.

Cole, T., & Leets, L. (1999). Attachment styles and intimate television viewing: Insecurely forming relationships in a parasocial way. *Journal of Social and Personal Relationships, 16*(4), 495–511.

Collings, B. (2014). #selfcontrol: @CAZWELLnyc and the role of the ironic selfie in transmedia celebrity self-promotion. *Celebrity Studies, 5*(4), 511–513.

Costall, A. (1995). Socialising affordances. *Theory & Psychology, 5*(4), 467–481.

Costall, A., & Morris, P. (2015). The "textbook Gibson": The assimilation of dissidence. *History of Psychology, 18*(1), 1–14.

Couldry, N. (2002). Playing for celebrity: *Big Brother* as ritual event. *Television and New Media, 3*(3), 283–293.

Couldry, N. (2003). *Media rituals*. London: Routledge.

Couldry, N. (2007). Media power: Some hidden dimensions. In S. Redmond & S. Holmes (Eds.), *A reader in stardom and celebrity* (pp. 353–359). London: Sage.

Couldry, N. (2009). Does 'the media' have a future? *European Journal of Communication, 24*(4), 437–449.

Couldry, N. (2015). The myth of 'us': Digital networks, political change and the production of collectivity. *Information, Communication & Society, 18*(6), 608–626.

Couldry, N., & van Dijck, J. (2015). Researching social media as if the 'social' mattered. *Social Media + Society, 1*(2), 1–7.

Crace, J. (2009, June 6). *Big Brother* beginners: 'These days we'd be far too dull to be on the show'. *The Guardian.* Retrieved from https://www.theguardian.com/media/2009/jun/06/bigbrother-reality-tv

Curnutt, H. (2011). Durable participants: A generational approach to reality TV's 'ordinary' labour pool. *Media Culture & Society, 33*(7), 1061–1076.

Dare-Edwards, H. (2014). 'Shipping bullshit': Twitter rumours, fan/celebrity interaction and questions of authenticity. *Celebrity Studies, 5*(4), 521–524.

Dawkins, R. (1976/1989). *The selfish gene.* Oxford: Oxford University Press.

De Cordova, R. (1990). *Picture personalities: The emergence of the star system in America.* Urbana, IL: University of Illinois Press.

Deller, R., & Murphy, K. (2016). 'As sugary as a frosted cupcake': Newspaper representations of a YouTube star. Presentation given at the 3rd Celebrity Studies Conference, University of Amsterdam, Amsterdam, 28–30 June.

Dibble, J. L., Hartmann, T., & Rosaen, S. F. (2016). Parasocial interaction and parasocial relationship: Conceptual classification and a critical assessment of measures. *Human Communication Research, 42*, 21–44.

Driessens, O. (2013a). The celebritization of society and culture: Understanding the structural dynamics of celebrity culture. *International Journal of Cultural Studies, 16*(6), 251–258.

Driessens, O. (2013b). Celebrity capital: Redefining celebrity using field theory. *Theory & Society, 42*(5), 543–560.

Driessens, O. (2015). On the epistemology and operationalization of celebrity. *Celebrity Studies*, 6(3), 370–373.

Driessens, O. (2016). The democratization of celebrity: Mediatization, promotion, and the body. In P. D. Marshall and S. Redmond (Eds.), *A Companion to Celebrity* (pp. 371–384). Chichester: Wiley.

Duckett, C. (2017, 7 November). Twitter opens floodgates on new 280-character tweets after few use it. *ZDNet*. Retrieved from http://www.zdnet.com/article/twitter-opens-floodgates-on-280-character-tweets-after-few-use-it/

Duffett, M. (2013). *Understanding fandom: An introduction to the study of media fan culture*. London: Bloomsbury.

Duguay, S. (2016). LGBTQ visibility through selfies: Comparing platform mediators across Ruby Rose's Instagram and Vine presence. *Social Media + Society*, 2(2), 1–12.

Dumont, G. (2017). The beautiful and the damned: The work of new media production in professional rock climbing. *Journal of Sport and Social Issues*, 41(2), 99–117.

Dunkley, D. (2017, August 27). Child gamers turned to gamblers in a click. *The Times*. Retrieved from https://www.thetimes.co.uk/article/child-gamers-turned-to-gamblers-in-a-click-p3k3k5z5m

Dyer, R. (1979). *Stars*. London: British Film Institute.

Edwards, D. (1997). *Discourse and cognition*. London: Sage.

Edwards, D., Ashmore, M., & Potter, J. (1995). Death and furniture: The rhetoric, politics and theology of bottom line arguments against relativism. *History of the Human Sciences*, 8(2), 25–49.

Edwards, D., & Potter, J. (1992). *Discursive psychology*. London: Sage.

Edwards, L., & Jeffreys, E. (Eds.). (2010). *Celebrity in China*. Hong Kong: Hong Kong University Press.

Ellis, J. (1982). *Visible fictions: Cinema, television, video*. London: Routledge.

Ellis, J. (2015). How to be in public: The case of an early television show. *Celebrity Studies*, 6(3), 355–369.

Engesser, S., Fawzi, N., & Larson, A. O. (2017). Populist online communication: Introduction to the special issue. *Information, Communication & Society, 20*(9), 1279–1292.

Ferguson, C. (2015). Do *Angry Birds* make for angry children? A meta-analysis of video game influences on children's and adolescents' aggression, mental health, prosocial behaviour and academic performance. *Perspectives on Psychological Science, 10*(5), 646–666.

Ferris, K. O. (2010). The next big thing: Local celebrity. *Society, 47*(5), 392–395.

Feuer, A. & George, J. (2005, February 26). Internet fame is cruel mistress for a dancer of the Numa Numa. *New York Times*. Retrieved from http://www.nytimes.com/2005/02/26/nyregion/internet-fame-is-cruel-mistress-for-a-dancer-of-the-numa-numa.html

Flood & Ellis-Petersen, H. (2014, December 8). YouTube star takes online break as she admits novel was 'not written alone'. *The Guardian*. Available at: http://www.theguardian.com/books/2014/dec/08/zoella-bestselling-girl-online-written-siobhan-curham-zoe-sugg

Foucault, M. (1988). Technologies of the self. In L. H. Martin, H. Gutman & P. H. Hutton (Eds.), *Technologies of the self: A seminar with Michel Foucault* (pp. 16–49). Cambridge, MA: MIT Press.

Foucault, M. (1993). About the beginning of the hermeneutics of the self: Two lectures at Dartmouth. *Political Theory, 21*(2), 198–227.

Freberg, K., Graham, K., McGaughey, K., & Freberg, L. (2011). Who are the social media influencers? A study of public perceptions of personality. *Public Relations Review, 37*, 90–92.

Friedman, L. M. (1999). *The horizontal society*. New Haven, CT: Yale University Press.

Frobenius, M. (2014). Beginning a monologue: The opening sequence of video blogs. *Journal of Pragmatics, 43*(3), 814–827.

Fuchs, C. (2014). *Social media: A critical introduction*. London: Sage.

Furness, H. (2015, April 27). Zoella writing Girl Online 2 without ghostwriter. *The Telegraph*. Retrieved from http://www.telegraph.co.uk/

news/celebritynews/11566781/Zoella-writing-Girl-Online-2-without-ghostwriter.html

Gallagher, P. (2017, October 13). GPs threaten to remove patients who visit 'Dr Google' first. *i News*. Retrieved from https://inews.co.uk/essentials/news/uk/doctors-gps-dr-google-patient-list/

Gamson, J. (1992). The assembly line of greatness: Celebrity in twentieth century America. *Critical Studies in Mass Communication, 9*(1), 1–24.

Gamson, J. (1994). *Claims to fame: Celebrity in contemporary America.* Berkeley, CA: University of California Press.

García-Rapp, F. (2016). The digital media phenomenon of YouTube beauty gurus: The case of Bubzbeauty. *International Journal of Web Based Communities, 12*(4), 360–375.

García-Rapp, F. (2017). Popularity markers on YouTube's attention economy: The case of Bubzbeauty. *Celebrity Studies, 8*(2), 228–245.

García-Rapp, F., & Roca-Cuberes, C. (2017). Being an online celebrity: Norms and expectations of YouTube's beauty community. *First Monday, 22*(7). Retrieved from http://dx.doi.org/10.5210/fm.v22i17.7788

Genz, S. (2015). My job is me: Postfeminist celebrity culture and the gendering of authenticity. *Feminist Media Studies, 15*(4), 545–561.

Geraghty, C. (2000). Re-examining stardom: Questions of texts, bodies and performance. In C. Gledhill and L. Williams (Eds.), *Reinventing Film Studies* (pp.183–201). London: Arnold.

Gergen, K. (1991). *The saturated self: Dilemmas of identity in contemporary life.* New York, NY: Basic.

Gibson, J. J. (1979). *The ecological approach to visual perception.* Houghton Mifflin: Boston, MA.

Gijón, M. M. (2014). The blogosphere in the Spanish literary field: Consequences and challenges to twenty-first century literature. *Hispanic Research Journal, 14*(4), 373–384.

Giles, D. C. (2000). *Illusions of immortality: A psychology of fame and celebrity.* Basingstoke: Macmillan.

Giles, D. C. (2002a). Keeping the public in their place: Audience participation in lifestyle television programming. *Discourse & Society*, *13*, 603–628.

Giles, D. C. (2002b). Parasocial interaction: A review of the literature and a model for future research. *Media Psychology*, *4*, 279–302.

Giles, D. C. (2013a). Animal celebrities. *Celebrity Studies*, *4*(2), 115–128.

Giles, D. C. (2013b). The extended self strikes back: Morrissey fans' reaction to public rejection by their idol. *Popular Communication*, *11*(2), 116–129.

Giles, D. C. (2015). Field migration, cultural mobility and celebrity: The case of Paul McCartney. *Celebrity Studies*, *6*(4), 538–552.

Giles, D. C. (2017a). The immortalisation of celebrities. In M. H. Jacobsen (Ed.), *Postmortal society: Multidisciplinary perspectives on death, survivalism and immortality in contemporary culture* (pp. 97–113). Abingdon: Routledge.

Giles, D. C. (2017b). How do fan and celebrity identities become established on Twitter? A study of 'social media natives' and their followers. *Celebrity Studies*, *8*(3), 445–460.

Giles, D. C., & Maltby, J. (2004). The role of media in adolescent development: Relations between autonomy, attachment, and interest in celebrities. *Personality and Individual Differences*, *36*, 813–822.

Giles, D. C., & Shaw, R. L. (2009). The psychology of news influence and the development of Media Framing Analysis. *Social and Personality Psychology Compass*, *3/4*, 375–393.

Goffman, E. (1959). *The presentation of self in everyday life*. New York, NY: Anchor.

Goffman, E. (1981). *Forms of talk*. Oxford: Blackwell.

Goldsmith, J. (2009). Celebrity and the spectacle of nation. In T. Mole (Ed.), *Romanticism and celebrity culture 1750–1850* (pp. 21–40). Cambridge: Cambridge University Press.

Gray, J. (2003). New audiences, new textualities: Anti-fans and non-fans. *International Journal of Cultural Studies*, *6*(1), 64–81.

Greene, A. L., & Adams-Price, C. (1990). Adolescents' secondary attachments to celebrity figures. *Sex Roles*, 23(7–8), 335–347.

Grint, K., & Woolgar, S. (1997). *The machine at work*. Cambridge: Polity.

Habermas, J. (1973). *Legitimation crisis*. Boston, MA: Beacon.

Halavais, A. (2014) 'Structure of Twitter: Social and technical', In K. Weller, A. Bruns, J. Burgess, M. Mahrt and C. Puschmann (Eds.), *Twitter and Society* (pp. 29–42). New York, NY: Peter Lang.

Hall, K. A. (2014). The authenticity of social-media performance: lonelygirl15 and the amateur brand of Young-Girlhood. *Women& Performance*, 25(2), 128–142.

Hall, S. (1980). Encoding/decoding, in S. Hall, D. Hobson , A. Lowe, & P. Willis (Eds.), *Culture, media, language: Working papers in Cultural Studies, 1972–79* (pp. 128–138). London: Hutchinson.

Hall, S. (1986). On postmodernism and articulation: An interview with Stuart Hall. In D. Morley & K. Chen (Eds.), *Stuart Hall: Critical dialogues in cultural studies*. New York, NY: Routledge.

Halpern, A. (2017, 10 June). Coolest travel jobs: What's it like to be a social media celebrity. *Afar*. Retrieved from https://www.afar.com/magazine/coolest-travel-jobs-what-its-like-to-be-a-social-media-celebrity

Handyside, S., & Ringrose, J. (2017). Snapchat memory and youth digital sexual cultures: Mediated temporality, duration and affect. *Journal of Gender Studies*, 26(3), 347–360.

Harmon, A. (2003, 19 May). Compressed data; Fame is no laughing matter for the 'Star Wars kid'. *New York Times*. Retrieved from http://www.nytimes.com/2003/05/19/business/compressed-data-fame-is-no-laughing-matter-for-the-star-wars-kid.html?pagewanted=1

Harré, R. (1983). *Personal being: A theory for individual psychology*. Oxford: Blackwell.

Harrington, C. L., & Bielby, D. D. (2010). A life course perspective on fandom. *International Journal of Cultural Studies*, 13(5), 429–450.

Hartmann, T., & Goldhoorn, C. (2011). Horton and Wohl revisited: Exploring viewers' experience of parasocial interaction. *Journal of Communication*, 61, 1104–1121.

Hawkes, R. (2016, May 4). Whatever happened to *Star Wars* kid? The sad but inspiring story behind one of the first victims of cyberbullying. *The Telegraph*. Retrieved from http://www.telegraph.co.uk/films/2016/05/04/whatever-happened-to-star-wars-kid-the-true-story-behind-one-of/

Haynes, J., & Marshall, L. (2017). Beats and tweets: Social media in the careers of independent musicians. *New Media & Society*. Retrieved from https://doi.org/10.1177/1461444817711404

Hellekson, K., & Busse, K. (Eds.). (2006). *Fan fiction and fan communities in the age of the internet*. Jefferson, NC: McFarland.

Hermes, J. (2009). Audience studies 2.0: On the theory, politics and method of qualitative audience research. *Interactions: Studies in Communication and Culture*, 1(1), 111–128.

Hern, A. (2017, March 10). How many Snapchat clones does it take for Facebook to lose its self-respect? *The Guardian*. Retrieved from https://www.theguardian.com/technology/2017/mar/10/snapchat-clones-facebook-copies

Herrman, J. (2017, February 17). YouTube's monster: PewdiePie and his populist revolt. *New York Times*. Retrieved from https://www.nytimes.com/2017/02/16/magazine/youtubes-monster-pewdiepie-and-his-populist-revolt.html

Hills, M. (2002). *Fan cultures*. London: Routledge.

Hills, M. (2003). Recognition in the eyes of the relevant beholder: Representing 'subcultural celebrity' and cult TV fans. *Mediactive*, 2, 59–75.

Hills, M. (2005). Patterns of surprise: The "aleatory object" in psycho-analytic ethnography and cyclical fandom. *American Behavioral Scientist*, 48(7), 801–821.

Hills, M. (2006) 'Not just another powerless elite? When media fans become subcultural celebrities', In S. Holmes and S. Redmond (Eds.), *Framing Celebrity* (pp. 101–118), London: Routledge.

Hills, M. (2016). From para-social to multisocial interaction: Theorising material/digital fandom and celebrity. In P. D. Marshall and S. Redmond (Eds.), *A Companion to Celebrity* (pp. 463–482), Chichester: Wiley.

Holmes, S. (2004). 'All you've got to worry about is the task, having a cup of tea, and doing a bit of sunbathing': Approaching celebrity in Big Brother.

In S. Holmes & D. Jermyn (Eds.), *Understanding reality television* (pp. 111–135). London: Routledge.

Holmes, S. (2006). It's a jungle out there! The game of fame in celebrity reality TV. In S. Holmes & S. Redmond (Eds.), *Framing celebrity: New directions in celebrity culture* (pp. 45–66). Abingdon: Routledge.

Holmes, S. (2011). Celebrity forum introduction: *Big Brother* RIP. *Celebrity Studies*, 2(2), 214–217.

Holmes, S., & Jermyn, D. (2004). Introduction: Understanding reality TV. In S. Holmes & D. Jermyn (Eds.), *Understanding reality television* (pp. 1–32). London: Routledge.

Holmes, S., Ralph, S., & Redmond, S. (2015). Swivelling the spotlight: Stardom, celebrity, and 'me'. *Celebrity Studies*, 6(1), 100–117.

Holmes, S., & Redmond, S. (2006). Introduction: Understanding celebrity culture. In S. Holmes & S. Redmond (Eds.), *Framing celebrity: New directions in celebrity culture* (pp. 1–16). Abingdon: Routledge.

Horton, D., & Wohl, R. R. (1956). Mass communication and para-social interaction. *Psychiatry*, 19, 215–229.

Hunt, E. (2015, 3 November). Essena O'Neill quits Instagram, claiming 'social media is not real life'. *The Guardian*. Retrieved from http://www.theguardian.com/media/2015/nov/03/instagram-star-essena-oneill-quits-2d-life-to-reveal-true-story-behind-images

Hutchby, I. (2001). Technologies, texts and affordances. *Sociology*, 35(2), 441–456.

Hutchby, I. (2014). Communicative affordances and participation frameworks in mediated interaction. *Journal of Pragmatics*, 72, 86–89.

Internet World Stats (2016). Retrieved from http://www.internetworldstats.com/

Jefferson, G. (2004). "At first I thought": A normalizing device for extraordinary events. In G. H. Lerner (Ed.), *Conversation analysis: Studies from the first generation* (pp. 131–167). Amsterdam: John Benjamins.

Jenkins, H. (1992). *Textual poachers: Television fans and participatory culture*. New York, NY: Routledge.

Jenkins, H. (2006). *Convergence culture: Where old and new media collide*. New York, NY: New York University Press.

Jenson, J. (1992). Fandom as pathology: The consequences of characterization. In L. Lewis (Ed.), *The adoring audience: Fan culture and popular media* (pp. 9–29). London: Routledge.

Jermyn, D. (2006). 'Bringing out the ★ in you': SJP, Carrie Bradshaw and the evolution of television stardom. In S. Holmes & S. Redmond (Eds.), *Framing Celebrity* (pp. 67–86). Abingdon: Routledge.

Jerslev, A. (2016). In the time of the microcelebrity: Celebrification and the YouTuber Zoella. *International Journal of Communication, 10*, 5233–5251.

Jimroglou, K. M. (1999). A camera with a view: JenniCAM, visual representation, and cyborg subjectivity. *Information, Communication & Society, 2*(4), 439–453.

Johansson, S. (2007). *Reading tabloids: Tabloid newspapers and their readers*. Stockholm: Sodertorns Hogskola.

Johnston, L. H. (2014, December 9). Zoella: Yes, using a ghostwriter matters when your whole brand is based on being authentic. *The Independent*. Retrieved from http://www.independent.co.uk/voices/comment/zoella-theres-nothing-wrong-with-hiring-a-ghost-writer-as-long-as-you-admit-it-9910453.html

Joinson, A. N. (2003). *Understanding the psychology of internet behaviour: Virtual worlds, real lives*. Basingstoke: Palgrave Macmillan.

Jones, O. (2011). *Chavs: The demonization of the working class*. London: Verso.

Jung, C. J. (1953). *Two essays on analytical psychology*. London: Routledge & Kegan Paul.

Katz, E., & Lazarsfeld, P. F. (1955). *Personal influence: The part played by people in the flow of mass communications*. New York, NY: The Free Press.

Kavka, M. (2012). *Reality TV*. Edinburgh: Edinburgh University Press.

Kavka, M., & West, A. (2004). Temporalities of the real: Conceptualising time in reality TV. In S. Holmes & D. Jermyn (Eds.), *Understanding reality television* (pp. 136–153). London: Routledge.

Kehrberg, A. K. (2015). 'I love you, please notice me': The hierarchical nature of Twitter fandom. *Celebrity Studies, 6*(1), 85–99.

Khamis, S., Ang, L., & Welling, R. (2017). Self-branding, 'micro-celebrity', and the rise of social media influencers. *Celebrity Studies, 8*(2), 191–208.

Khaira-Hanks, P. (2017, October 4). Rupi Kaur: The inevitable backlash against Instagram's favourite poet. *The Guardian*. Retrieved from https://www.theguardian.com/books/booksblog/2017/oct/04/rupi-kaur-instapoets-the-sun-and-her-flowers

Khomami, N. (2015, May 25). Fat-shamed 'dancing man' gets own back at star-studded Hollywood party. *The Guardian*. Retrieved from http://www.theguardian.com/technology/2015/may/25/dancing-man-fat-shamed-cyberbullies-hollywood-party

King, B. (1985). Articulating stardom. *Screen, 26*(5), 27–45.

King, B. (2016). Stardom, celebrity and the moral economy of pretending. In P. D. Marshall and S. Redmond (Eds.), *A Companion to Celebrity* (pp. 315–332). Chichester: Wiley.

Knight, S. (2010). *Crime fiction since 1800: Detection, death, diversity.* New York, NY: Palgrave Macmillan.

Koliska, M., & Roberts, J. (2015). Selfies: Witnessing and participatory journalism with a point of view. *International Journal of Communication, 9*, 1672–1685.

Kuss, D., & Griffiths, M. (2015). *Internet addiction in psychotherapy.* Basingstoke: Palgrave.

Langer, J. (1981). Television's 'personality system'. *Media, Culture & Society, 4*(4), 351–365.

Levy, M. R. (1979). Watching TV news as para-social interaction. *Journal of Broadcasting, 23*, 69–80.

Lister, M. et al. (2009). *New media: A critical introduction* (2nd ed.). Abingdon: Routledge.

Liu, H. (2007). Social network profiles as taste performances. *Journal of Computer-Mediated Communication, 13*(1), 252–275.

Livingstone, S. (2013). The participation paradigm in audience research. *The Communication Review*, *16*, 21–30.

Livingstone, S., & Lunt, P. (1994). *Talk on television: Audience participation and public debate*. London: Routledge.

Lo, A. (2008, November 8). Bus Uncle returns to limelight looking for companionship. *South China Morning Post*. Retrieved from http://www.scmp.com/article/659364/bus-uncle-returns-limelight-looking-companionship

Lovelock, M. (2017). 'Is every YouTuber going to make a coming out video eventually?' YouTube celebrity video bloggers and lesbian and gay identity. *Celebrity Studies*, *8*(1), 87–103.

Lowbridge, C. (2015, October 23). The UK YouTube stars with fans across the world. *BBC News*. Retrieved from http://www.bbc.co.uk/news/uk-england-34504053

Luckhurst, M., & Moody, J. (2005). Introduction: The singularity of theatrical celebrity. In M. Luckhurst & J. Moody (Eds.), *Theatre and Celebrity in Britain 1660-2000* (pp. 1–14). Basingstoke: Palgrave.

Lury, K. (1995). Television performance: Being, acting and corpsing. *New Formations*, *28*, 114–127.

MacKenzie, D., & Wajcman, L. (1999). *The social shaping of technology* (2nd ed.). Buckingham: Open University Press.

Maguire, E. (2015). Self-branding, hotness and girlhood in the video blogs of Jenna Marbles. *Biography*, *38*(1), 72–86.

Mahdavi, A. (2017, 15 February). PewDiePie thinks 'Death to All Jews' is a joke. Are you laughing yet? *The Guardian*. Retrieved from https://www.theguardian.com/commentisfree/2017/feb/15/youtube-pewdiepie-thinks-death-to-all-jews-joke-laughing-yet

Maloney, M., Roberts, S., & Caruso, A. (2017). 'Mmm…I love it bro!' Performances of masculinity in YouTube gaming. *New Media & Society*. Retrieved from https://doi.org/10.1177/1461444817703368

Maltby, J., Day, L., McCutcheon, L. E., Houran, J., & Ashe, D. (2006). Extreme celebrity worship, fantasy proneness and dissociation. Developing the measurement and understanding of celebrity worship in a clinical personality context. *Personality & Individual Differences*, 40, 273–283.

Maltby, J., Houran, J., Lange, R., Ashe, D. D., & McCutcheon, L. E. (2001). Thou shalt worship no other gods: unless they are celebrities: The relationship between celebrity worship and religious orientation. *Personality and Individual Differences*, 32, 1157–1172.

Maltby, J., McCutcheon, L. E., Ashe, D. D., & Houran, J. (2001). The self-reported psychological well-being of celebrity worshippers. *North American Journal of Psychology*, 3(3), 441–452.

Manning, N., Penfold-Mounce, R., Loader, B. D., Vromen, A., & Xenos, M. (2017). Politicians, celebrities and social media: A case of informalisation? *Journal of Youth Studies*, 20(2), 127–144.

Marriott, S. (1996). Time and time again: 'Live' television commentary and the construction of replay talk. *Media, Culture & Society*, 18(1), 69–86.

Marsh, S. (2017, 5 October). Social media stars breaching rules on promoting brands, watchdog says. *The Guardian*. Retrieved from https://www.theguardian.com/media/2017/oct/05/social-media-stars-breaching-rules-on-promoting-brands-watchdog-says-instagram-twitter

Marshall, P. D. (1997). *Celebrity and power: Fame in contemporary culture*. Minneapolis, MN: University of Minnesota Press.

Marshall, P. D. (2010). The promotion and presentation of the self: Celebrity as a marker of presentational media. *Celebrity Studies*, 1(1), 35–48.

Marshall, P. D. (2014). Persona studies: Mapping the proliferation of the public self. *Journalism*, 15(2), 153–170.

Marshall, P. D., & Henderson, N. (2016). Political persona – an introduction. *Persona Studies*, 2(2), 1–18.

Marshall, P. D., Moore, C., & Barbour, K. (2015). Persona as method: Exploring celebrity and the public self through persona studies. *Celebrity Studies*, 6(3), 288–305.

Marshall, P. D. and Redmond, S. (Eds.), (2015). *A Companion to Celebrity*. Chichester: Wiley.

Marwick, A. E. (2013). *Status update: Celebrity, publicity and branding in the social media age*. New Haven, CT: Yale University Press.

Marwick, A. E. (2015). Instafame: Luxury selfies in the attention economy. *Public Culture, 27*(1), 137–160.

Marwick, A. E. (2016). You may know me from YouTube: (Micro)-celebrity in social media. In P. D. Marshall and S. Redmond (Eds.), *A Companion to Celebrity* (pp. 333–350). Chichester: Wiley.

Marwick, A. E., & Boyd, D. (2011). To see and be seen: Celebrity practice on Twitter. *Convergence, 17*(2), 139–158.

Maslow, A. H. (1943). A theory of human motivation. *Psychological Review, 50*(4), 370–396.

Maton, K. (2010). Last night we dreamt that somebody loved us: Smiths fans (and me) in the late 1980s. In S. Campbell & C. Coulter (Eds.), *Why pamper life's complexities? Essays on the Smiths* (pp. 179–194). Manchester: Manchester University Press.

Matney, L. (2017, 22 June). YouTube has 1.5 billion logged-in monthly users watching a ton of mobile video. *Tech Crunch*. Retrieved from: https://techcrunch.com/2017/06/22/youtube-has-1-5-billion-logged-in-monthly-users-watching-a-ton-of-mobile-video/

Mavroudis, J., & Milne, E. (2016). Researching microcelebrity: Methods, access and labour. *First Monday, 21*(7). Available at: http://firstmonday.org/ojs/index.php/fm/article/view/6401

McCutcheon, L. E., Lange, R., & Houran, J. (2002). Conceptualization and measurement of celebrity worship. *British Journal of Psychology, 93*, 67–87.

McCutcheon, L. E., Scott, V. B., Aruguete, M. S., & Parker, J. S. (2006). Exploring the link between attachment and the inclination to obsess about or stalk celebrities. *North American Journal of Psychology, 8*(2), 289–300.

McLuhan, M. (1964). *Understanding media: The extensions of man*. Cambridge, MA: MIT Press.

Macrae, S. (2017). 'Get off my internets': How anti-fans deconstruct lifestyle bloggers' authenticity work. *Persona Studies*, 3(1), 13–27.

McRoberts, S., Ma, H., Hall, A., & Yarosh, S. (2017). Share first, save later: Performance of self through Snapchat stories. *Proceedings of the 2017 CHI Conference on Human Factors in Computing Systems*, 6902–6911.

Miller, D., Costa, E., Haynes, N., Tom, M., Nicolescu, R., Sinanan, J., ... Wang, X. (2016). *How the world changed social media*. London: UCL Press.

Mole, T. (2007). *Byron's romantic celebrity: Industrial culture and the hermeneutic of intimacy*. Basingstoke: Palgrave.

Molyneaux, M., & Osborne, T. (2017). Populism: A deflationary view. *Economy and Society*, 46(1), 1–19.

Monaco, J. (1978). *Celebrity*. New York, NY: Delta.

Montgomery, M. (2001). Defining 'fresh talk'. *Discourse Studies*, 3(4), 397–405.

Moran, J. (2000). *Star authors: Literary celebrity in America*. London: Pluto.

Morris, M., & Ogan, C. (1996). The Internet as mass medium. *Journal of Computer-Mediated Communication 1*(4). doi:10.1111/j.1083-6101.1996.tb00174.x

Moseley, R. (2000). Makeover takeover on British television. *Screen*, 41(3), 299–314.

Murray, S., & Ouelette, L. (2009). Introduction. In S. Murray & L. Ouelette (Eds.), *Reality TV: Remaking television culture* (2nd ed., pp. 1–22). New York, NY: New York University Press.

NeeHao. (2011, January 14). 'YouTube superstar Bubzbeauty', *NeeHao*. Retrieved from http://www.neehao.co.uk/2011/01/youtube-superstar-bubzbeauty/

Neuman, W. R. (2016). *The digital difference: Evolving media technology and the theory of communication effects*. Cambridge, MA: Harvard University Press.

Newman, J. (2016). Stampylongnose and the rise of the celebrity videogame player. *Celebrity Studies*, 7(2), 285–288.

Nkadi, A. (2015, February 10). Are YouTubers celebrities? *Live Mag UK*. Retrieved from: http://www.livemaguk.com/are-youtubers-celebrities/

Norman, D. A. (1988). *The psychology of everyday things*. New York, NY: Basic.

Oh, D. C. (2017). K-pop fans react: Hybridity and the white celebrity-fan on YouTube. *International Journal of Communication, 11*, 2270–2287.

Olczyk, T., & Wasilewski, J. (2016). From rock star to political star: curious case of Paweł Kukiz's persona power. *Persona Studies, 2*(2), 57–70.

Oppenheim, M. (2016, June 9). Overly Attached Girlfriend: The story of the girl behind the meme. *The Independent*. Retrieved from http://www.independent.co.uk/news/people/overly-attached-girlfriend-the-story-of-the-girl-behind-the-meme-a7072451.html

Osterhout, J. E. (2010, April 18). Stealth marketing: When you're being pitched and you don't even know it. *NY Daily News*. Retrieved from http://www.nydailynews.com/life-style/stealth-marketing-pitched-don-article-1.165278

Parkinson, H. J. (2017, 22 November). Jeremy Hunt gets into Twitter row over the NHS with actor Ralf Little. *The Guardian*. Retrieved from https://www.theguardian.com/politics/2017/nov/22/jeremy-hunt-gets-into-twitter-row-over-nhs-with-actor-ralf-little

Pedroni, M. (2016). Meso-celebrities, fashion and the media: How digital influencers struggle for visibility. *Film, Fashion & Consumption, 5*(1), 103–121.

Perse, E. M., & Rubin, R. B. (1989). Attribution in social and parasocial relationships. *Communication Research, 16*, 59–77.

Peterson, K. M. (2016). Beyond fashion tips and Hijab tutorials: The aesthetic style of Islamic lifestyle videos. *Film Criticism, 40*(2). Retrieved from https://quod.lib.umich.edu/f/fc/13761232.0040.203/--beyond-fashion-tips-and-hijab-tutorials-the-aesthetic-style?rgn=main;view=fulltext

Pisch, A. (2016). *The personality cult of Stalin in Soviet posters, 1929–1953: Archetypes, inventions and fabrications*. Acton: ANU Press.

Postman, N. (1985). *Amusing ourselves to death: Public discourse in the age of show business*. New York, NY: Penguin.

Potter, A. (2010). *The authenticity hoax: Why the real things we seek don't make us happy*. New York, NY: Harper Perennial.

Potter, J. (1996). *Representing reality: Discourse, rhetoric and social construction*. London: Sage.

Potter, J., & Reicher, S. (1987). Discourses of community and conflict: The organisation of social categories in accounts of a 'riot'. *British Journal of Social Psychology, 26*, 25–40.

Qureshi, H. (2015, November 23). How do I love thee? Let me Instagram it. *The Guardian*. Retrieved from http://www.theguardian.com/books/2015/nov/23/instapoets-instagram-twitter-poetry-lang-leav-rupi-kaur-tyler-knott-gregson

Rainey, S. (2012, September 14). YouTube videos funded our gap year travels. *The Telegraph*. Retrieved from http://www.telegraph.co.uk/lifestyle/9544479/YouTube-videos-funded-our-gap-year-travels.html

Rein, I. J., Kotler, P., & Stoller, M. R. (1987). *High visibility*. New York, NY: Dodd, Mead & Co.

Ricoeur, P. (1970). *Freud and philosophy: An essay on interpretation*. New Haven, CT: Yale University Press.

Rockwell, D., & Giles, D.C. (2009). Being-in-the-world of celebrity: The phenomenology of fame. *Journal of Phenomenological Psychology, 40*, 178–210.

Rogers, R. (2014). Foreword: Debanalising Twitter: The transformation of an object of study. In K. Weller, A. Bruns, J. Burgess, M. Mahrt & C. Puschmann (Eds.), *Twitter and Society*. (pp. ix–xxvi). New York, NY: Peter Lang.

Rojek, C. (2001) *Celebrity*, London: Reaktion.

Rojek, C. (2012). *Fame attack: The inflation of celebrity and its consequences*. London: Bloomsbury.

Rojek, C. (2016). *Presumed intimacy: Para-social relationships in media, society and celebrity culture*. Cambridge: Polity.

Rosengren, K. E. (1974). Uses and gratifications: A paradigm outlined. In J. G. Blumler & E. Katz (Eds.), *The uses of mass communications: Current perspectives on gratifications research* (pp. 269–286). Beverly Hills, CA: Sage.

Rubin, A. M., Perse, E. M., & Powell, R. A. (1985). Loneliness, parasocial interaction, and local television news viewing. *Human Communication Research, 12,* 155–80.

Ruddock, A. (2006). Invisible centres: Boris Johnson, authenticity, cultural citizenship and a centrifugal model of media power. *Social Semiotics, 16*(2), 263–282.

Rudulph, H. W. (2015, June 8). Cyrene Quiamco can make $10,000 for 1 snap on Snapchat. *Cosmopolitan.* Retrieved from http://www.cosmopolitan.com/career/a40043/cyrene-quiamco-internets-most-fascinating/

Sacks, H. (1984). On doing 'being ordinary'. In J. M. Atkinson & J. Heritage (Eds.), *Structures of social action: Studies in conversation analysis* (pp. 413–429). Cambridge: Cambridge University Press.

Samadder, R. (2014). Alfie Deyes, the 21-year-old king of YouTube: 'He's normal, not like celebrities.' *The Guardian.* Retrieved from http://www.theguardian.com/lifeandstyle/shortcuts/2014/sep/28/alfie-deyes-youtube-pointlessblog-videos-book

Sandvoss, C. (2005). *Fans: The mirror of consumption.* Cambridge: Polity.

Saul, H. (2015, March 30). Menstruation-themed photo series artist 'censored by Instagram' says images are to demystify taboos around periods. *The Independent.* Retrieved from https://www.independent.co.uk/arts-entertainment/art/menstruation-themed-photo-series-artist-censored-by-instagram-says-images-are-to-demystify-taboos-10144331.html

Saul, H. (2016, March 27). Instafamous: Meet the social media influencers redefining celebrity. *The Independent.* Retrieved from http://www.independent.co.uk/news/people/instagram-model-natasha-oakley-iskra-lawrence-kayla-itsines-kendall-jenner-jordyn-woods-a6907551.html

Scannell, P. (1996). *Radio, television and modern life.* Oxford: Wiley.

Scannell, P. (2001). Authenticity and experience. *Discourse Studies, 3*(4), 405–411.

Schickel, R. (1985) *Intimate strangers: The culture of celebrity*, New York, NY: Fromm International.

Schimmel, K. S., Harrington, C. L., & Bielby, D. D. (2007). Keep your fans to yourself: The disjuncture between sport studies' and pop culture studies' perspectives on fandom. *Sport in Society*, *10*(4), 580–600.

Sconce, J. (2004). See you in hell Johnny Bravo! In S. Murray & L. Ouelette (Eds.), *Reality TV: Remaking television culture* (pp. 251–276). New York, NY: New York University Press.

Scott, K. (2015). The pragmatics of hashtags: Inference and conversational style on Twitter. *Journal of Pragmatics*, *81*, 8–20.

Sehdev, J. (2014) 'YouTube stars are more popular than mainstream celebrities among US teens', *Variety*. Retrieved from http://variety.com/2014/digital/news/survey-youtube-stars-more-popular-than-mainstream-celebs-among-u-s-teens-1201275245/

Senft, T. (2008). *Camgirls: Celebrity and community in the age of social networks*. New York, NY: Peter Lang.

Sheridan, L., North, A., Maltby, J., & Gillett, R. (2007). Celebrity worship, addiction and criminality. *Psychology, Crime & Law*, *13*(6), 559–571.

Shifman, L. (2012). An anatomy of a YouTube meme. *New Media & Society*, *14*, 187–203.

Shingler, M. (2012). *Star studies: A critical guide*. London: BFI.

Shrayne, J. (2010). 'A small utopia': *Unterstützer* not *anhänger*. Einsturzende Neubaten's supporter initiative. *Popular Music*, *29*(3), 373–96.

Siegel, J., Dubrovsky, V., Kiesler, S., & McGuire, T. W. (1986). Group processes in computer-mediated communication. *Organizational Behavior and Human Decision Processes*, *37*(2), 157–187.

Singh, K., Fox, J. R. E., & Brown, R. J. (2016). Health anxiety and Internet use: A thematic analysis. *Cyberpsychology: Journal of psychosocial research on Cyberspace, 10*(2), article 1. doi: 10.5817/CP2016-2-4

Smith, A. (2010) 'Lifestyle television programmes and the construction of the expert host', *European Journal of Cultural Studies*, *13*(2): 191–205.

Smith, D. (2014). Charlie is so "English"-like: Nationality and the branded celebrity person in the age of YouTube. *Celebrity Studies*, *5*(3), 256–274.

Smith, D. R. (2016) "Imagining others more complexly': Celebrity and the ideology of fame among YouTube's 'Nerdfighteria', *Celebrity Studies*, 7(3): 339–353.

Snowsell, C. (2011). Fans, apostles and NMEs. In E. Devereux, A. Dillane, & M. J. Power (Eds.), *Morrissey: Fandom, representations and identities* (pp. 73–94). Bristol: Intellect.

Solon, O. (2013, 20 June). Richard Dawkins on the Internet's 'hijacking' of the word 'meme'. *Wired*. Retrieved from http://www.wired.co.uk/article/richard-dawkins-memes

Stampler, L. (2014, July 24). Meet the first viral snap chat stars. *Time*. Retrieved from: http://time.com/3002803/snapchat-stars/

Steiner, A. (2010). Personal readings and public texts: Book blogs and online writing about literature. *Culture Unbound, 2,* 471–494.

Sternberg, R. J. (1996). Love stories. *Personal Relationships, 3*(1), 59–79.

Stevenson, N. (1995). *Understanding media cultures: Social theory and mass communication.* London: Sage.

Stevenson, N. (2009). Talking to Bowie fans: Masculinity, ambivalence and cultural citizenship. *European Journal of Cultural Studies, 12*(1), 79–98.

Stever, G. S. (1991). The celebrity appeal questionnaire. *Psychological Reports, 68,* 859–866.

Stever, G. S. (2011). Celebrity worship: Critiquing a construct. *Journal of Applied Social Psychology, 41*(6), 1356–1370.

Stever, G. S. & Hughes, E. (2013). *What role Twitter? Celebrity conversations with fans.* Paper presented at Social Media: The Fourth Annual Transforming Audiences conference, University of Westminster, 2–3 September.

Stever, G. S., & Lawson, K. (2013). Twitter as a way for celebrities to communicate with fans: Implications for the study of parasocial interaction. *North American Journal of Psychology, 15*(2), 339–354.

Stommel, W., & te Molder, H. (2015). Counselling online and over the phone: When pre-closing questions fail as a closing device. *Language in Social Interaction, 48*(3), 281–300.

Strangelove, M. (2010). *Watching YouTube: Extraordinary videos made by ordinary people.* Toronto: University of Toronto Press.

Street, J. (2004). Celebrity politicians: Popular culture and political representation. *British Journal of Politics & International Relations*, 6(4), 435–452.

Studlar, G. (2015). The changing face of celebrity and the emergence of motion picture stardom. In P. D. Marshall and S. Redmond (Eds.), *A Companion to Celebrity* (pp. 58–78). Chichester: Wiley.

The Telegraph (2011, August 3). Paul Daniels injured in Sooty pizza-throwing incident. Retrieved from http://www.telegraph.co.uk/news/picturegalleries/celebritynews/8678482/Paul-Daniels-injured-in-Sooty-pizza-throwing-accident.html

The Telegraph (2011, December 3). Fenton owner unmasked as editorial consultant Max Findlay. Retrieved from http://www.telegraph.co.uk/lifestyle/pets/8953661/Fenton-owner-unmasked-as-editorial-consultant-Max-Findlay.html

Thomas, S. (2014). Celebrity in the 'Twitterverse': History, Authenticity and the Multiplicity of Stardom. *Celebrity Studies*, 5(3), 242–55.

Thornborrow, J. (2017). Styling the 'ordinary': Tele-factual genres and participant identities. In J. Mortensen, N. Coupland & J. Thogersen (Eds.), *Style, mediation and change: Sociolinguistic perspectives on talking media* (pp. 143–164). Oxford: Oxford University Press.

Time (2016). The 100 most influential people. Retrieved from http://time.com/collection/2016-time-100/artists/

Tolson, A. (1991). Televised chat and the synthetic personality. In P. Scannell (Ed.), *Broadcast talk* (pp. 178–200). London: Sage.

Tolson, A. (2001). 'Being yourself': The pursuit of authentic celebrity. *Discourse Studies*, 3(4), 443–457.

Tolson, A. (2010). A new authenticity? Communicative practices on YouTube. *Critical Discourse Studies*, 7(4), 277–289.

Tolson, A. (2015). The history of television celebrity: A discursive approach. *Celebrity Studies*, 6(3), 341–354.

Treem, J. W., & Leonardi, P. M. (2012). Social media use in organizations: Exploring the affordances of visibility, editability, persistence and association. *Communication Yearbook*, 36, 143–189.

Trilling, L. (1972). *Sincerity and authenticity*. Cambridge, MA: Harvard University Press.

Turner, G. (2004). *Understanding celebrity*. London: Sage.

Turner, G. (2006). The mass production of celebrity: 'Celetoids', reality TV and the 'demotic turn'. *International Journal of Cultural Studies, 9*(2). 153–165.

Turner, G. (2010). *Ordinary people and the media: The demotic turn*. London: Sage.

Turner, G. (2014). *Understanding celebrity* (2nd ed.). London: Sage.

Tyler, I., & Bennett, B. (2010). 'Celebrity chav': Fame, femininity and social class. *International Journal of Cultural Studies, 13*(3), 375–393.

Usher, B. (2015). Twitter and the celebrity interview. *Celebrity Studies, 6*(3), 306–321.

Ussher, J. (1997). *Body talk: The material and discursive regulation of sexuality, madness and reproduction*. London: Routledge.

Valente, T. W. (1995). *Network models of the diffusion of innovations*. Creskill, NJ: Hampton Press.

van de Rijt, A., Shor, E., Ward, C., & Skiena, S. (2013). Only 15 minutes? The social stratification of fame in printed media. *American Sociological Review, 78*(2), 266–289.

Van den Bulck, H., Claessens, N., & Bels, A. (2014). 'By working she means tweeting': Online celebrity gossip media and audience readings of celebrity Twitter behaviour. *Celebrity Studies, 5*(4), 514–517.

Van Doren, C. (2008, July 28). All the answers: The quiz show scandal - and its aftermath. *The New Yorker*. Retrieved from http://www.newyorker.com/magazine/2008/07/28/all-the-answers

Van Gorp, B. (2014). It takes two to tango: The relationship between the press and celebrities in Belgium. *Celebrity Studies, 5*(4), 423–437.

Van Leeuwen, T. (2001). What is authenticity? *Discourse Studies, 3*(4), 392–397.

Van Syckle, K. (2016, 21 January). 'It put me on anti-depressants': Welcome to GOMI, the cruel site for female snark. *The Guardian*. Retrieved from https://www.theguardian.com/lifeandstyle/2016/jan/21/gomi-blog-internet-comments-women

Van Zoonen, L. (2005). *Entertaining the citizen: When politics and popular culture converge*. Boulder, CO: Rowman & Littlefield.

Waddell, T. F. (2016). The allure of privacy or the desire for self-expression? Identifying users' gratifications for ephemeral, photograph-based communication. *Cyberpsychology, Behavior and Social Networking*, *19*(7), 441–445.

Walker, A. (1970). *Stardom: The Hollywood phenomenon*. New York, NY: Stein & Day.

Wedgwood, S. (2017, October 24). 'I view the hurtful messages as sadism': What it's like to be Instagram famous. *The Guardian*. Retrieved from https://www.theguardian.com/technology/2017/oct/24/instagram-influencers-hurtful-messages-sadism-famous

Wiggins, B. E., & Bowers, G. B. (2015). Memes as genre: A structurational analysis of the memescape. *New Media & Society*, *17*(11), 1886–1906.

Williams, R. (1974). *Television: Technology and cultural form*. New York, NY: Schocken.

Williams, R. (2016). Localebrities, adopted residents and local characters: Audience and celebrity in a small nation. *Celebrity Studies*, *7*(2), 154–168.

Winnicott, D. W. (1971). *Playing and reality*. London: Penguin.

Wood, H. (2017). The politics of hyperbole on *Geordie Shore*: Class, gender, youth and excess. *European Journal of Cultural Studies*, *20*(1), 39–55.

Wood, M., Corbett, J., & Flinders, M. (2016). Just like us: Everyday celebrity politicians and the pursuit of popularity in an age of anti-politics. *The British Journal of Politics and International Relations*, *18*(3), 581–599.

Xu, W. W., Park, J. Y., Kim, J. Y., & Park, H. W. (2016). Networked cultural diffusion and creation on YouTube: An analysis of YouTube memes. *Journal of Broadcasting and Electronic Media*, *60*(1), 104–122.

Yardley, L. (1996). Reconciling discursive and materialist perspectives in health and illness: A reconstruction of the biopsychosocial approach. *Theory & Psychology*, 6(3), 485–508.

York, L. M. (2007). *Literary celebrity in Canada*. Toronto: University of Toronto Press.

Zappavigna, M. (2012). Searchable talk: The linguistic function of hashtags. *Social Semiotics*, 25(3), 274–291.

INDEX

www.ingramcontent.com/pod-product-compliance
Lightning Source LLC
Chambersburg PA
CBHW071239050326
40690CB00011B/2186